RICK AND MORTY
vs.
DUNGEONS & DRAGONS
II: PAINSCAPE

ONI PRESS

IDW

OFFICIAL LICENSED PRODUCT

[adult swim]

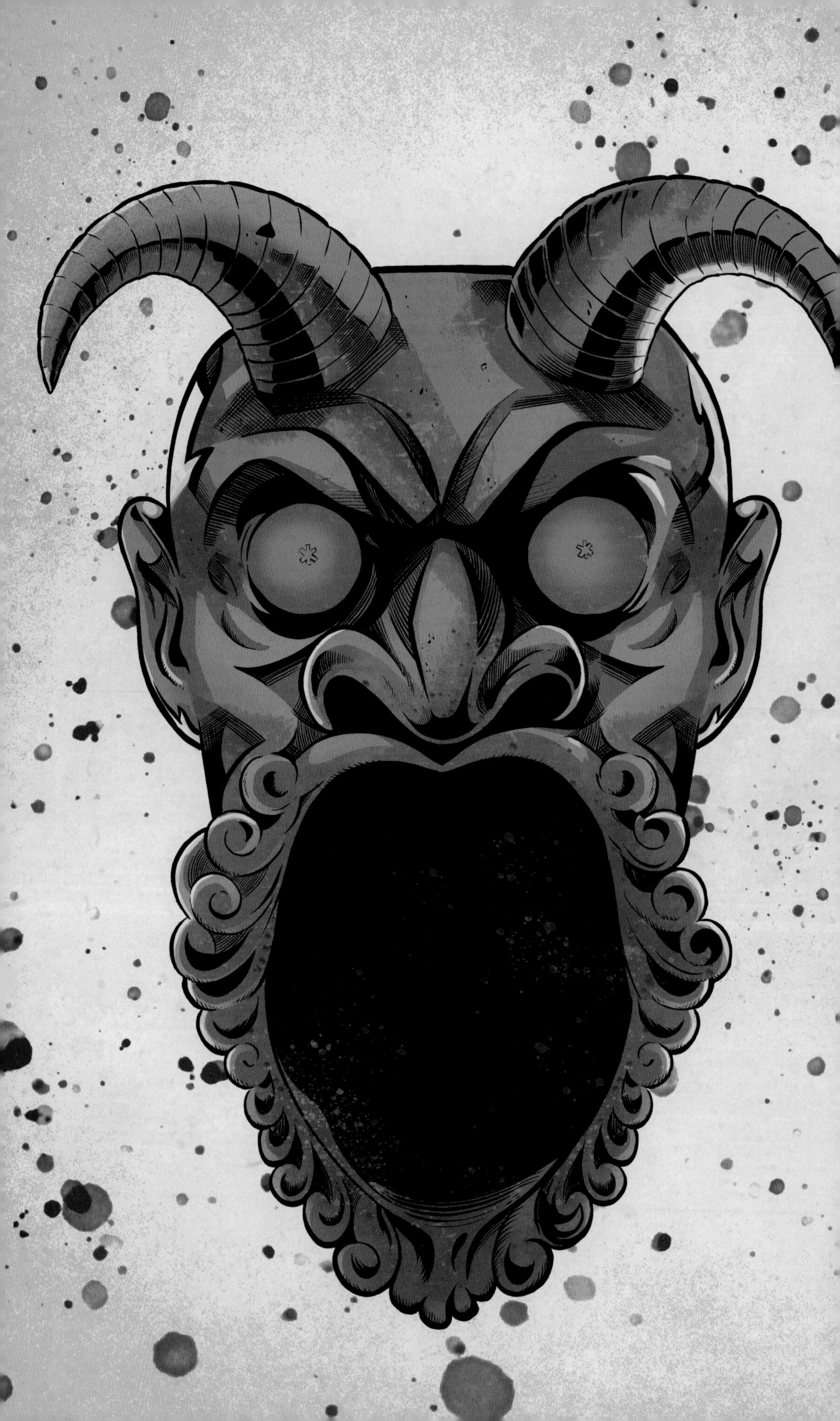

RICK AND MORTY

vs.

DUNGEONS & DRAGONS

II: PAINSCAPE

Rick and Morty™ created by Dan Harmon and Justin Roiland

written by **Jim Zub**

illustrated by **Troy Little**

colored by **Leonardo Ito**

lettered by **Crank!** with additional hand lettering by **Troy Little**

retail cover by **Troy Little** after **Cynthia Sheppard**

oni exclusive cover By **Julieta Colás**

edited By **Sarah Gaydos** for oni press
Chase Marotz for idw publishing

designed by **Sarah Rockwell**

Published by Oni-Lion Forge Publishing Group, llc

JAMES LUCAS JONES, *president & publisher*

SARAH GAYDOS, *editor in chief*

CHARLIE CHU, *e.v.p. of creative & business development*

BRAD ROOKS, *director of operations*

AMBER O'NEILL, *special projects manager*

HARRIS FISH, *events manager*

MARGOT WOOD, *director of marketing & sales*

JEREMY ATKINS, *director of brand communications*

DEVIN FUNCHES, *sales & marketing manager*

KATIE SAINZ, *marketing manager*

TARA LEHMANN, *marketing & publicity associate*

TROY LOOK, *director of design & production*

KATE Z. STONE, *senior graphic designer*

SONJA SYNAK, *graphic designer*

HILARY THOMPSON, *graphic designer*

SARAH ROCKWELL, *junior graphic designer*

ANGIE KNOWLES, *digital prepress lead*

VINCENT KUKUA, *digital prepress technician*

SHAWNA GORE, *senior editor*

ROBIN HERRERA, *senior editor*

AMANDA MEADOWS, *senior editor*

JASMINE AMIRI, *editor*

GRACE BORNHOFT, *editor*

ZACK SOTO, *editor*

STEVE ELLIS, *vice president of games*

BEN EISNER, *game developer*

MICHELLE NGUYEN, *executive assistant*

JUNG LEE, *logistics coordinator*

JOE NOZEMACK, *publisher emeritus*

IDW — **CHRIS RYALL,** *president & publisher/cco*, **CARA MORRISON,** *chief financial officer*, **MATTHEW RUZICKA,** *chief accounting officer*, **DAVID HEDGECOCK,** *associate publisher*, **JOHN BARBER,** *editor-in-chief*, **JUSTIN EISINGER,** *editorial director, graphic novels & collections*, **JERRY BENNINGTON,** *vp of new product development*, **LORELEI BUNJES,** *vp of technology & information services*, **JUD MEYERS,** *sales director*, **ANNA MORROW,** *marketing director*, **TARA McCRILLIS,** *director of design & production*, **MIKE FORD,** *director of operations*, **REBEKAH CAHALIN,** *general manager*, **TED ADAMS AND ROBBIE ROBBINS,** *IDW founders*

ONIPRESS.COM | LIONFORGE.COM | ADULTSWIM.COM
FACEBOOK.COM/ONIPRESS | FACEBOOK.COM/LIONFORGE | TWITTER.COM/RICKANDMORTY
TWITTER.COM/ONIPRESS | TWITTER.COM/LIONFORGE | DND.WIZARDS.COM
INSTAGRAM.COM/ONIPRESS | INSTAGRAM.COM/LIONFORGE | TWITTER.COM/WIZARDS_DND

First edition: March 2020

ISBN 978-1-62010-690-7
eISBN 978-1-62010-702-7
Oni Exclusive ISBN 978-1-62010-710-2

PRINTED IN USA.

Library of Congress Control Number: 2019940886

1 2 3 4 5 6 7 8 9 10

   [adult swim]™

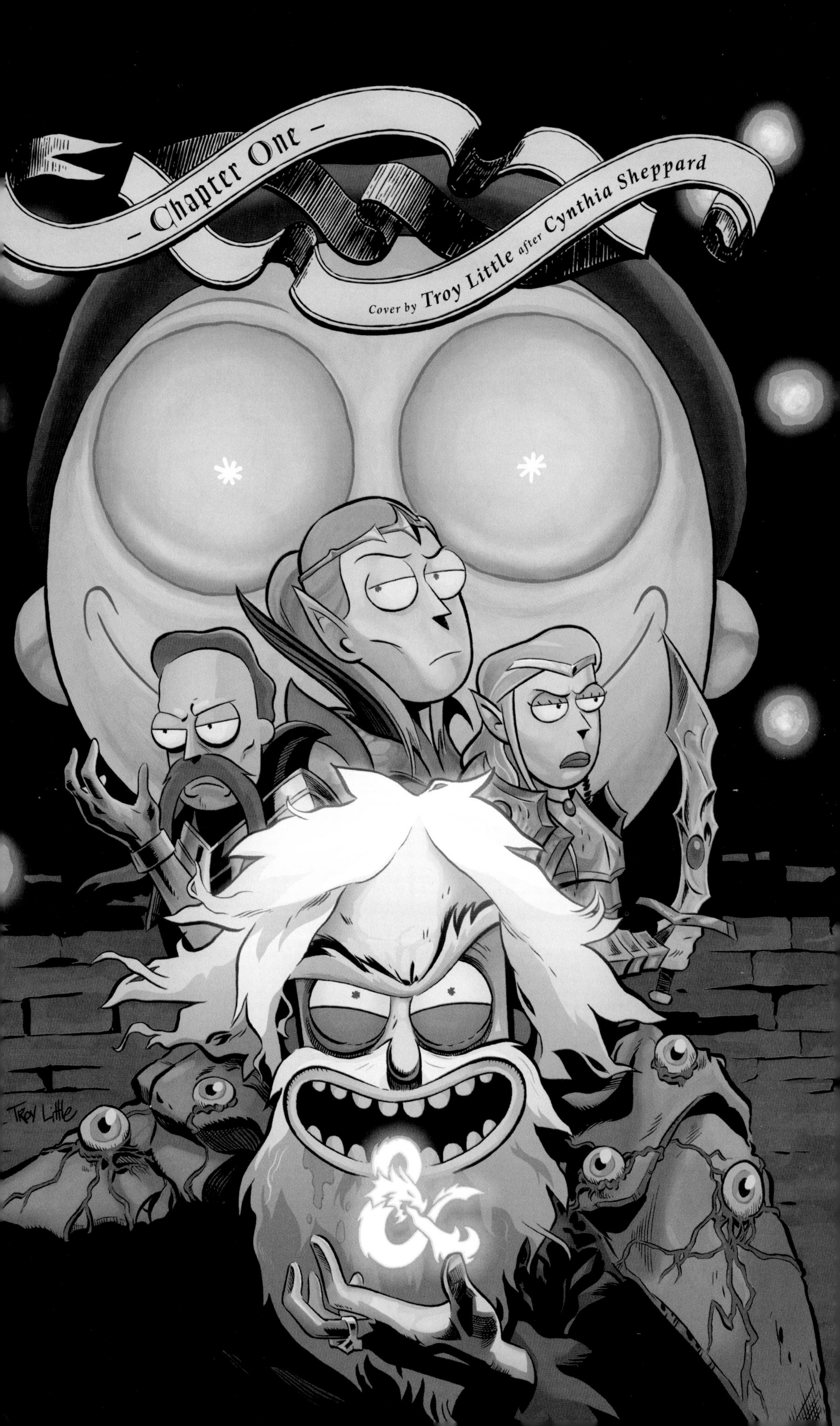

– Chapter One –
Cover by Troy Little after Cynthia Sheppard
TROY LITTLE

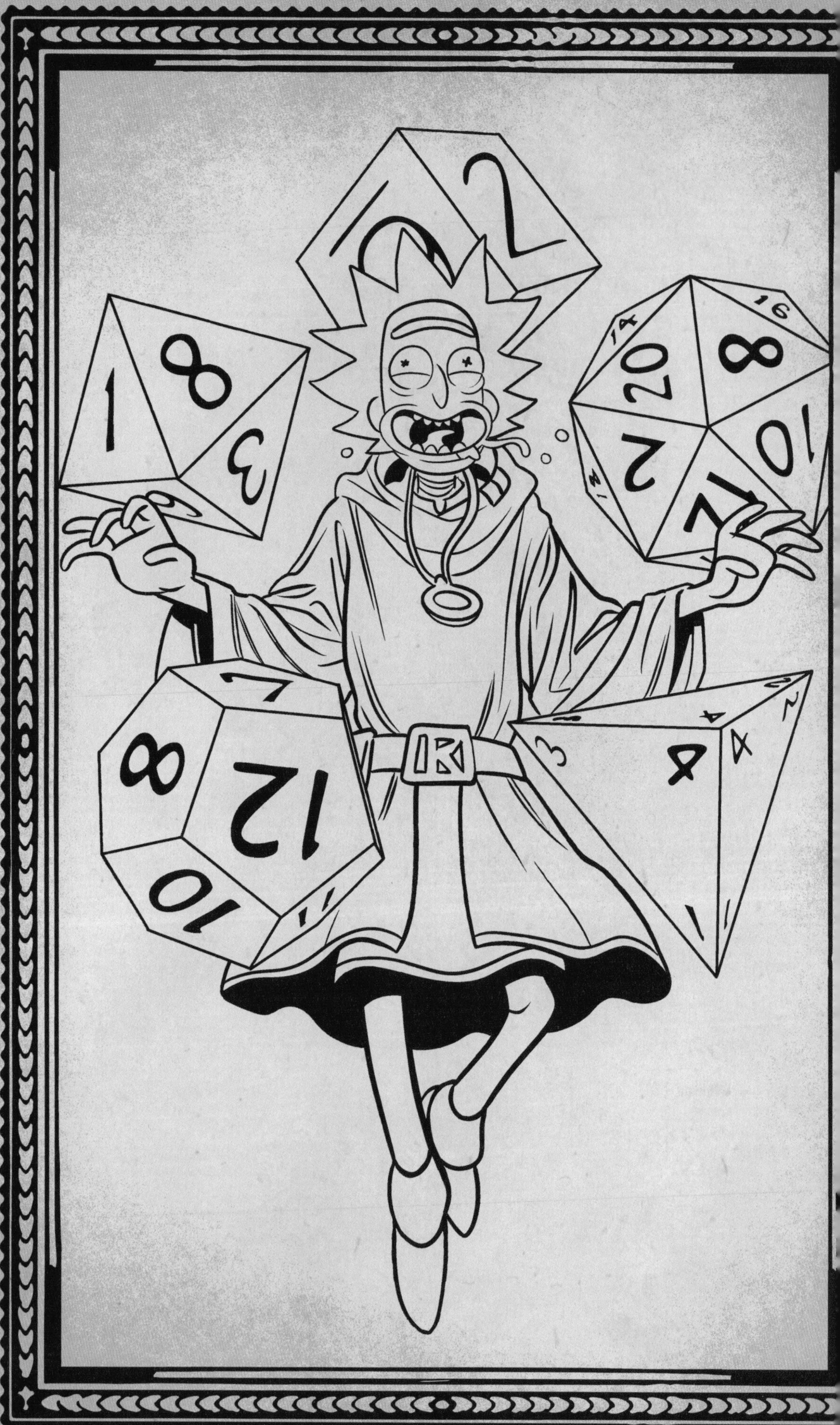

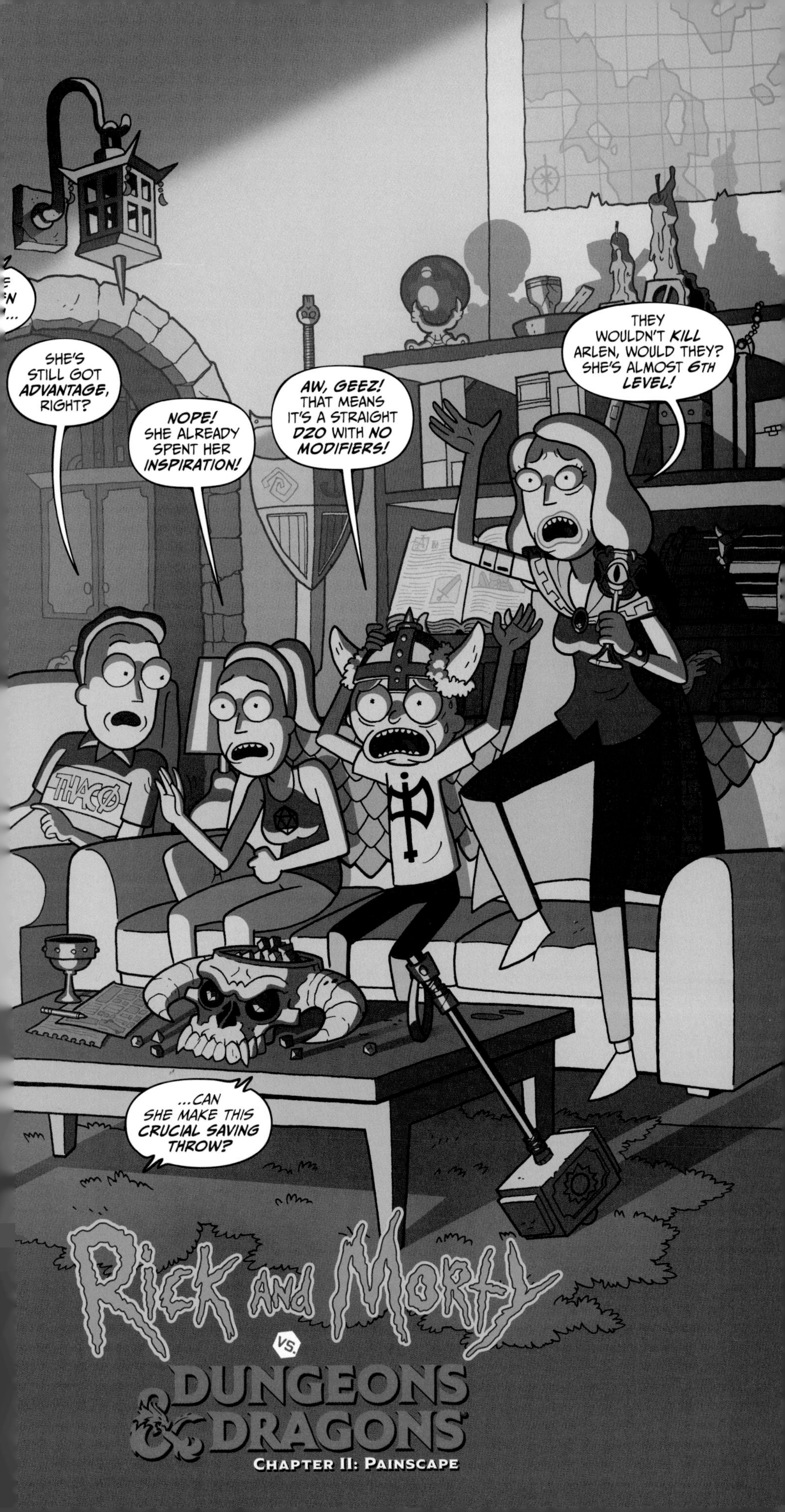
SHE'S STILL GOT ADVANTAGE, RIGHT?
NOPE! SHE ALREADY SPENT HER INSPIRATION!
AW, GEEZ! THAT MEANS IT'S A STRAIGHT D20 WITH NO MODIFIERS!
THEY WOULDN'T KILL ARLEN, WOULD THEY? SHE'S ALMOST 6TH LEVEL!
...CAN SHE MAKE THIS CRUCIAL SAVING THROW?
THAC0
Rick and Morty
VS.
DUNGEONS & DRAGONS
CHAPTER II: PAINSCAPE

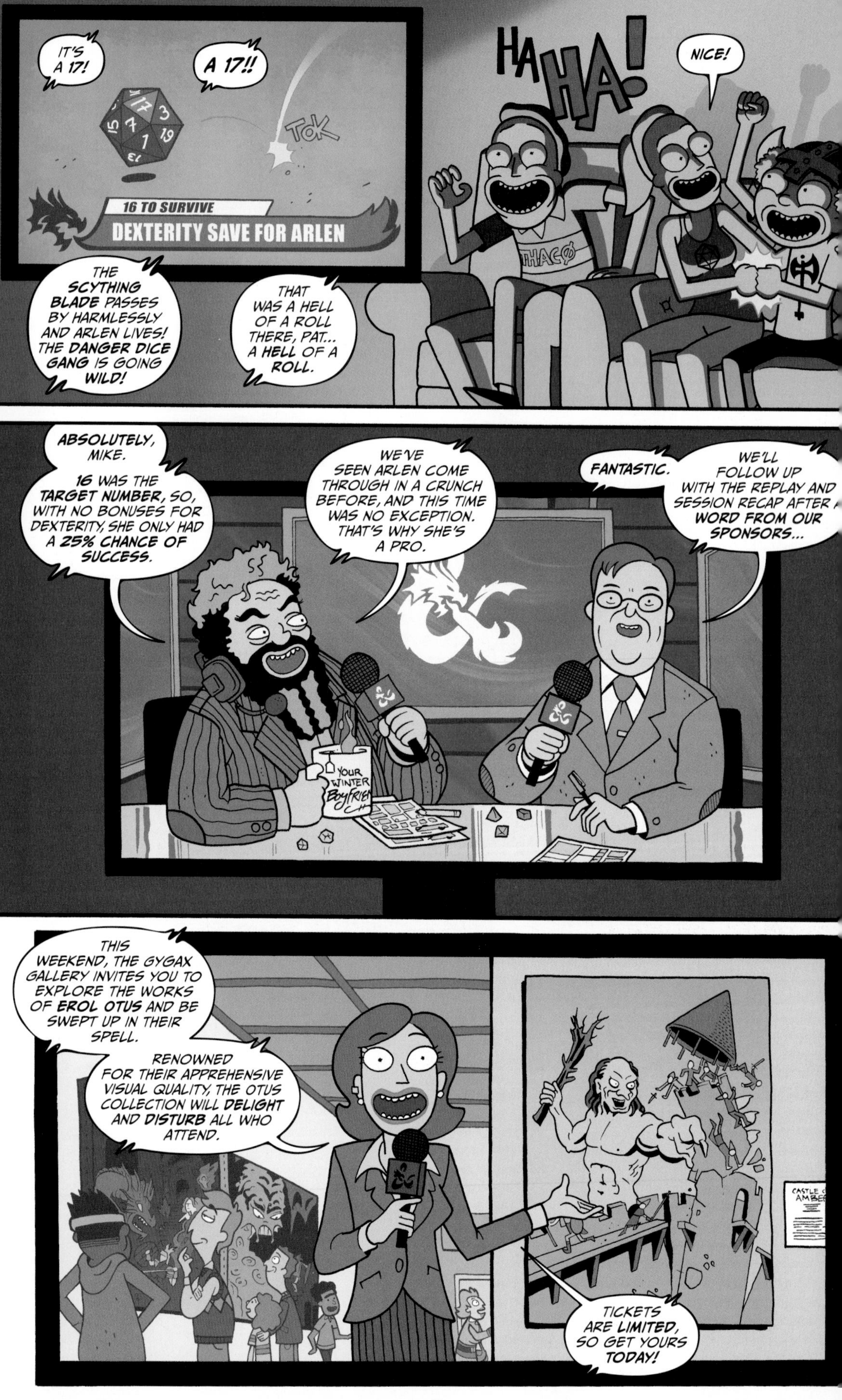

IT'S A 17!
A 17!!
TOK
16 TO SURVIVE
DEXTERITY SAVE FOR ARLEN
HAHA!
NICE!
THACØ
THE SCYTHING BLADE PASSES BY HARMLESSLY AND ARLEN LIVES! THE DANGER DICE GANG IS GOING WILD!
THAT WAS A HELL OF A ROLL THERE, PAT... A HELL OF A ROLL.
ABSOLUTELY, MIKE.
16 WAS THE TARGET NUMBER, SO, WITH NO BONUSES FOR DEXTERITY, SHE ONLY HAD A 25% CHANCE OF SUCCESS.
WE'VE SEEN ARLEN COME THROUGH IN A CRUNCH BEFORE, AND THIS TIME WAS NO EXCEPTION. THAT'S WHY SHE'S A PRO.
FANTASTIC.
WE'LL FOLLOW UP WITH THE REPLAY AND SESSION RECAP AFTER A WORD FROM OUR SPONSORS...
THIS WEEKEND, THE GYGAX GALLERY INVITES YOU TO EXPLORE THE WORKS OF EROL OTUS AND BE SWEPT UP IN THEIR SPELL.
RENOWNED FOR THEIR APPREHENSIVE VISUAL QUALITY, THE OTUS COLLECTION WILL DELIGHT AND DISTURB ALL WHO ATTEND.
TICKETS ARE LIMITED, SO GET YOURS TODAY!

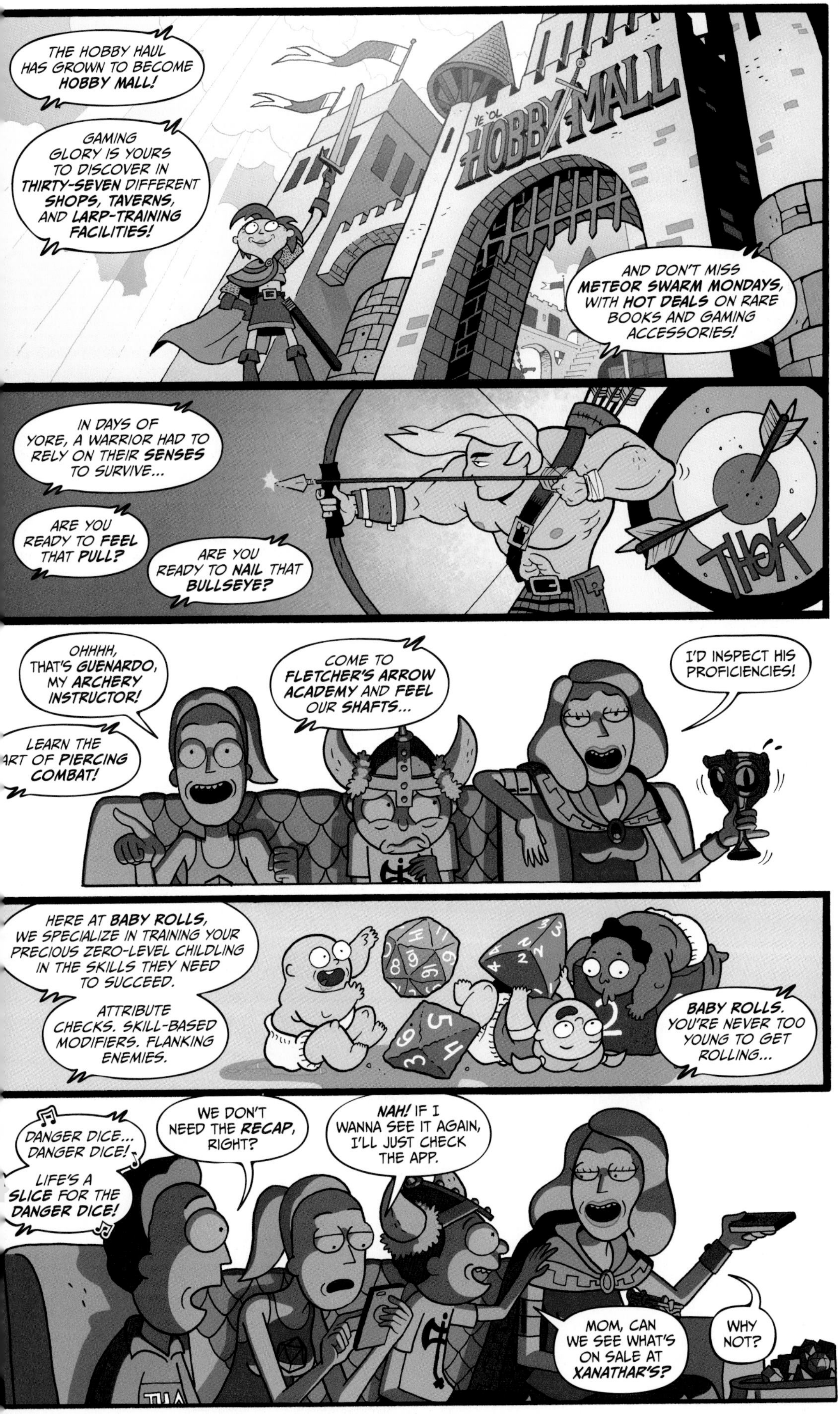
THE HOBBY HAUL HAS GROWN TO BECOME HOBBY MALL!
GAMING GLORY IS YOURS TO DISCOVER IN THIRTY-SEVEN DIFFERENT SHOPS, TAVERNS, AND LARP-TRAINING FACILITIES!
YE 'OL HOBBY MALL
AND DON'T MISS METEOR SWARM MONDAYS, WITH HOT DEALS ON RARE BOOKS AND GAMING ACCESSORIES!
IN DAYS OF YORE, A WARRIOR HAD TO RELY ON THEIR SENSES TO SURVIVE...
ARE YOU READY TO FEEL THAT PULL?
ARE YOU READY TO NAIL THAT BULLSEYE?
THOK
OHHHH, THAT'S GUENARDO, MY ARCHERY INSTRUCTOR!
LEARN THE ART OF PIERCING COMBAT!
COME TO FLETCHER'S ARROW ACADEMY AND FEEL OUR SHAFTS...
I'D INSPECT HIS PROFICIENCIES!
HERE AT BABY ROLLS, WE SPECIALIZE IN TRAINING YOUR PRECIOUS ZERO-LEVEL CHILDLING IN THE SKILLS THEY NEED TO SUCCEED.
ATTRIBUTE CHECKS. SKILL-BASED MODIFIERS. FLANKING ENEMIES.
BABY ROLLS. YOU'RE NEVER TOO YOUNG TO GET ROLLING...
DANGER DICE... DANGER DICE!
LIFE'S A SLICE FOR THE DANGER DICE!
WE DON'T NEED THE RECAP, RIGHT?
NAH! IF I WANNA SEE IT AGAIN, I'LL JUST CHECK THE APP.
MOM, CAN WE SEE WHAT'S ON SALE AT XANATHAR'S?
WHY NOT?

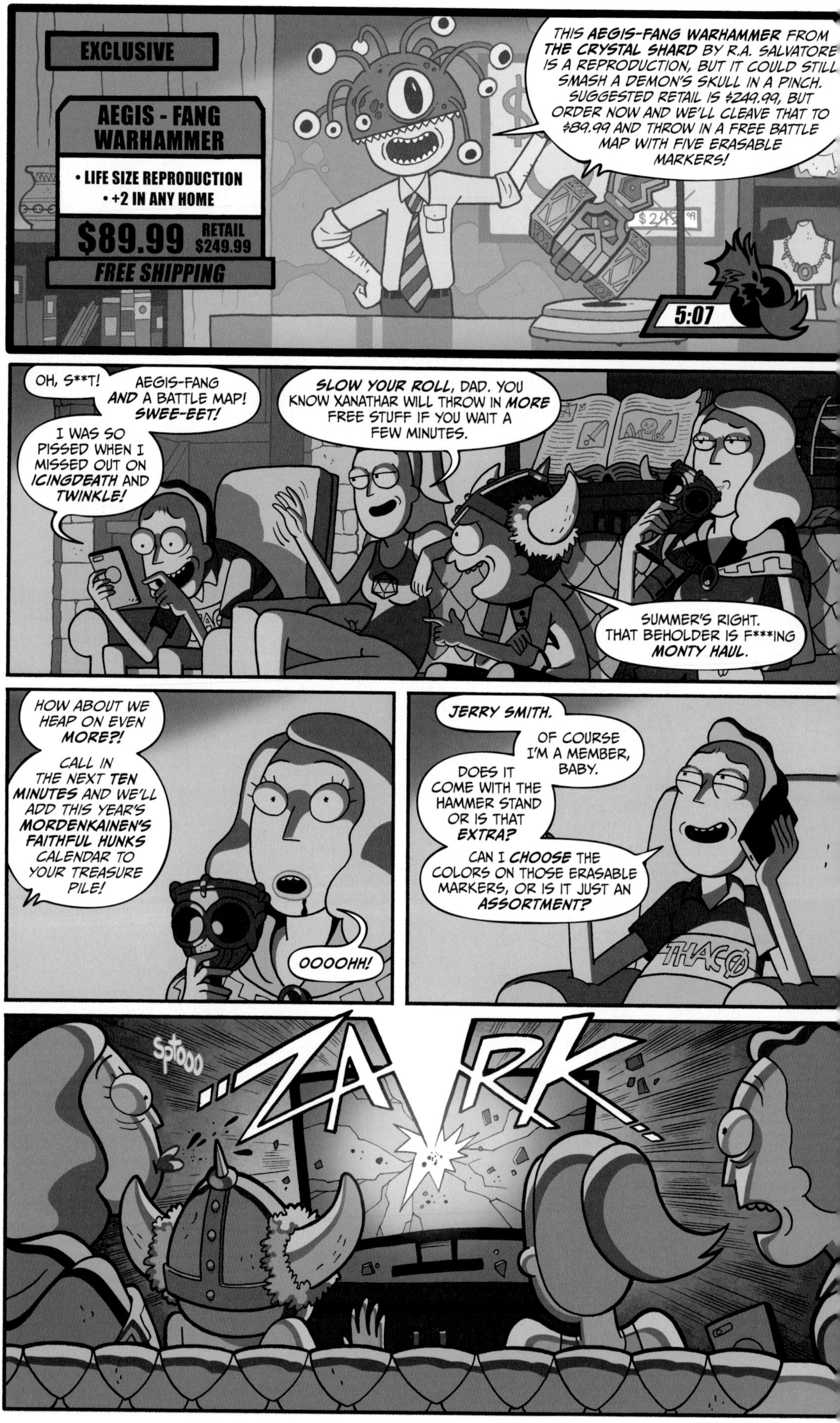
EXCLUSIVE
AEGIS - FANG WARHAMMER
• LIFE SIZE REPRODUCTION
• +2 IN ANY HOME
$89.99 RETAIL $249.99
FREE SHIPPING
THIS AEGIS-FANG WARHAMMER FROM THE CRYSTAL SHARD BY R.A. SALVATORE IS A REPRODUCTION, BUT IT COULD STILL SMASH A DEMON'S SKULL IN A PINCH. SUGGESTED RETAIL IS $249.99, BUT ORDER NOW AND WE'LL CLEAVE THAT TO $89.99 AND THROW IN A FREE BATTLE MAP WITH FIVE ERASABLE MARKERS!
5:07
OH, S**T!
AEGIS-FANG AND A BATTLE MAP! SWEE-EET!
I WAS SO PISSED WHEN I MISSED OUT ON ICINGDEATH AND TWINKLE!
SLOW YOUR ROLL, DAD. YOU KNOW XANATHAR WILL THROW IN MORE FREE STUFF IF YOU WAIT A FEW MINUTES.
SUMMER'S RIGHT. THAT BEHOLDER IS F***ING MONTY HAUL.
HOW ABOUT WE HEAP ON EVEN MORE?!
CALL IN THE NEXT TEN MINUTES AND WE'LL ADD THIS YEAR'S MORDENKAINEN'S FAITHFUL HUNKS CALENDAR TO YOUR TREASURE PILE!
OOOOHH!
JERRY SMITH.
OF COURSE I'M A MEMBER, BABY.
DOES IT COME WITH THE HAMMER STAND OR IS THAT EXTRA?
CAN I CHOOSE THE COLORS ON THOSE ERASABLE MARKERS, OR IS IT JUST AN ASSORTMENT?
THACØ
SPTOOO
...ZARK...

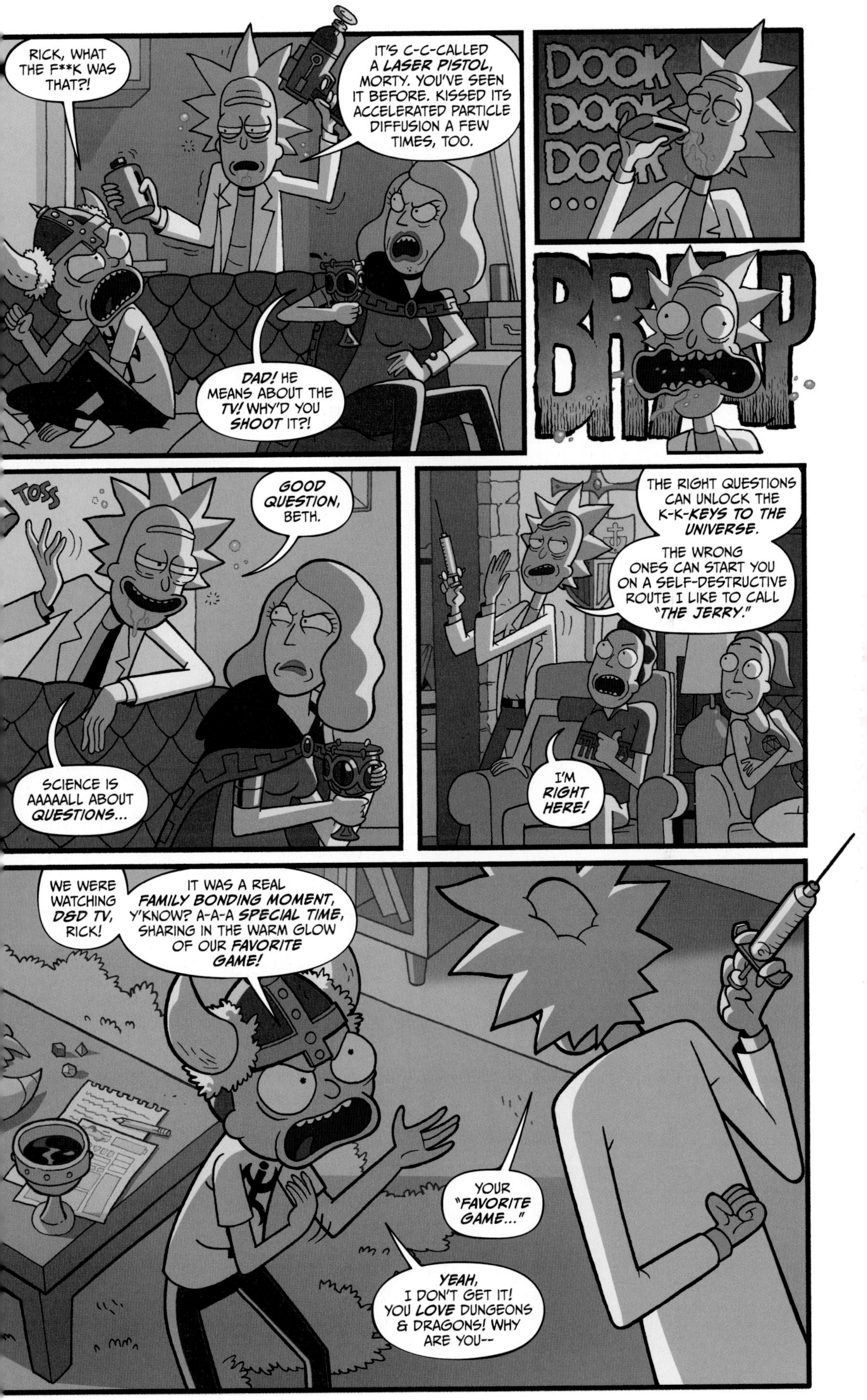
RICK, WHAT THE F**K WAS THAT?!
IT'S C-C-CALLED A *LASER PISTOL*, MORTY. YOU'VE SEEN IT BEFORE. KISSED ITS ACCELERATED PARTICLE DIFFUSION A FEW TIMES, TOO.
DAD! HE MEANS ABOUT THE *TV!* WHY'D YOU *SHOOT* IT?!
DOOK DOOK DOOK...
BRAP
TOSS
GOOD QUESTION, BETH.
SCIENCE IS AAAAALL ABOUT *QUESTIONS...*
THE RIGHT QUESTIONS CAN UNLOCK THE K-K-*KEYS TO THE UNIVERSE.*
THE WRONG ONES CAN START YOU ON A SELF-DESTRUCTIVE ROUTE I LIKE TO CALL *"THE JERRY."*
I'M *RIGHT HERE!*
WE WERE WATCHING *D&D TV,* RICK!
IT WAS A REAL *FAMILY BONDING MOMENT,* Y'KNOW? A-A-A *SPECIAL TIME,* SHARING IN THE WARM GLOW OF OUR *FAVORITE GAME!*
YOUR *"FAVORITE GAME..."*
YEAH, I DON'T GET IT! YOU *LOVE* DUNGEONS & DRAGONS! WHY ARE YOU--

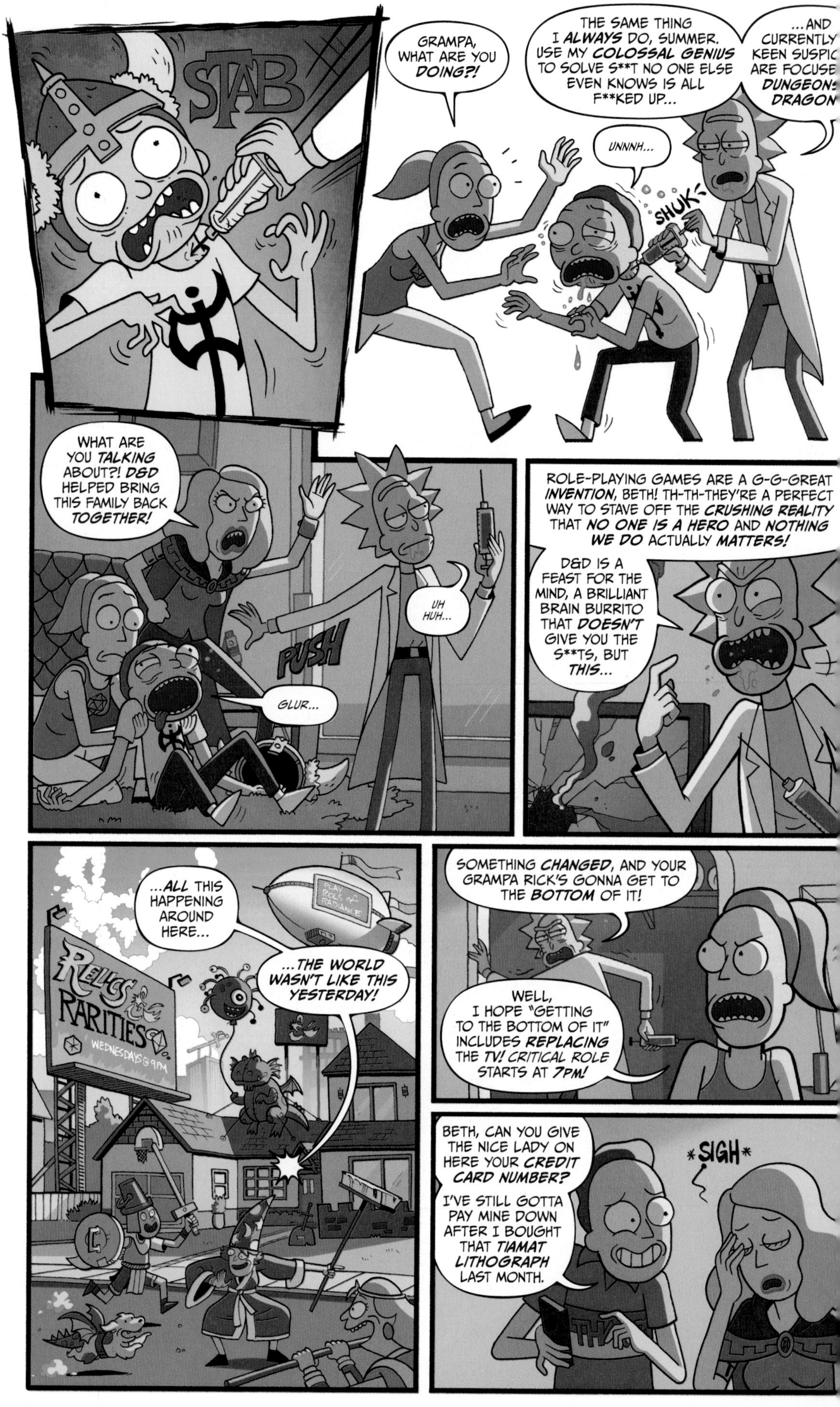
STAB
GRAMPA, WHAT ARE YOU DOING?!
THE SAME THING I ALWAYS DO, SUMMER. USE MY COLOSSAL GENIUS TO SOLVE S**T NO ONE ELSE EVEN KNOWS IS ALL F**KED UP...
...AND CURRENTLY KEEN SUSPIC ARE FOCUSE DUNGEONS DRAGON
UNNNH...
SHUK
WHAT ARE YOU TALKING ABOUT?! D&D HELPED BRING THIS FAMILY BACK TOGETHER!
UH HUH...
PUSH
GLUR...
ROLE-PLAYING GAMES ARE A G-G-GREAT INVENTION, BETH! TH-TH-THEY'RE A PERFECT WAY TO STAVE OFF THE CRUSHING REALITY THAT NO ONE IS A HERO AND NOTHING WE DO ACTUALLY MATTERS!
D&D IS A FEAST FOR THE MIND, A BRILLIANT BRAIN BURRITO THAT DOESN'T GIVE YOU THE S**TS, BUT THIS...
...ALL THIS HAPPENING AROUND HERE...
...THE WORLD WASN'T LIKE THIS YESTERDAY!
PLAY POOLS of RADIANCE
RARITIES
WEDNESDAYS @ 9PM
SOMETHING CHANGED, AND YOUR GRAMPA RICK'S GONNA GET TO THE BOTTOM OF IT!
WELL, I HOPE "GETTING TO THE BOTTOM OF IT" INCLUDES REPLACING THE TV! CRITICAL ROLE STARTS AT 7PM!
BETH, CAN YOU GIVE THE NICE LADY ON HERE YOUR CREDIT CARD NUMBER?
I'VE STILL GOTTA PAY MINE DOWN AFTER I BOUGHT THAT TIAMAT LITHOGRAPH LAST MONTH.
SIGH

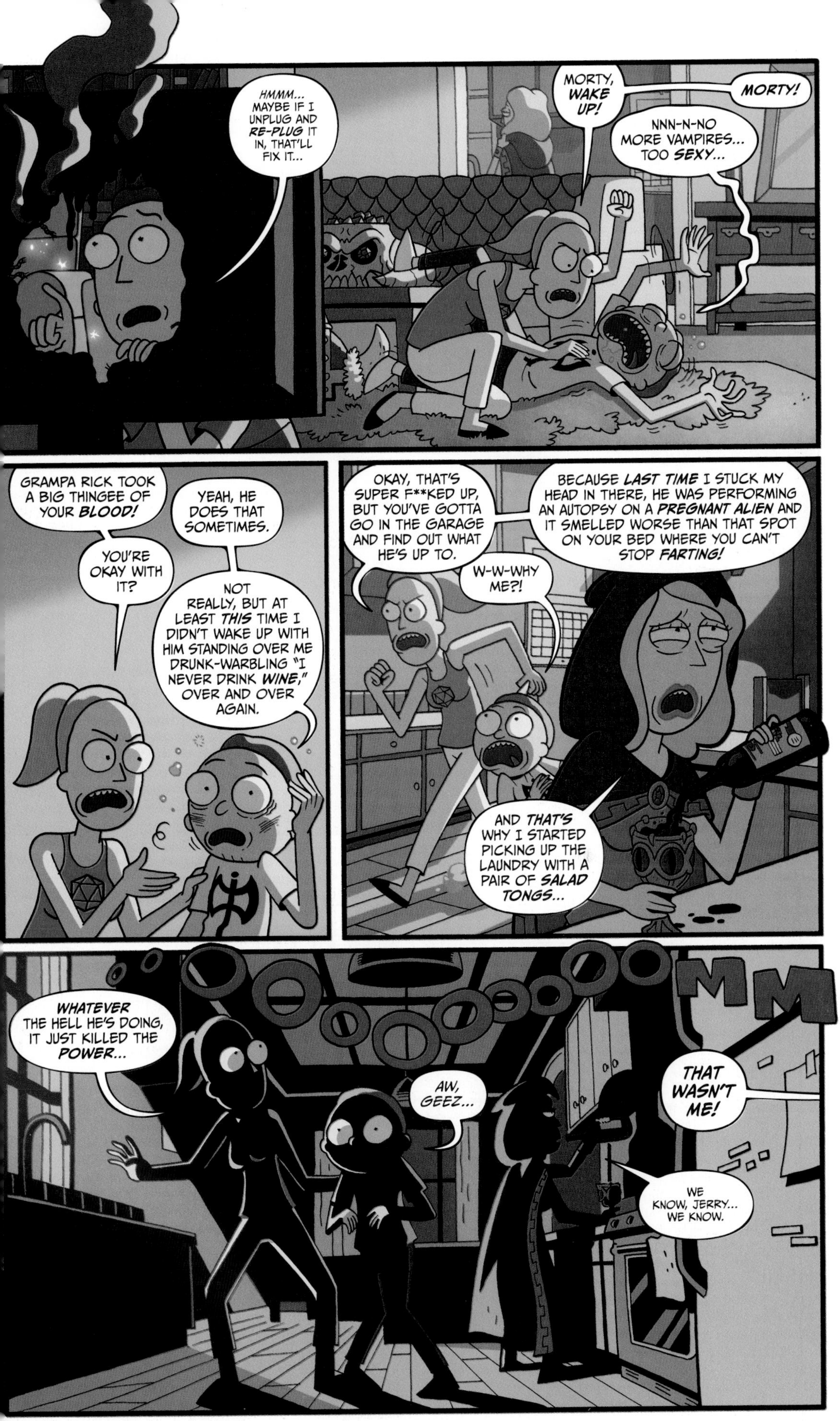
HMMM... MAYBE IF I UNPLUG AND RE-PLUG IT IN, THAT'LL FIX IT...
MORTY, WAKE UP!
MORTY!
NNN-N-NO MORE VAMPIRES... TOO SEXY...
GRAMPA RICK TOOK A BIG THINGEE OF YOUR BLOOD!
YEAH, HE DOES THAT SOMETIMES.
YOU'RE OKAY WITH IT?
NOT REALLY, BUT AT LEAST THIS TIME I DIDN'T WAKE UP WITH HIM STANDING OVER ME DRUNK-WARBLING "I NEVER DRINK WINE," OVER AND OVER AGAIN.
OKAY, THAT'S SUPER F**KED UP, BUT YOU'VE GOTTA GO IN THE GARAGE AND FIND OUT WHAT HE'S UP TO.
BECAUSE LAST TIME I STUCK MY HEAD IN THERE, HE WAS PERFORMING AN AUTOPSY ON A PREGNANT ALIEN AND IT SMELLED WORSE THAN THAT SPOT ON YOUR BED WHERE YOU CAN'T STOP FARTING!
W-W-WHY ME?!
AND THAT'S WHY I STARTED PICKING UP THE LAUNDRY WITH A PAIR OF SALAD TONGS...
OOOOOOOOOOOOOOOMM
WHATEVER THE HELL HE'S DOING, IT JUST KILLED THE POWER...
AW, GEEZ...
THAT WASN'T ME!
WE KNOW, JERRY... WE KNOW.

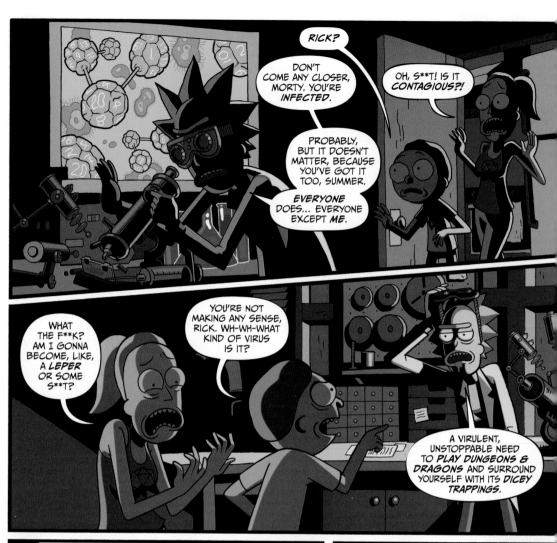

RICK?

DON'T COME ANY CLOSER, MORTY. YOU'RE INFECTED.

OH, S**T! IS IT CONTAGIOUS?!

PROBABLY, BUT IT DOESN'T MATTER, BECAUSE YOU'VE GOT IT TOO, SUMMER.

EVERYONE DOES... EVERYONE EXCEPT ME.

WHAT THE F**K? AM I GONNA BECOME, LIKE, A LEPER OR SOME S**T?

YOU'RE NOT MAKING ANY SENSE, RICK. WH-WH-WHAT KIND OF VIRUS IS IT?

A VIRULENT, UNSTOPPABLE NEED TO PLAY DUNGEONS & DRAGONS AND SURROUND YOURSELF WITH ITS DICEY TRAPPINGS.

D&D WAS ASCENDING THE POP CULTURE LADDER, MORTY.

IT GOT A BIT OF PLAY ON LATE-NIGHT TALK SHOWS AND ARTICLES IN HIGH-PROFILE MAGAZINES. EVEN A FEW CELEBRITIES F**KED THE BANDWAGON FOR A BIT.

IT WAS WEIRD AND UNEXPECTED, BUT STILL WITHIN THE PRACTICAL LIMITS OF GEEK REALITY WE COULD COMPREHEND.

BUT, THIS? THIS S**T IS BANANAS. B-A-N-A-NANAS.

LARP S**T

ARE YOU SURE?

WHAT'S YOUR FAVORITE BOOK, MORTY?

DRAGONS OF AUTUMN TWILIGHT.

BEST VIDEO GAME?

BALDUR'S GATE II: SHADOWS OF AMN.

WHAT'D YOU HAVE FOR BREAKFAST?

DROW FLAKES WITH LOLTH-BERRIES.

YUP. A D20 DEPENDENCE OUTBREAK, AND IT'S NOT FROM OUR DIMENSION...

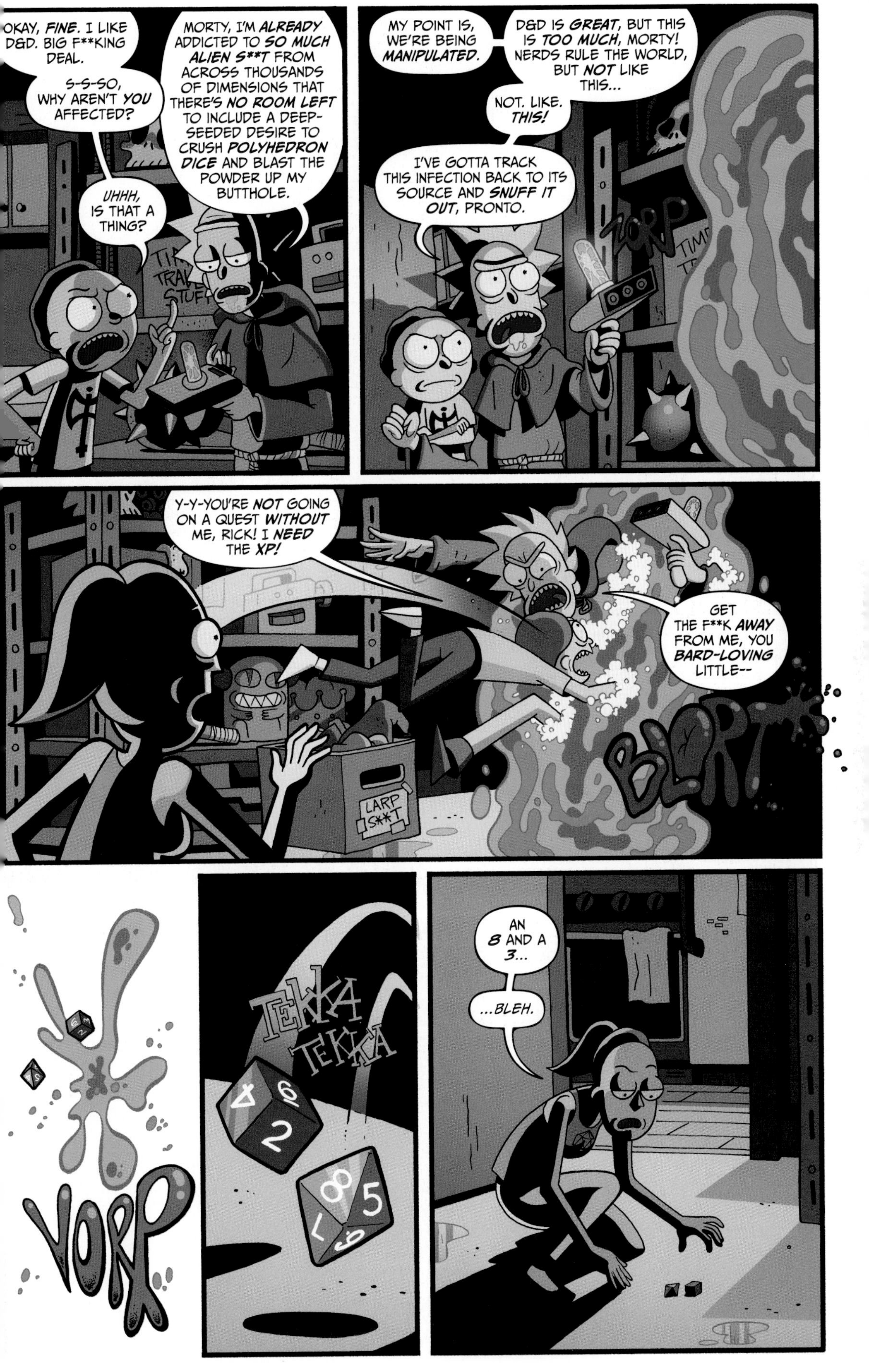
OKAY, FINE. I LIKE D&D. BIG F**KING DEAL.
S-S-SO, WHY AREN'T YOU AFFECTED?
MORTY, I'M ALREADY ADDICTED TO SO MUCH ALIEN S**T FROM ACROSS THOUSANDS OF DIMENSIONS THAT THERE'S NO ROOM LEFT TO INCLUDE A DEEP-SEEDED DESIRE TO CRUSH POLYHEDRON DICE AND BLAST THE POWDER UP MY BUTTHOLE.
UHHH, IS THAT A THING?
MY POINT IS, WE'RE BEING MANIPULATED.
D&D IS GREAT, BUT THIS IS TOO MUCH, MORTY! NERDS RULE THE WORLD, BUT NOT LIKE THIS...
NOT. LIKE. THIS!
I'VE GOTTA TRACK THIS INFECTION BACK TO ITS SOURCE AND SNUFF IT OUT, PRONTO.
ZORP
Y-Y-YOU'RE NOT GOING ON A QUEST WITHOUT ME, RICK! I NEED THE XP!
GET THE F**K AWAY FROM ME, YOU BARD-LOVING LITTLE--
BLORT
LARP S**T
VORP
TEKKA TEKKA
AN 8 AND A 3...
...BLEH.

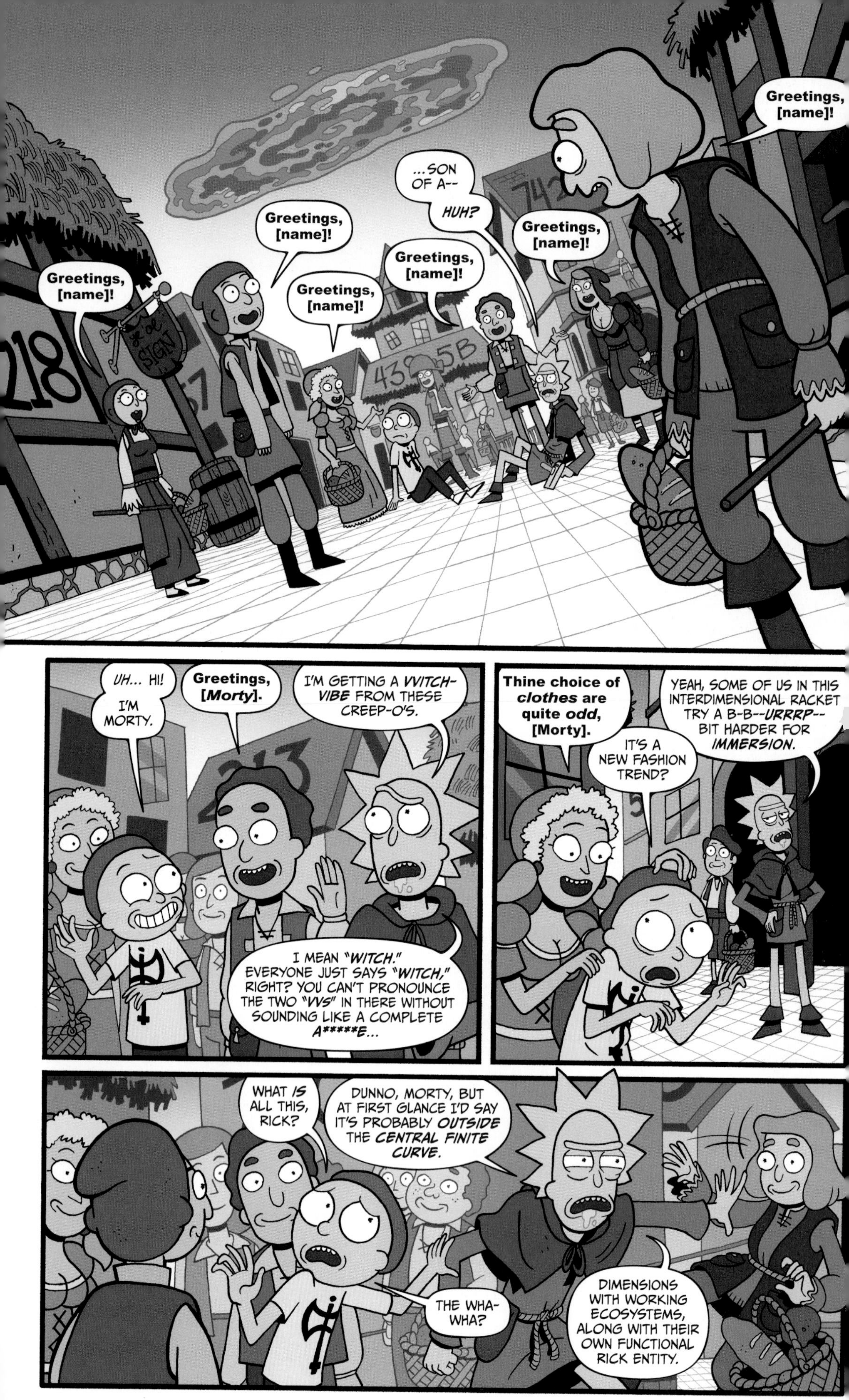
Greetings, [name]!
Greetings, [name]!
Greetings, [name]!
Greetings, [name]!
...SON OF A--
HUH?
Greetings, [name]!
Greetings, [name]!
UH... HI! I'M MORTY.
Greetings, [Morty].
I'M GETTING A VVITCH-VIBE FROM THESE CREEP-O'S.
I MEAN "WITCH." EVERYONE JUST SAYS "WITCH," RIGHT? YOU CAN'T PRONOUNCE THE TWO "VVS" IN THERE WITHOUT SOUNDING LIKE A COMPLETE A*****E...
Thine choice of clothes are quite odd, [Morty].
IT'S A NEW FASHION TREND?
YEAH, SOME OF US IN THIS INTERDIMENSIONAL RACKET TRY A B-B--URRRP-- BIT HARDER FOR IMMERSION.
WHAT IS ALL THIS, RICK?
DUNNO, MORTY, BUT AT FIRST GLANCE I'D SAY IT'S PROBABLY OUTSIDE THE CENTRAL FINITE CURVE.
THE WHA-WHA?
DIMENSIONS WITH WORKING ECOSYSTEMS, ALONG WITH THEIR OWN FUNCTIONAL RICK ENTITY.

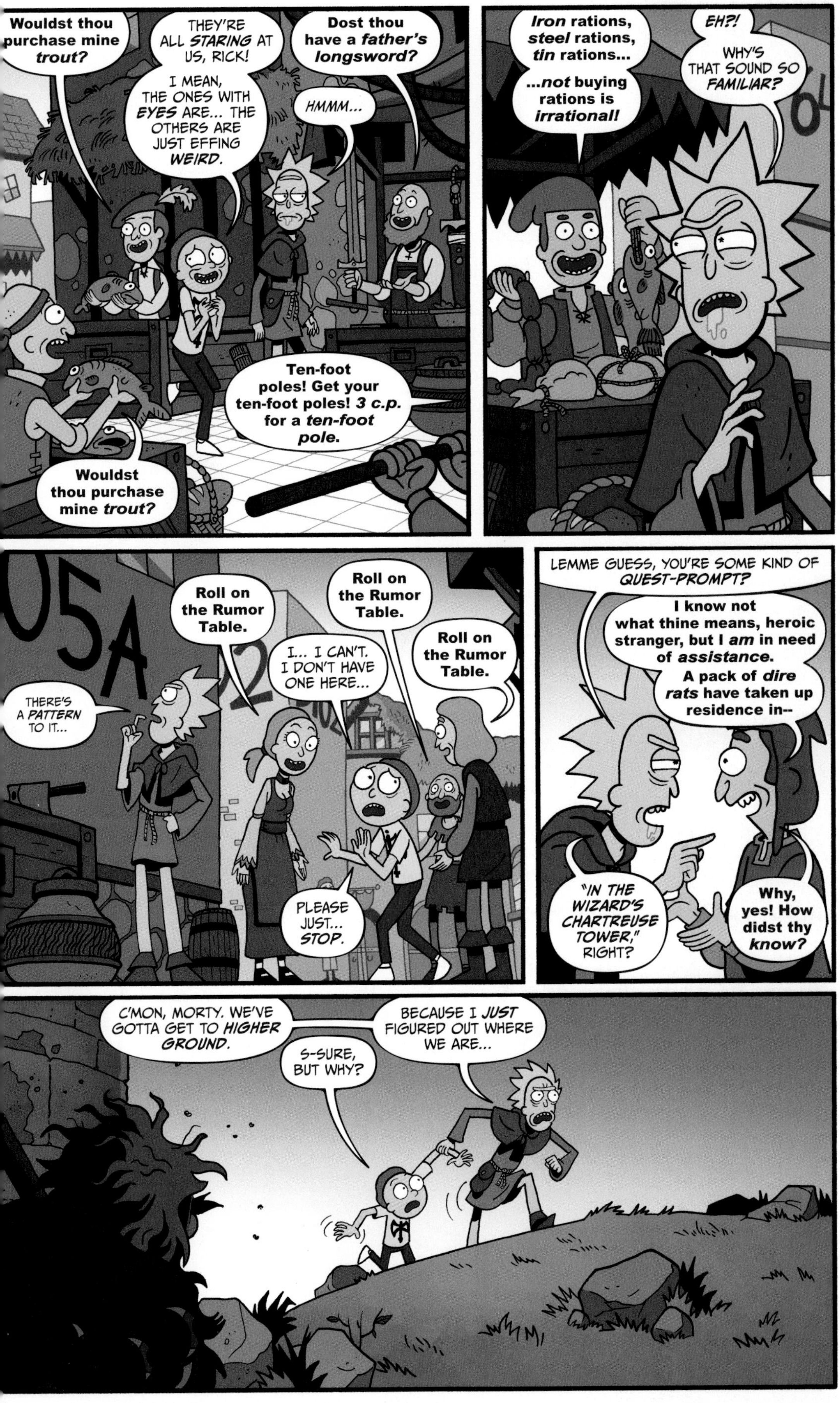

Wouldst thou purchase mine *trout?*
THEY'RE ALL *STARING* AT US, RICK!
I MEAN, THE ONES WITH *EYES* ARE... THE OTHERS ARE JUST EFFING *WEIRD.*
Dost thou have a *father's longsword?*
HMMM...
Ten-foot poles! Get your ten-foot poles! *3 c.p.* for a *ten-foot pole.*
Wouldst thou purchase mine *trout?*
Iron rations, *steel* rations, *tin* rations...
...*not* buying rations is *irrational!*
EH?!
WHY'S THAT SOUND SO *FAMILIAR?*
THERE'S A *PATTERN* TO IT...
Roll on the Rumor Table.
Roll on the Rumor Table.
I... I CAN'T. I DON'T HAVE ONE HERE...
Roll on the Rumor Table.
PLEASE JUST... *STOP.*
LEMME GUESS, YOU'RE SOME KIND OF *QUEST-PROMPT?*
I know not what thine means, heroic stranger, but I *am* in need of *assistance.*
A pack of *dire rats* have taken up residence in--
"IN THE WIZARD'S CHARTREUSE TOWER," RIGHT?
Why, yes! How didst thy *know?*
C'MON, MORTY. WE'VE GOTTA GET TO *HIGHER GROUND.*
S-SURE, BUT WHY?
BECAUSE I *JUST* FIGURED OUT WHERE WE ARE...

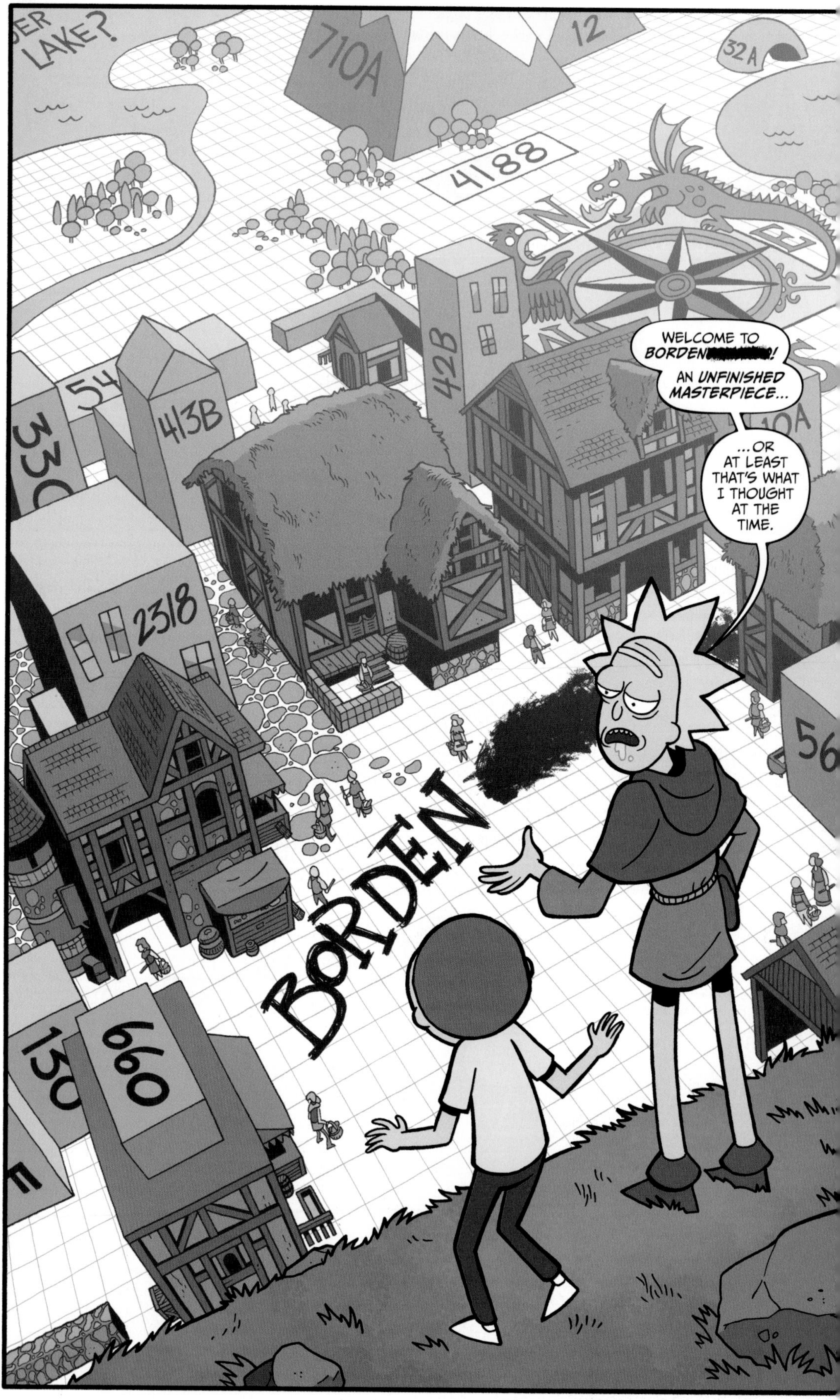
LAKE?
710A
12
32A
4188
42B
413B
2318
WELCOME TO BORDEN[redacted]! AN *UNFINISHED MASTERPIECE*...
...OR AT LEAST THAT'S WHAT I THOUGHT AT THE TIME.
BORDEN

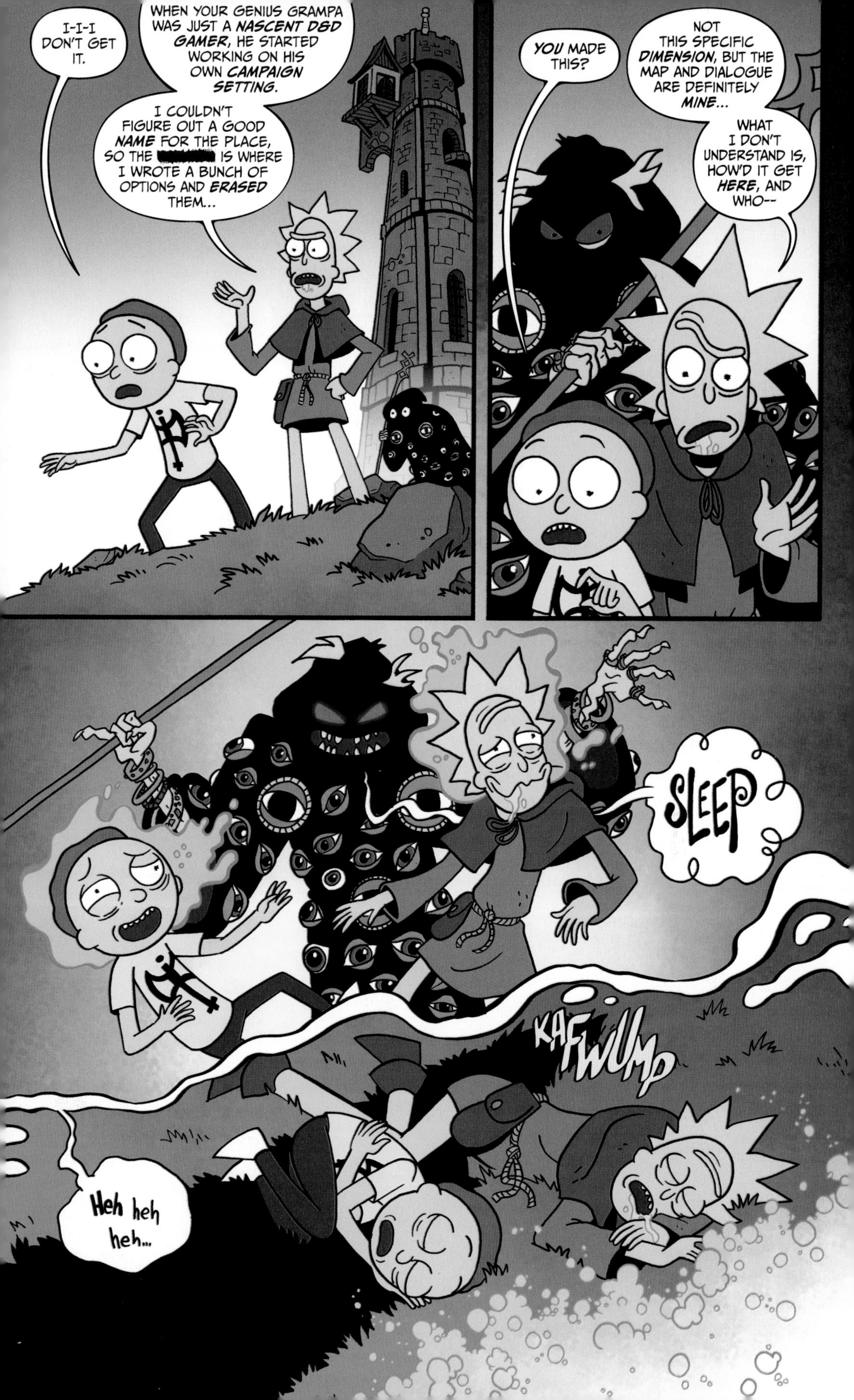
I-I-I DON'T GET IT.
WHEN YOUR GENIUS GRAMPA WAS JUST A NASCENT D&D GAMER, HE STARTED WORKING ON HIS OWN CAMPAIGN SETTING.
I COULDN'T FIGURE OUT A GOOD NAME FOR THE PLACE, SO THE [redacted] IS WHERE I WROTE A BUNCH OF OPTIONS AND ERASED THEM...
YOU MADE THIS?
NOT THIS SPECIFIC DIMENSION, BUT THE MAP AND DIALOGUE ARE DEFINITELY MINE...
WHAT I DON'T UNDERSTAND IS, HOW'D IT GET HERE, AND WHO--
SLEEP
KAFWUMP
Heh heh heh...

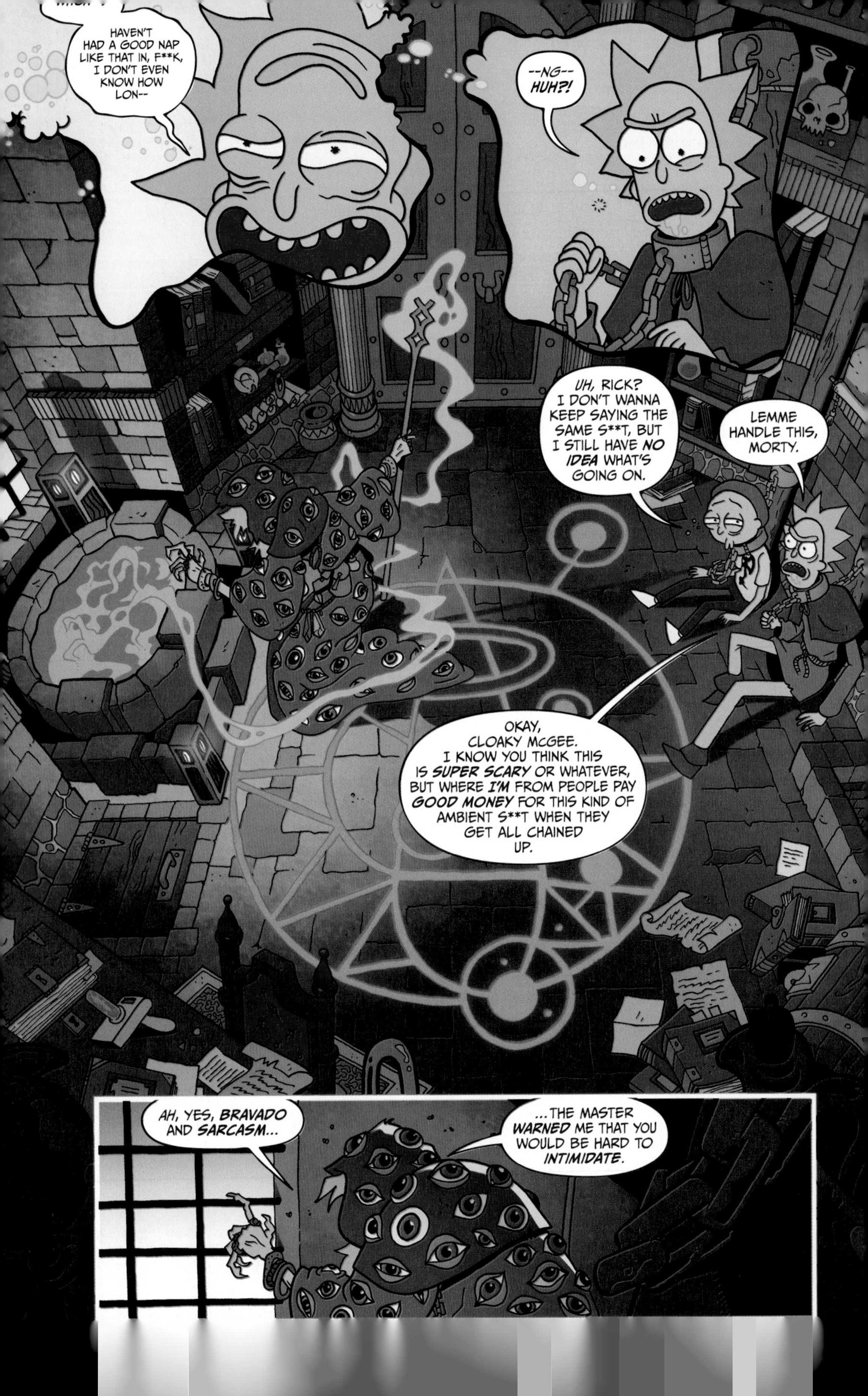
HAVEN'T HAD A GOOD NAP LIKE THAT IN, F**K, I DON'T EVEN KNOW HOW LON--
--NG-- HUH?!
UH, RICK? I DON'T WANNA KEEP SAYING THE SAME S**T, BUT I STILL HAVE NO IDEA WHAT'S GOING ON.
LEMME HANDLE THIS, MORTY.
OKAY, CLOAKY McGEE. I KNOW YOU THINK THIS IS SUPER SCARY OR WHATEVER, BUT WHERE I'M FROM PEOPLE PAY GOOD MONEY FOR THIS KIND OF AMBIENT S**T WHEN THEY GET ALL CHAINED UP.
AH, YES, BRAVADO AND SARCASM...
...THE MASTER WARNED ME THAT YOU WOULD BE HARD TO INTIMIDATE.

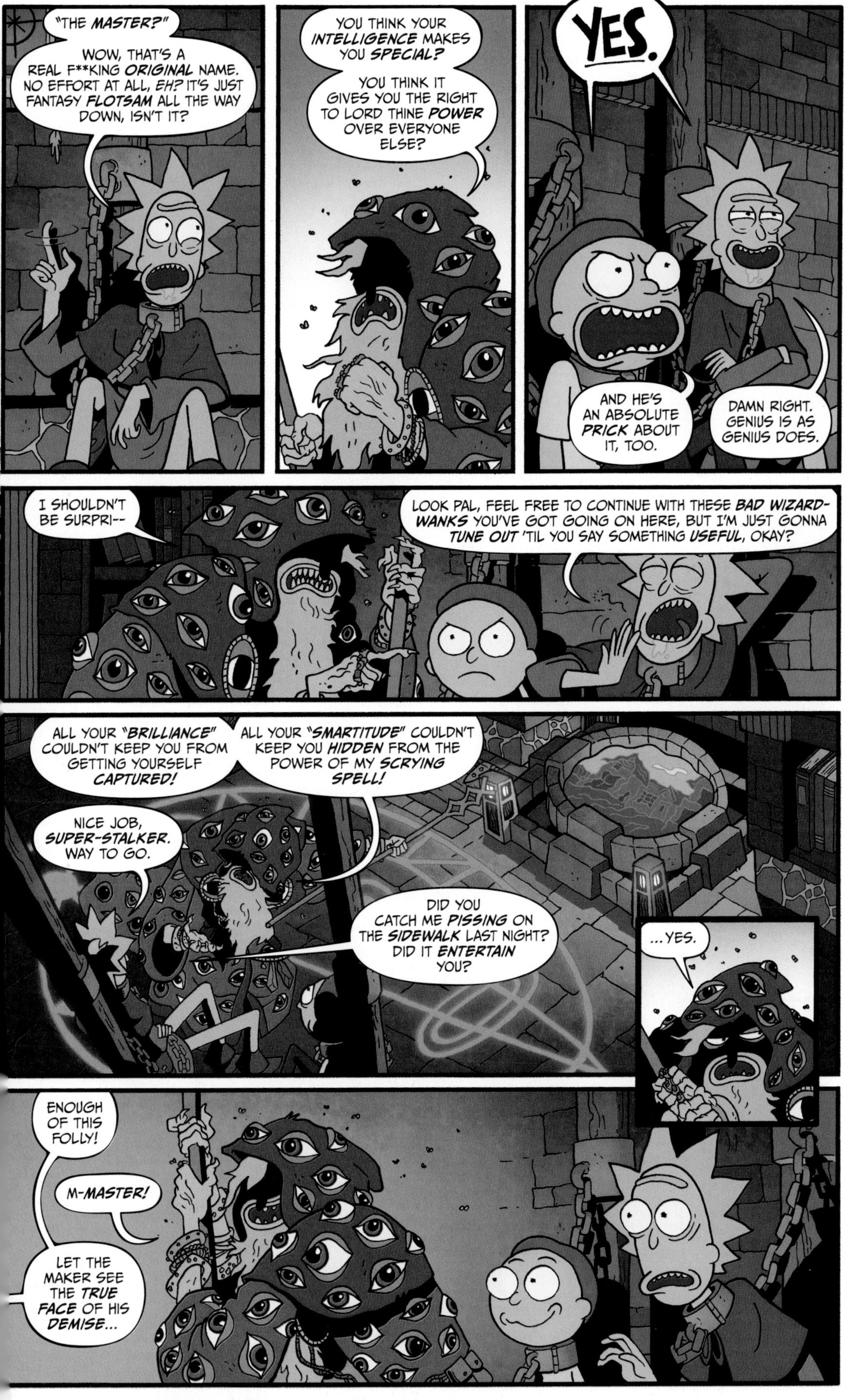
"THE MASTER?"
WOW, THAT'S A REAL F**KING ORIGINAL NAME. NO EFFORT AT ALL, EH? IT'S JUST FANTASY FLOTSAM ALL THE WAY DOWN, ISN'T IT?
YOU THINK YOUR INTELLIGENCE MAKES YOU SPECIAL?
YOU THINK IT GIVES YOU THE RIGHT TO LORD THINE POWER OVER EVERYONE ELSE?
YES.
AND HE'S AN ABSOLUTE PRICK ABOUT IT, TOO.
DAMN RIGHT. GENIUS IS AS GENIUS DOES.
I SHOULDN'T BE SURPRI--
LOOK PAL, FEEL FREE TO CONTINUE WITH THESE BAD WIZARD-WANKS YOU'VE GOT GOING ON HERE, BUT I'M JUST GONNA TUNE OUT 'TIL YOU SAY SOMETHING USEFUL, OKAY?
ALL YOUR "BRILLIANCE" COULDN'T KEEP YOU FROM GETTING YOURSELF CAPTURED!
ALL YOUR "SMARTITUDE" COULDN'T KEEP YOU HIDDEN FROM THE POWER OF MY SCRYING SPELL!
NICE JOB, SUPER-STALKER. WAY TO GO.
DID YOU CATCH ME PISSING ON THE SIDEWALK LAST NIGHT? DID IT ENTERTAIN YOU?
...YES.
ENOUGH OF THIS FOLLY!
M-MASTER!
LET THE MAKER SEE THE TRUE FACE OF HIS DEMISE...

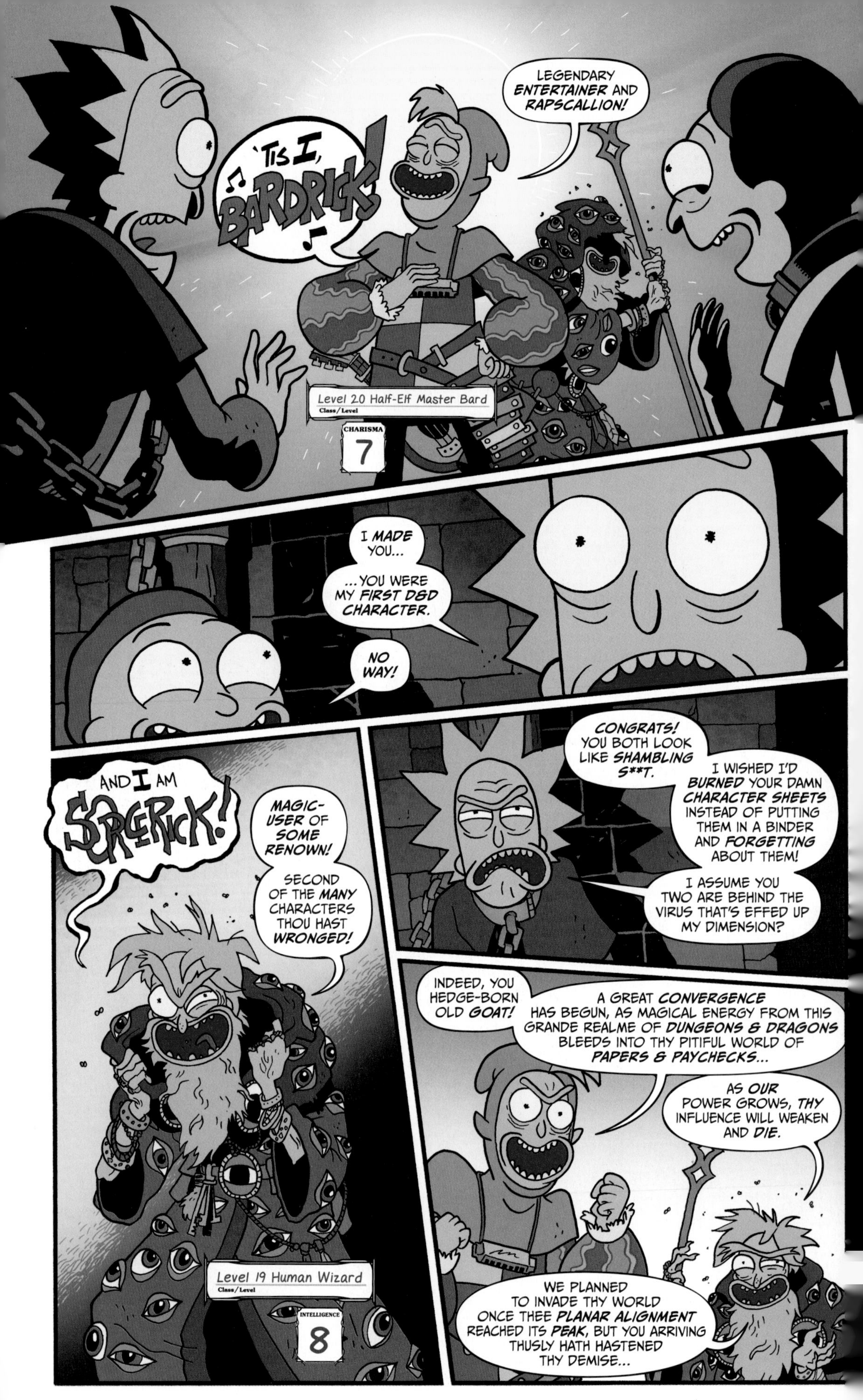
'TIS I, BARDRICK!
LEGENDARY ENTERTAINER AND RAPSCALLION!
Level 20 Half-Elf Master Bard
Class/Level
CHARISMA
7
I MADE YOU...
...YOU WERE MY FIRST D&D CHARACTER.
NO WAY!
AND I AM SORCERICK!
MAGIC-USER OF SOME RENOWN!
SECOND OF THE MANY CHARACTERS THOU HAST WRONGED!
Level 19 Human Wizard
Class/Level
INTELLIGENCE
8
CONGRATS! YOU BOTH LOOK LIKE SHAMBLING S**T.
I WISHED I'D BURNED YOUR DAMN CHARACTER SHEETS INSTEAD OF PUTTING THEM IN A BINDER AND FORGETTING ABOUT THEM!
I ASSUME YOU TWO ARE BEHIND THE VIRUS THAT'S EFFED UP MY DIMENSION?
INDEED, YOU HEDGE-BORN OLD GOAT!
A GREAT CONVERGENCE HAS BEGUN, AS MAGICAL ENERGY FROM THIS GRANDE REALME OF DUNGEONS & DRAGONS BLEEDS INTO THY PITIFUL WORLD OF PAPERS & PAYCHECKS...
AS OUR POWER GROWS, THY INFLUENCE WILL WEAKEN AND DIE.
WE PLANNED TO INVADE THY WORLD ONCE THEE PLANAR ALIGNMENT REACHED ITS PEAK, BUT YOU ARRIVING THUSLY HATH HASTENED THY DEMISE...

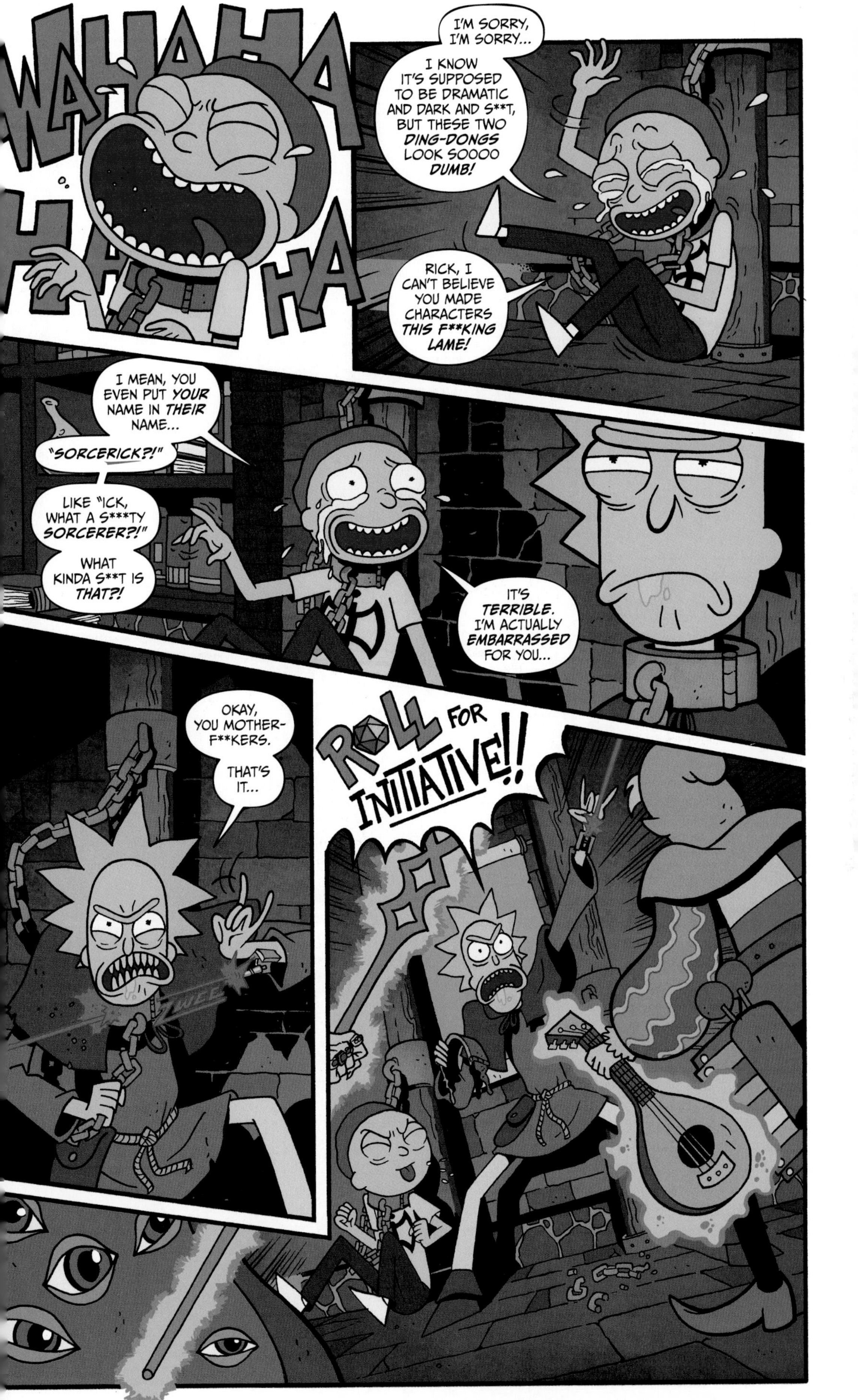
WAHAHA HA HA HA
I'M SORRY, I'M SORRY...
I KNOW IT'S SUPPOSED TO BE DRAMATIC AND DARK AND S**T, BUT THESE TWO DING-DONGS LOOK SOOOO DUMB!
RICK, I CAN'T BELIEVE YOU MADE CHARACTERS THIS F**KING LAME!
I MEAN, YOU EVEN PUT YOUR NAME IN THEIR NAME...
"SORCERICK?!"
LIKE "ICK, WHAT A S***TY SORCERER?!"
WHAT KINDA S**T IS THAT?!
IT'S TERRIBLE. I'M ACTUALLY EMBARRASSED FOR YOU...
OKAY, YOU MOTHER-F**KERS.
THAT'S IT...
ROLL FOR INITIATIVE!!

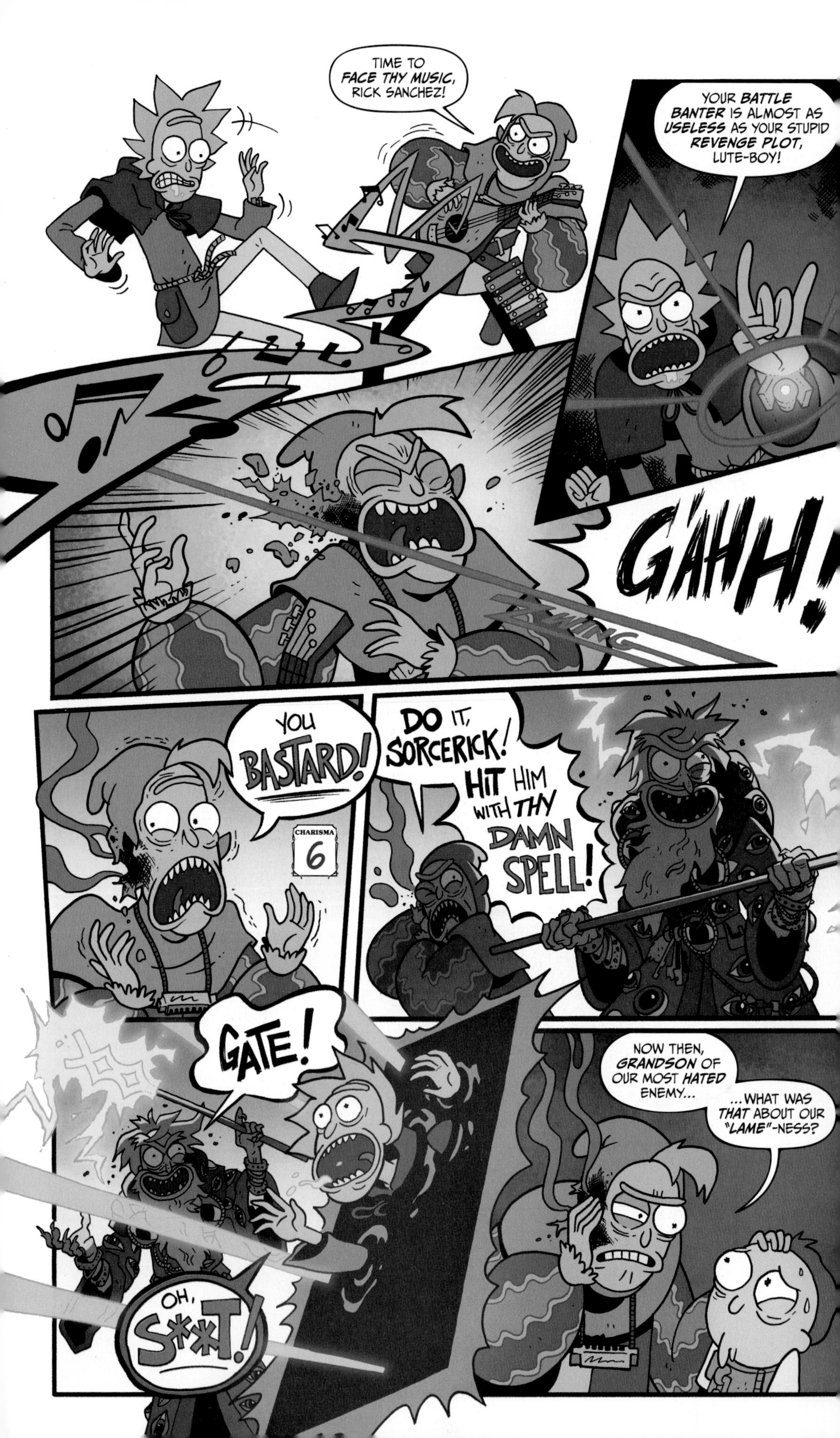

TIME TO FACE THY MUSIC, RICK SANCHEZ!
YOUR BATTLE BANTER IS ALMOST AS USELESS AS YOUR STUPID REVENGE PLOT, LUTE-BOY!
GAHH!
ZWING
YOU BASTARD!
CHARISMA
6
DO IT, SORCERICK!
HIT HIM WITH THY DAMN SPELL!
GATE!
OH, S**T!
NOW THEN, GRANDSON OF OUR MOST HATED ENEMY...
...WHAT WAS THAT ABOUT OUR "LAME"-NESS?

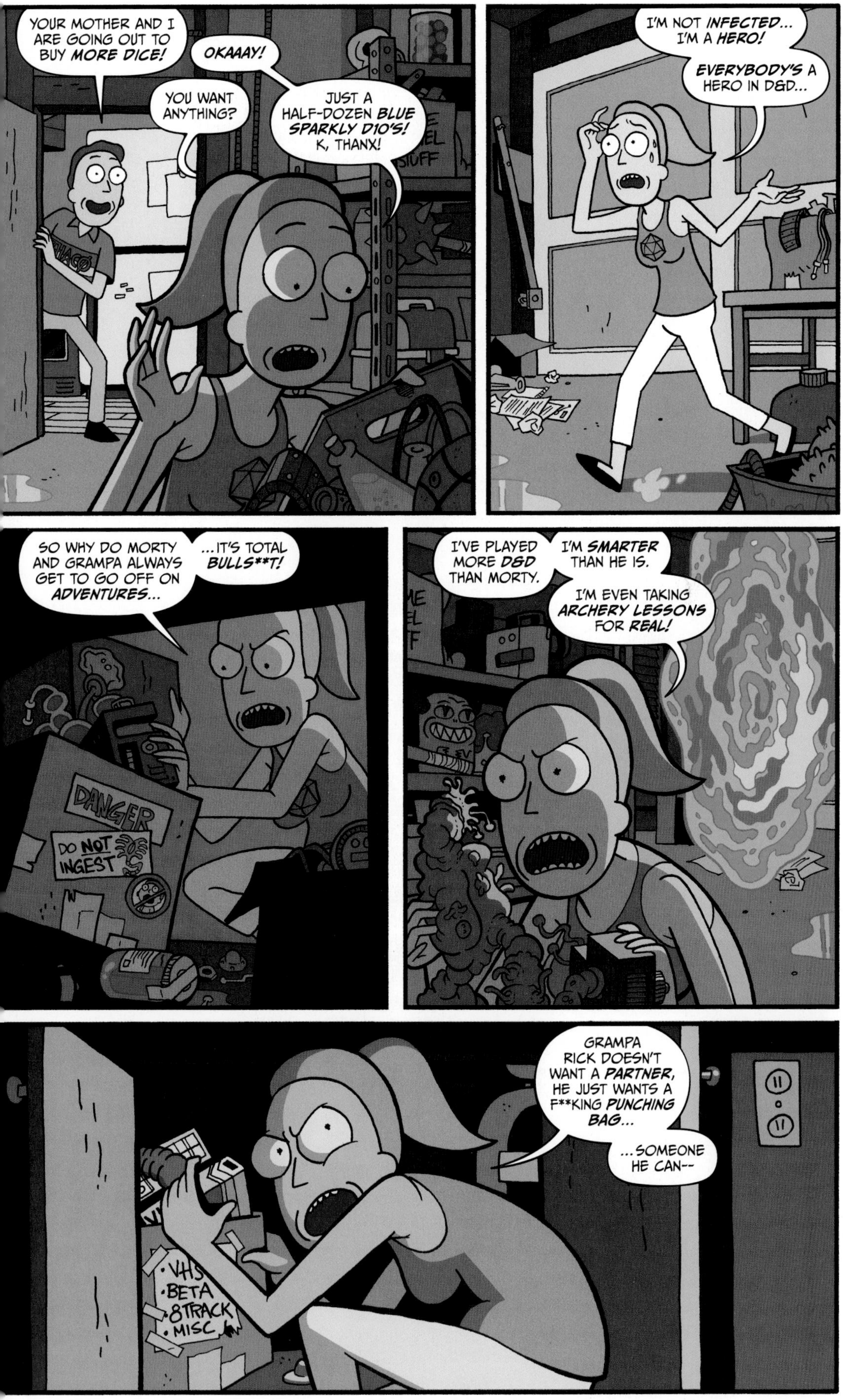
YOUR MOTHER AND I ARE GOING OUT TO BUY MORE DICE!
OKAAAY!
YOU WANT ANYTHING?
JUST A HALF-DOZEN BLUE SPARKLY D10'S! K, THANX!
I'M NOT INFECTED... I'M A HERO!
EVERYBODY'S A HERO IN D&D...
SO WHY DO MORTY AND GRAMPA ALWAYS GET TO GO OFF ON ADVENTURES...
...IT'S TOTAL BULLS**T!
DANGER
DO NOT INGEST
I'VE PLAYED MORE D&D THAN MORTY.
I'M SMARTER THAN HE IS.
I'M EVEN TAKING ARCHERY LESSONS FOR REAL!
GRAMPA RICK DOESN'T WANT A PARTNER, HE JUST WANTS A F**KING PUNCHING BAG...
...SOMEONE HE CAN--
VHS
BETA
8TRACK
MISC

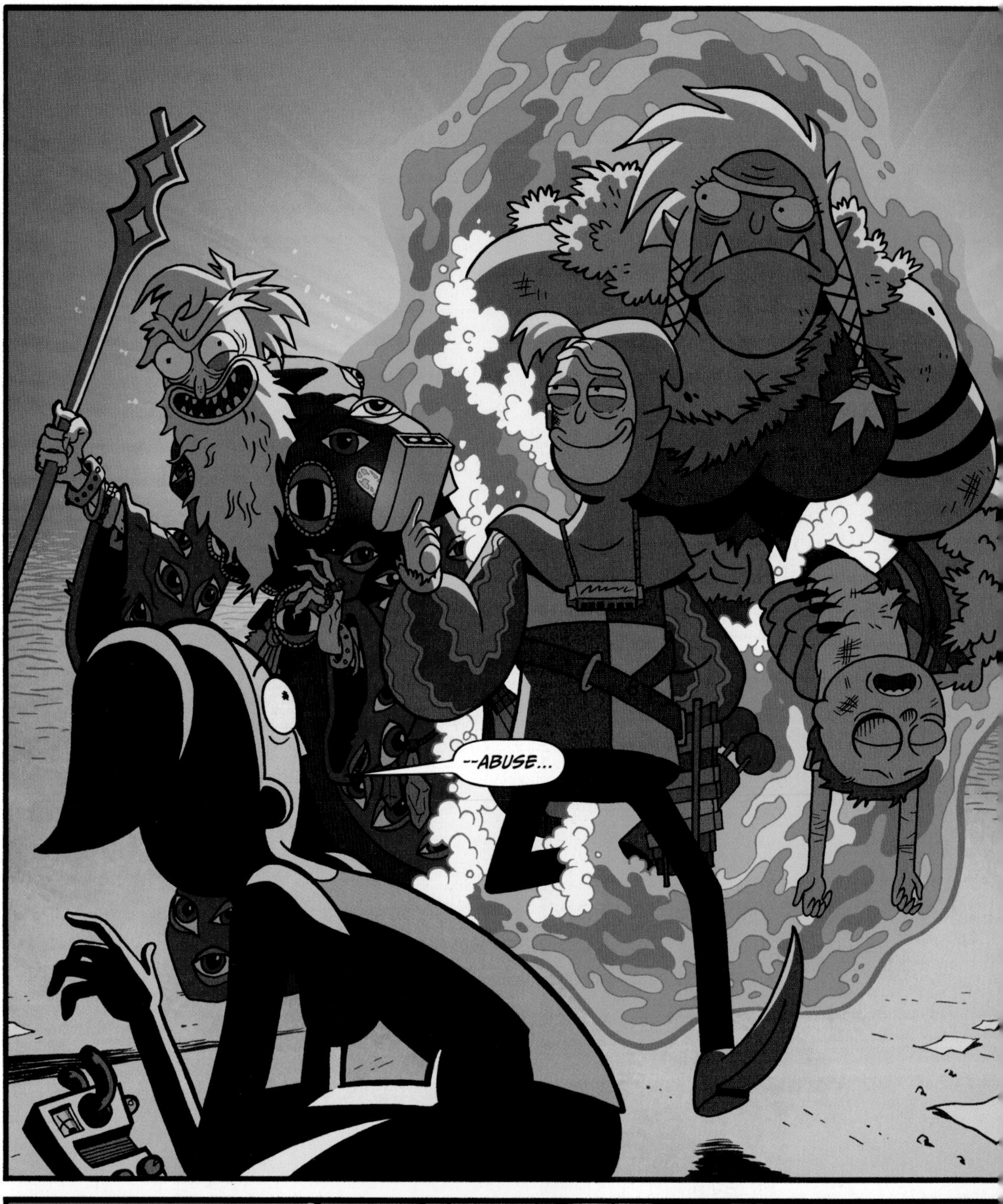
--ABUSE...

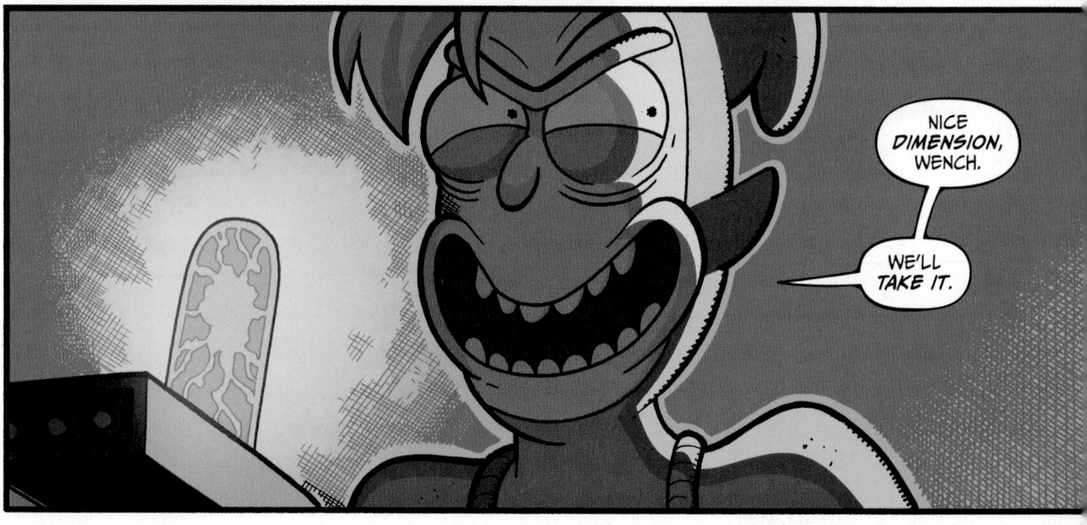
NICE DIMENSION, WENCH.
WE'LL TAKE IT.

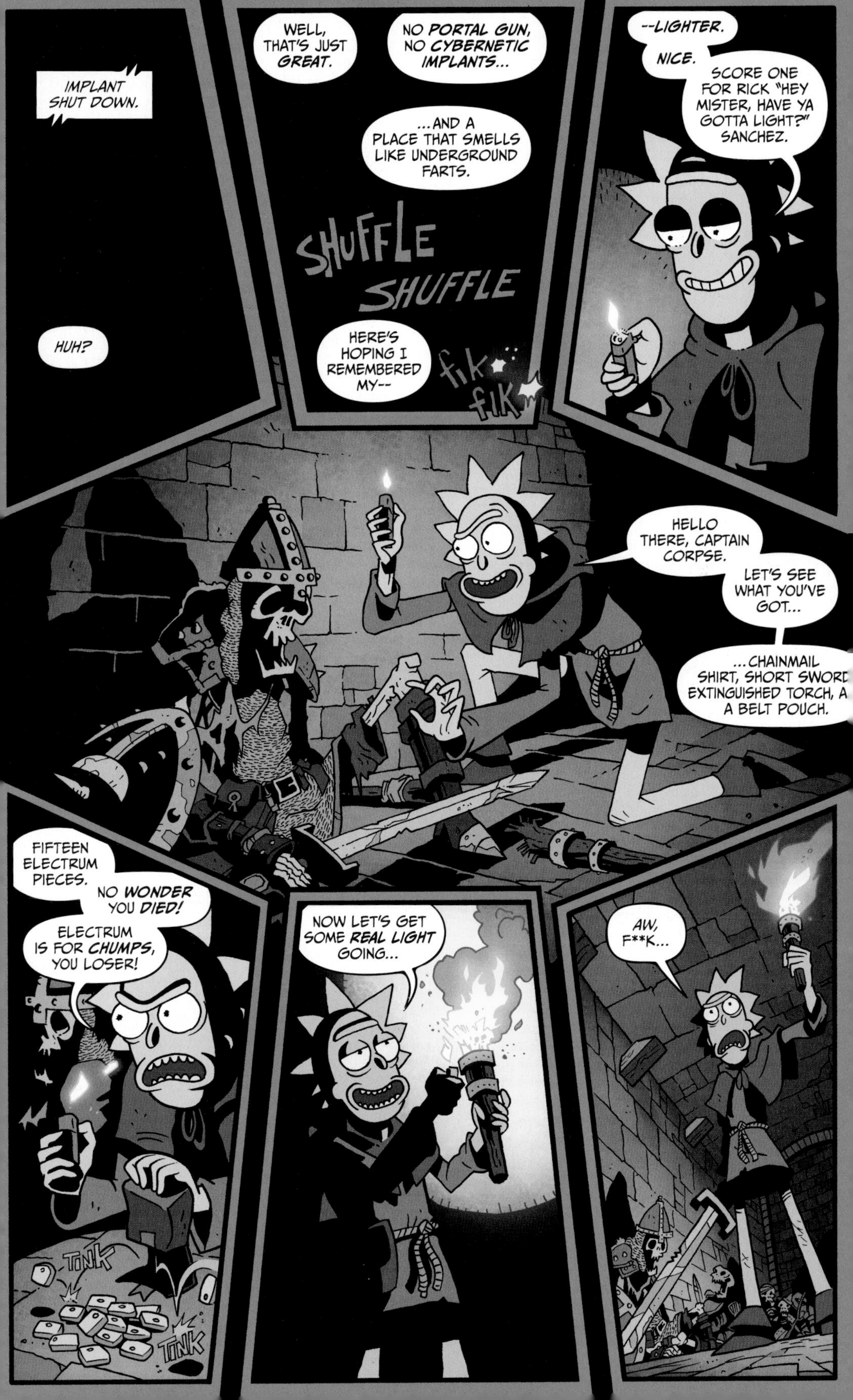

IMPLANT SHUT DOWN.
HUH?
WELL, THAT'S JUST GREAT.
NO PORTAL GUN, NO CYBERNETIC IMPLANTS...
...AND A PLACE THAT SMELLS LIKE UNDERGROUND FARTS.
SHUFFLE SHUFFLE
HERE'S HOPING I REMEMBERED MY--
FIK FIK
--LIGHTER.
NICE.
SCORE ONE FOR RICK "HEY MISTER, HAVE YA GOTTA LIGHT?" SANCHEZ.
HELLO THERE, CAPTAIN CORPSE.
LET'S SEE WHAT YOU'VE GOT...
...CHAINMAIL SHIRT, SHORT SWORD, EXTINGUISHED TORCH, A A BELT POUCH.
FIFTEEN ELECTRUM PIECES.
NO WONDER YOU DIED!
ELECTRUM IS FOR CHUMPS, YOU LOSER!
TINK
TINK
NOW LET'S GET SOME REAL LIGHT GOING...
AW, F**K...

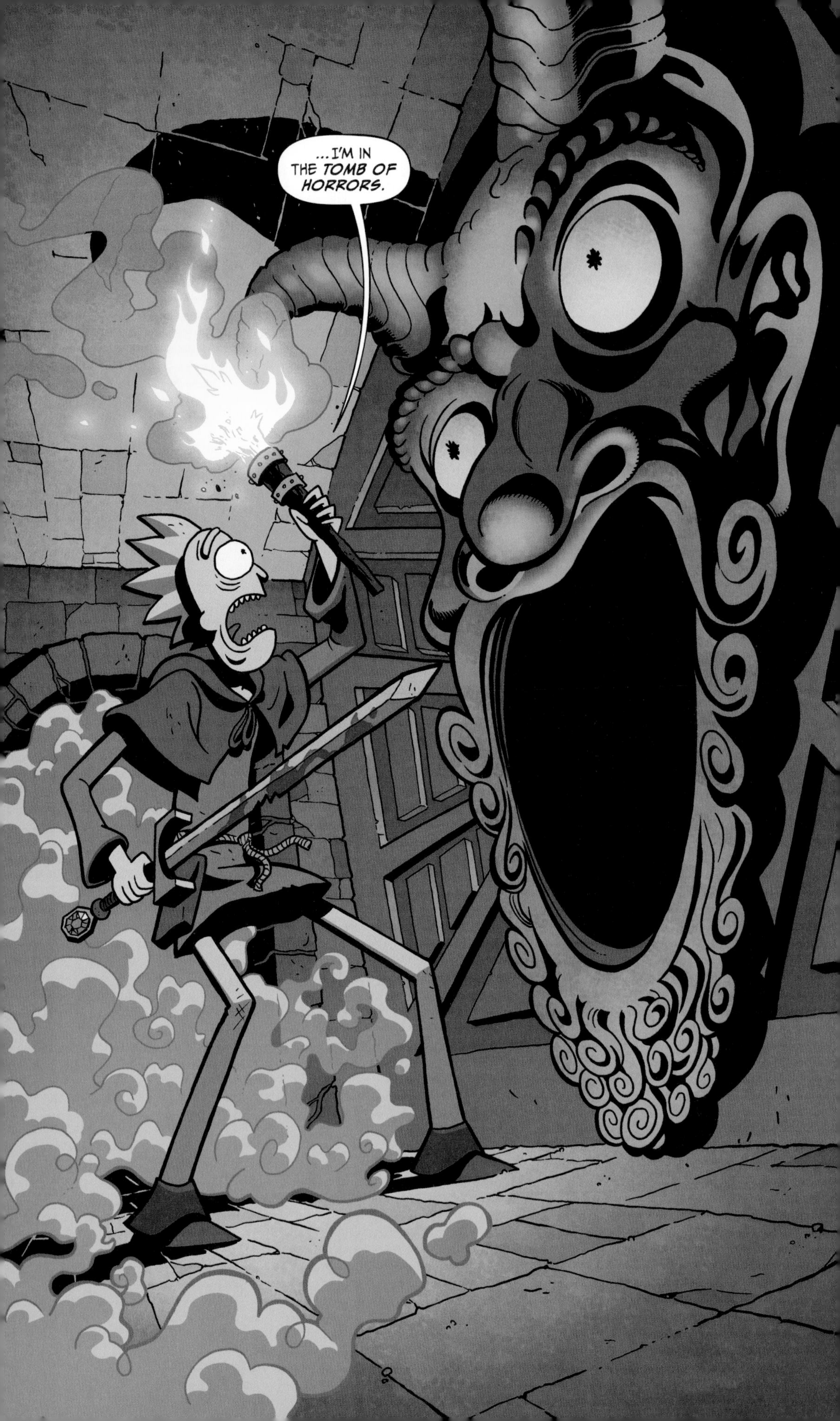
...I'M IN THE TOMB OF HORRORS.

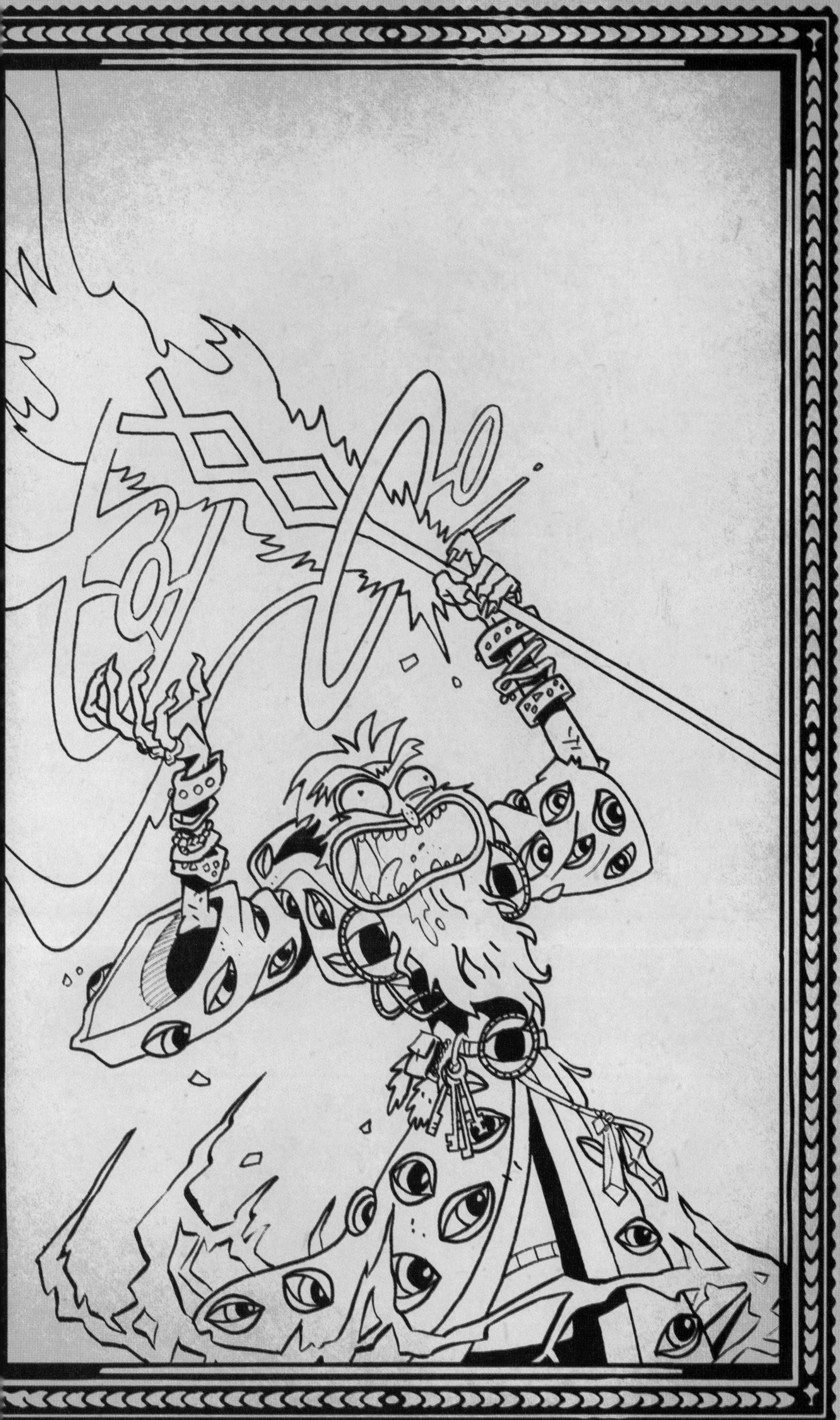

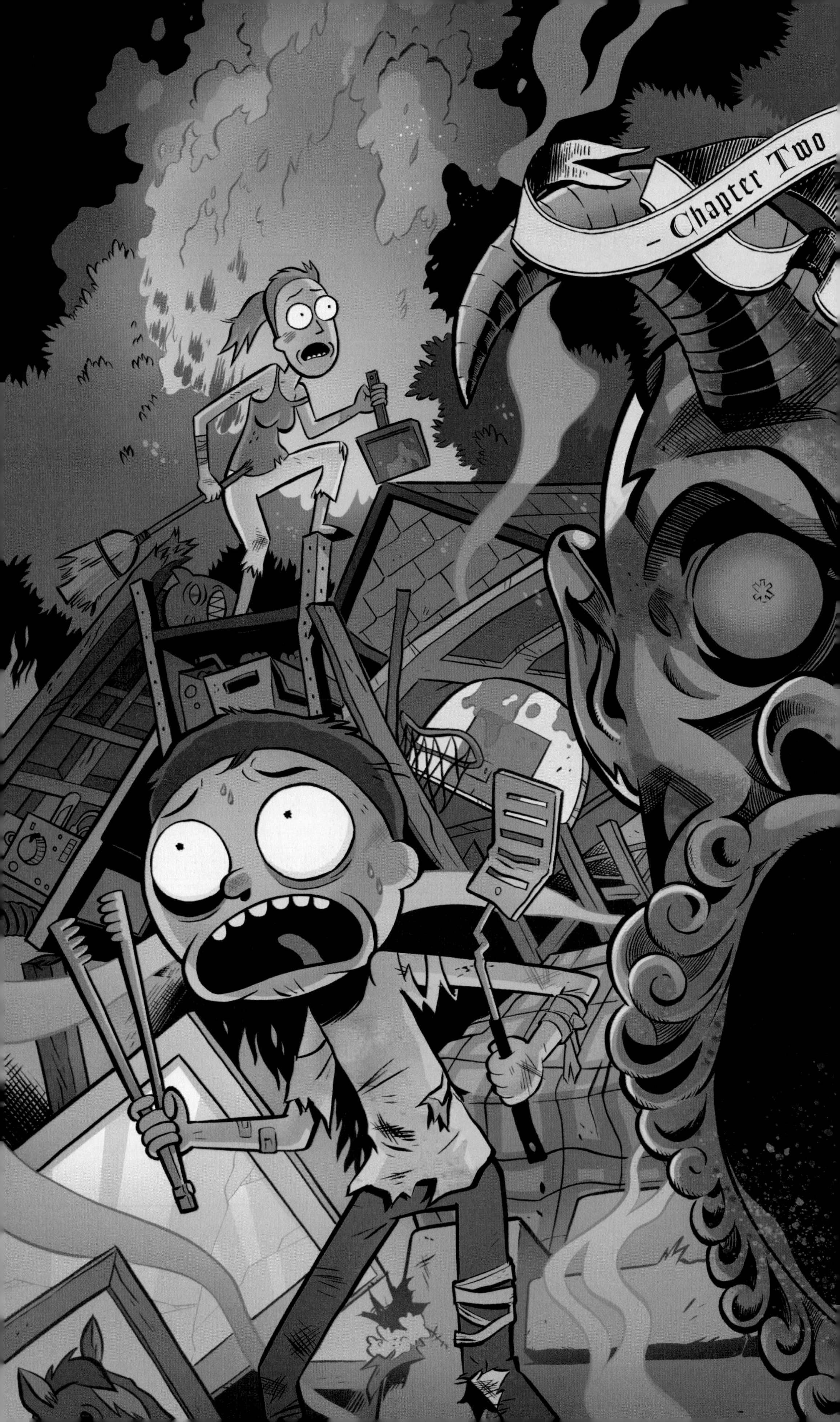
Chapter Two

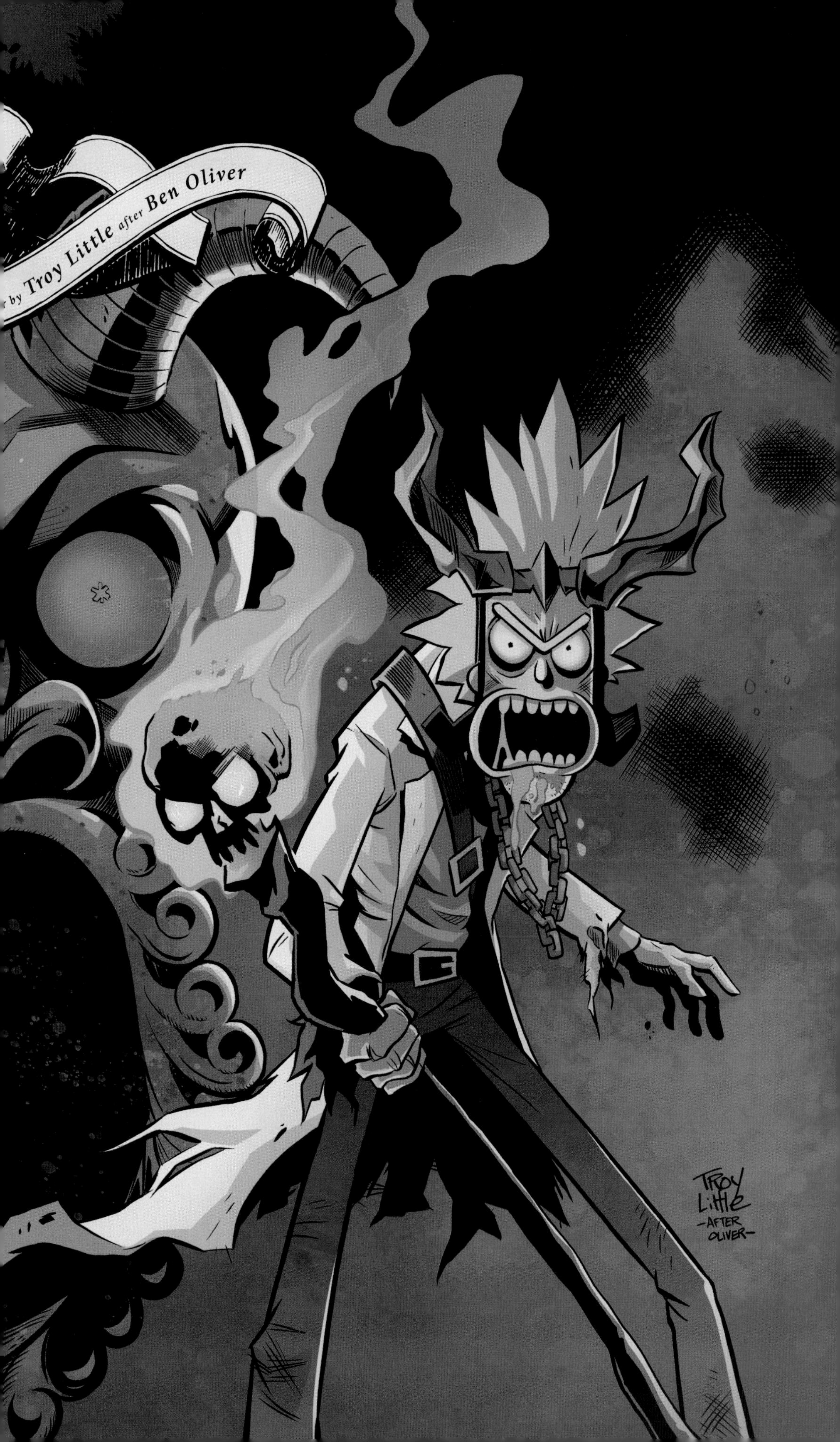

by Troy Little after Ben Oliver
TROY LITTLE -AFTER OLIVER-

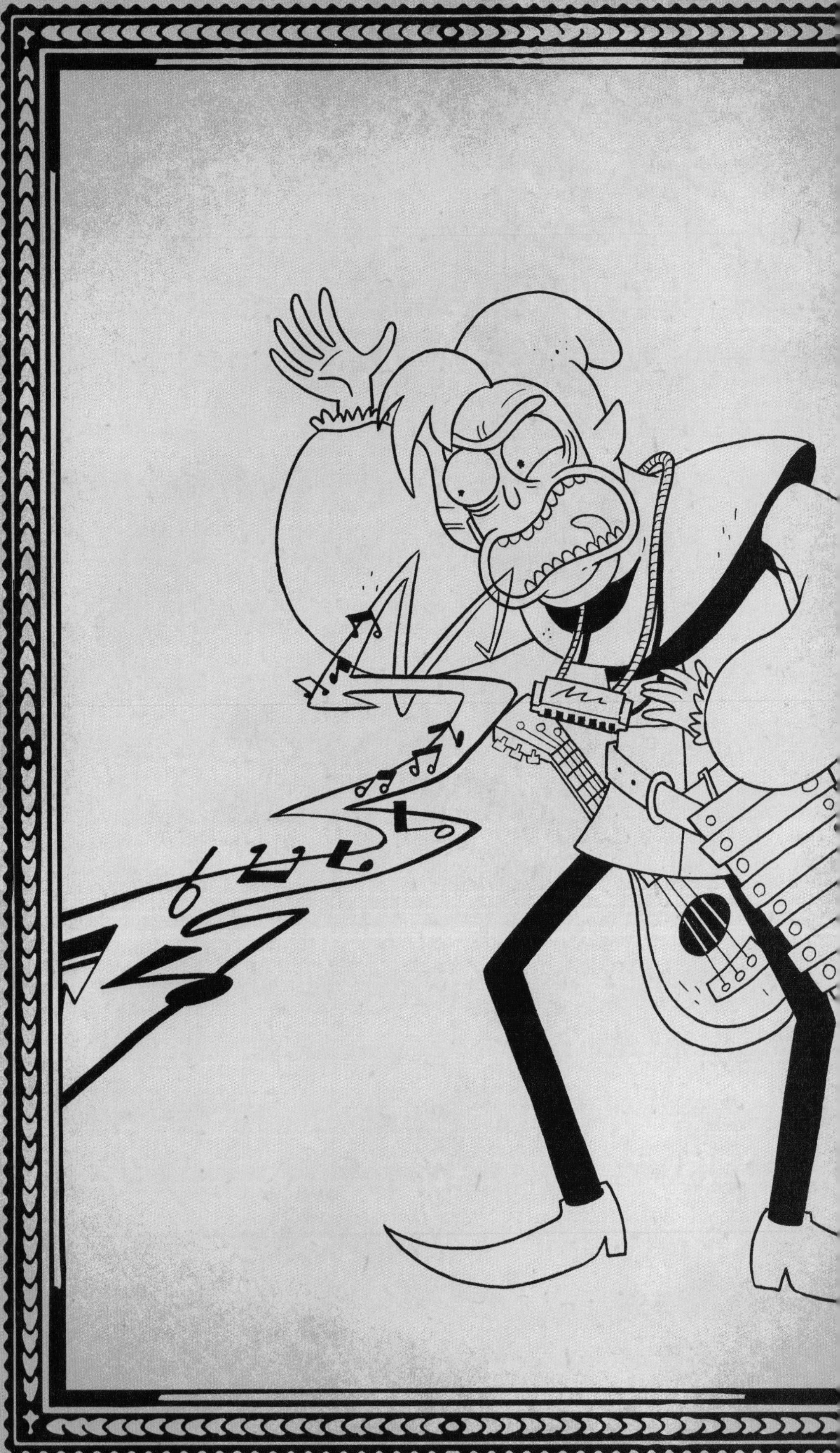

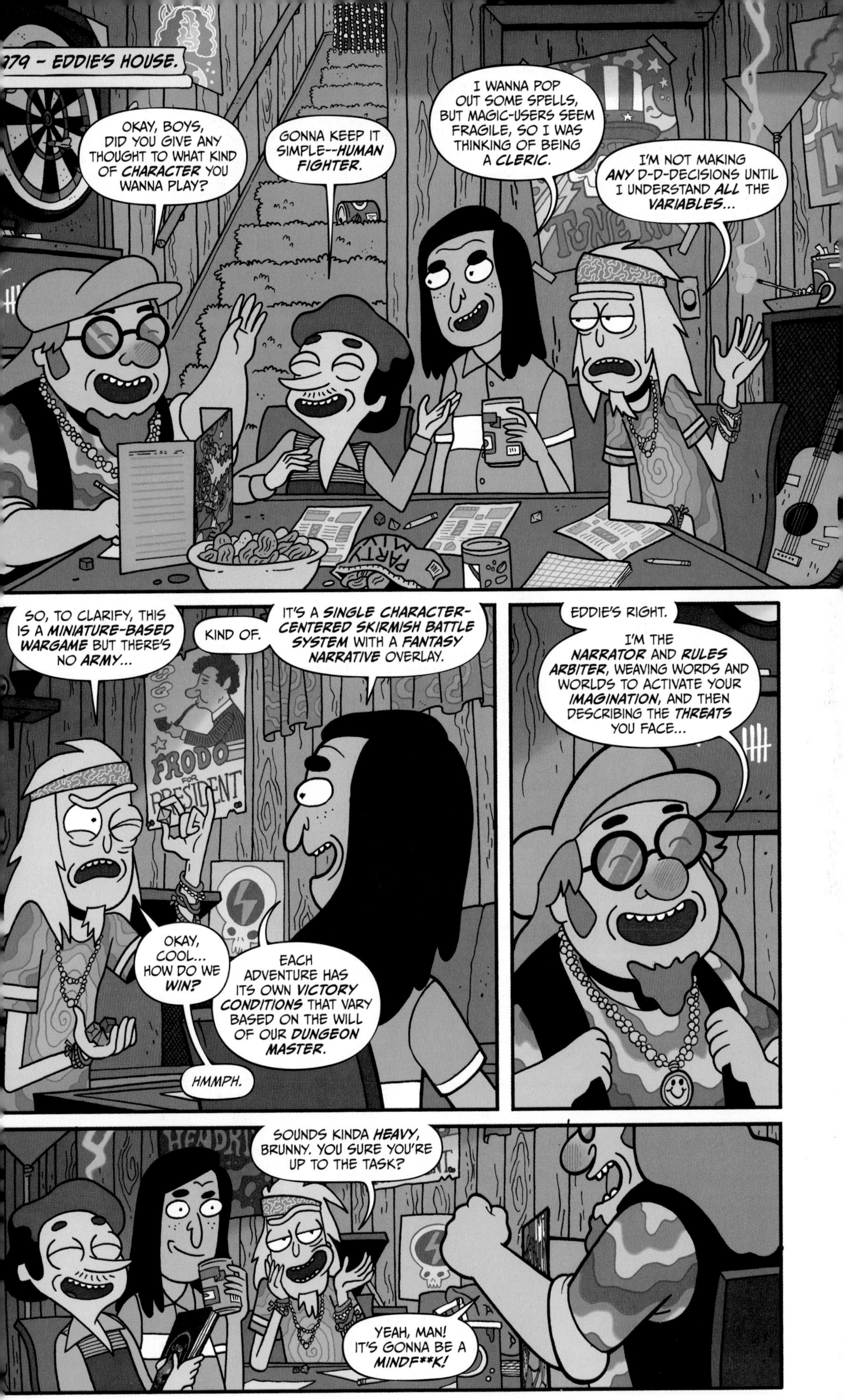
979 – EDDIE'S HOUSE.
OKAY, BOYS, DID YOU GIVE ANY THOUGHT TO WHAT KIND OF CHARACTER YOU WANNA PLAY?
GONNA KEEP IT SIMPLE--HUMAN FIGHTER.
I WANNA POP OUT SOME SPELLS, BUT MAGIC-USERS SEEM FRAGILE, SO I WAS THINKING OF BEING A CLERIC.
I'M NOT MAKING ANY D-D-DECISIONS UNTIL I UNDERSTAND ALL THE VARIABLES...
SO, TO CLARIFY, THIS IS A MINIATURE-BASED WARGAME BUT THERE'S NO ARMY...
KIND OF.
IT'S A SINGLE CHARACTER-CENTERED SKIRMISH BATTLE SYSTEM WITH A FANTASY NARRATIVE OVERLAY.
FRODO FOR PRESIDENT
OKAY, COOL... HOW DO WE WIN?
EACH ADVENTURE HAS ITS OWN VICTORY CONDITIONS THAT VARY BASED ON THE WILL OF OUR DUNGEON MASTER.
HMMPH.
EDDIE'S RIGHT.
I'M THE NARRATOR AND RULES ARBITER, WEAVING WORDS AND WORLDS TO ACTIVATE YOUR IMAGINATION, AND THEN DESCRIBING THE THREATS YOU FACE...
SOUNDS KINDA HEAVY, BRUNNY. YOU SURE YOU'RE UP TO THE TASK?
YEAH, MAN! IT'S GONNA BE A MINDF**K!

I NEED THE, WHAT'S IT CALLED, THE "PLAYER'S HANDBOOK..."

WAIT YOUR *TURN*, RICKIE! WE'VE ONLY GOT ONE OF THESE TO SHARE RIGHT NOW.

≠SNORT≠

FINE, WHATEVER. JUST TELL ME, WHAT'S THE MOST *POWERFUL* CHARACTER TYPE?

THAT DEPENDS ON YOUR *DEFINITION* OF "POWER."

NICE ONE, I-I-*IMMANUEL KANT*, BUT THIS IS A F*****G GAME, AND THAT MEANS THERE ARE *STATISTICS* AND *PROBABILITIES*... S**T WE CAN *MEASURE* AND O-O-*OPTIMIZE*.

RICK, YOU CAN'T OPTIMIZE *STORYTELLING*...

WANNA BET?

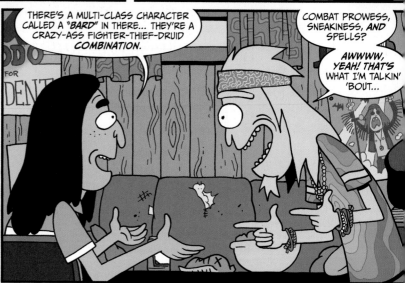

THERE'S A MULTI-CLASS CHARACTER CALLED A "BARD" IN THERE... THEY'RE A CRAZY-ASS FIGHTER-THIEF-DRUID *COMBINATION*.

COMBAT PROWESS, SNEAKINESS, *AND* SPELLS?

AWWWW, YEAH! THAT'S WHAT I'M TALKIN' 'BOUT...

IT'S TRUE, BUT BARDS ARE ONLY ALLOWED AT THE DM'S *DISCRETION*.

FINE, THEN YOU SHOULD D-D-*DISCRETIFY* IT!

I WANNA PLAY A *BARD*!

I--

BARD!

THE *REQUIREMENTS* ARE *RIDICULOUSLY HIGH*, RICK... YOU'LL HAVE TO ROLL--

FINE. JUST GIMME THE F*****G DICE.

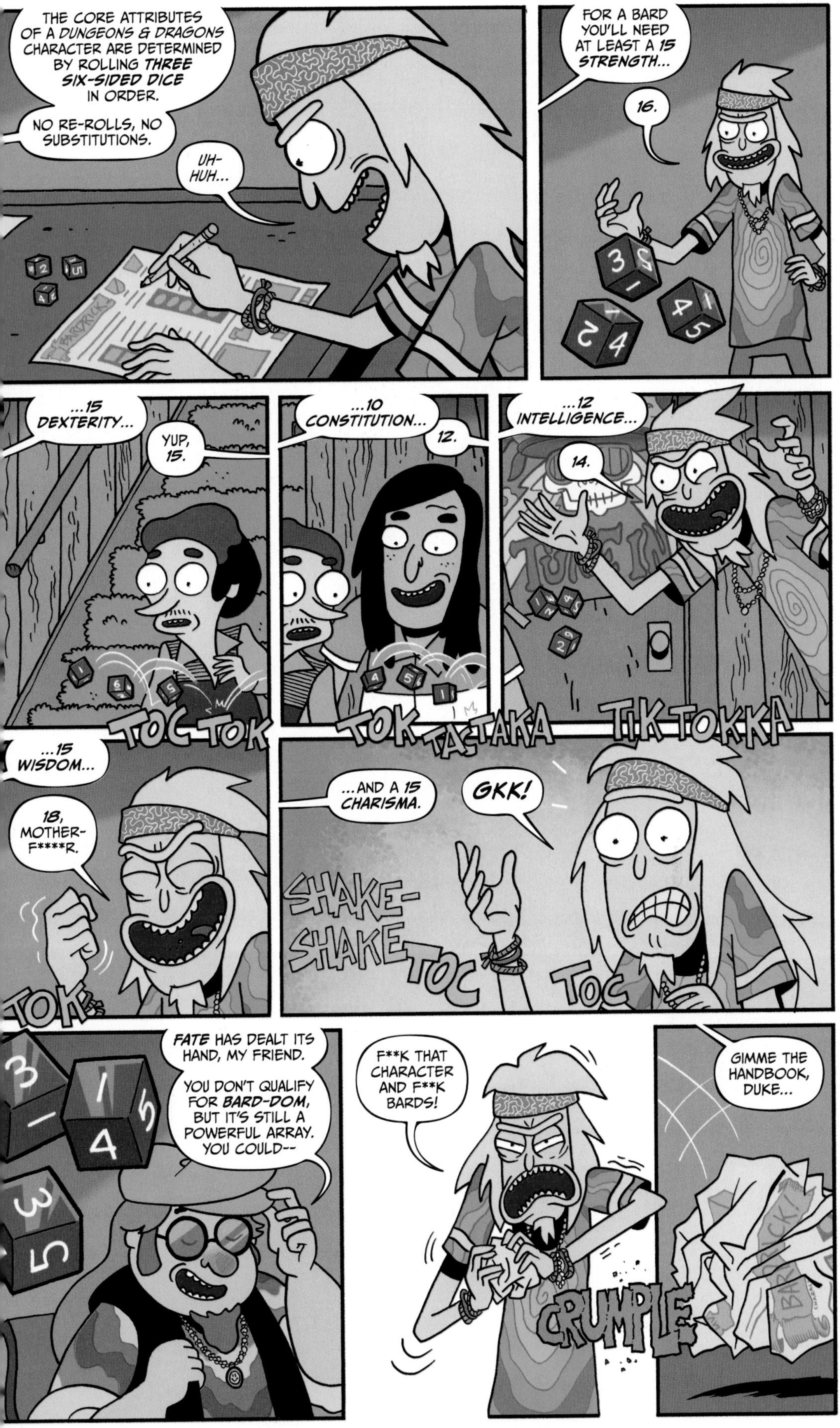
THE CORE ATTRIBUTES OF A DUNGEONS & DRAGONS CHARACTER ARE DETERMINED BY ROLLING THREE SIX-SIDED DICE IN ORDER.
NO RE-ROLLS, NO SUBSTITUTIONS.
UH-HUH...
FOR A BARD YOU'LL NEED AT LEAST A 15 STRENGTH...
16.
...15 DEXTERITY...
YUP, 15.
...10 CONSTITUTION...
12.
...12 INTELLIGENCE...
14.
TOC TOK
TOK TA TAKA
TIK TOKKA
...15 WISDOM...
18, MOTHER-F****R.
TOK
...AND A 15 CHARISMA.
GKK!
SHAKE-SHAKE TOC
TOC
FATE HAS DEALT ITS HAND, MY FRIEND.
YOU DON'T QUALIFY FOR BARD-DOM, BUT IT'S STILL A POWERFUL ARRAY. YOU COULD--
F**K THAT CHARACTER AND F**K BARDS!
GIMME THE HANDBOOK, DUKE...
CRUMPLE

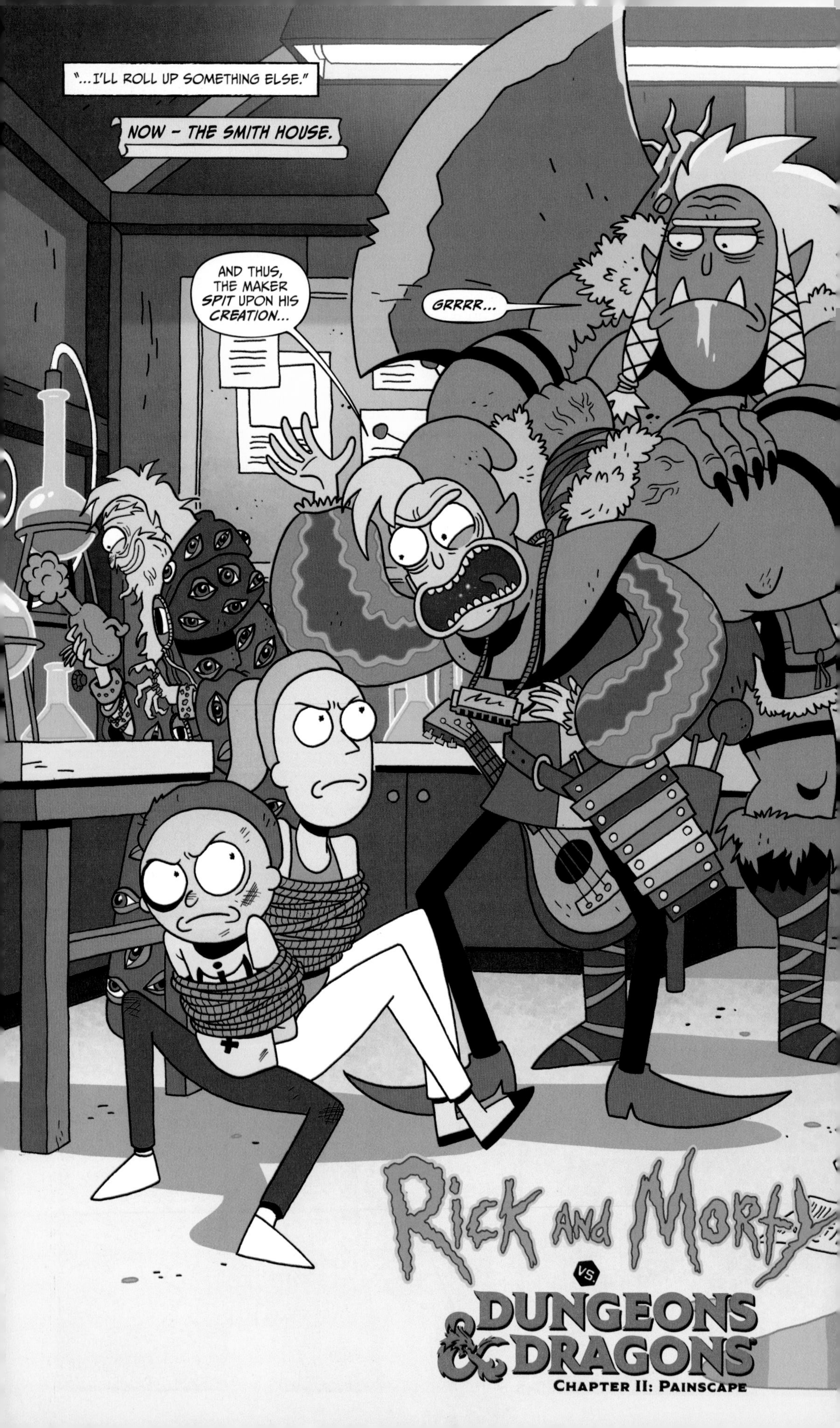

"...I'LL ROLL UP SOMETHING ELSE."
NOW - THE SMITH HOUSE.
AND THUS, THE MAKER SPIT UPON HIS CREATION...
GRRRR...
RICK AND MORTY
VS.
DUNGEONS & DRAGONS
CHAPTER II: PAINSCAPE

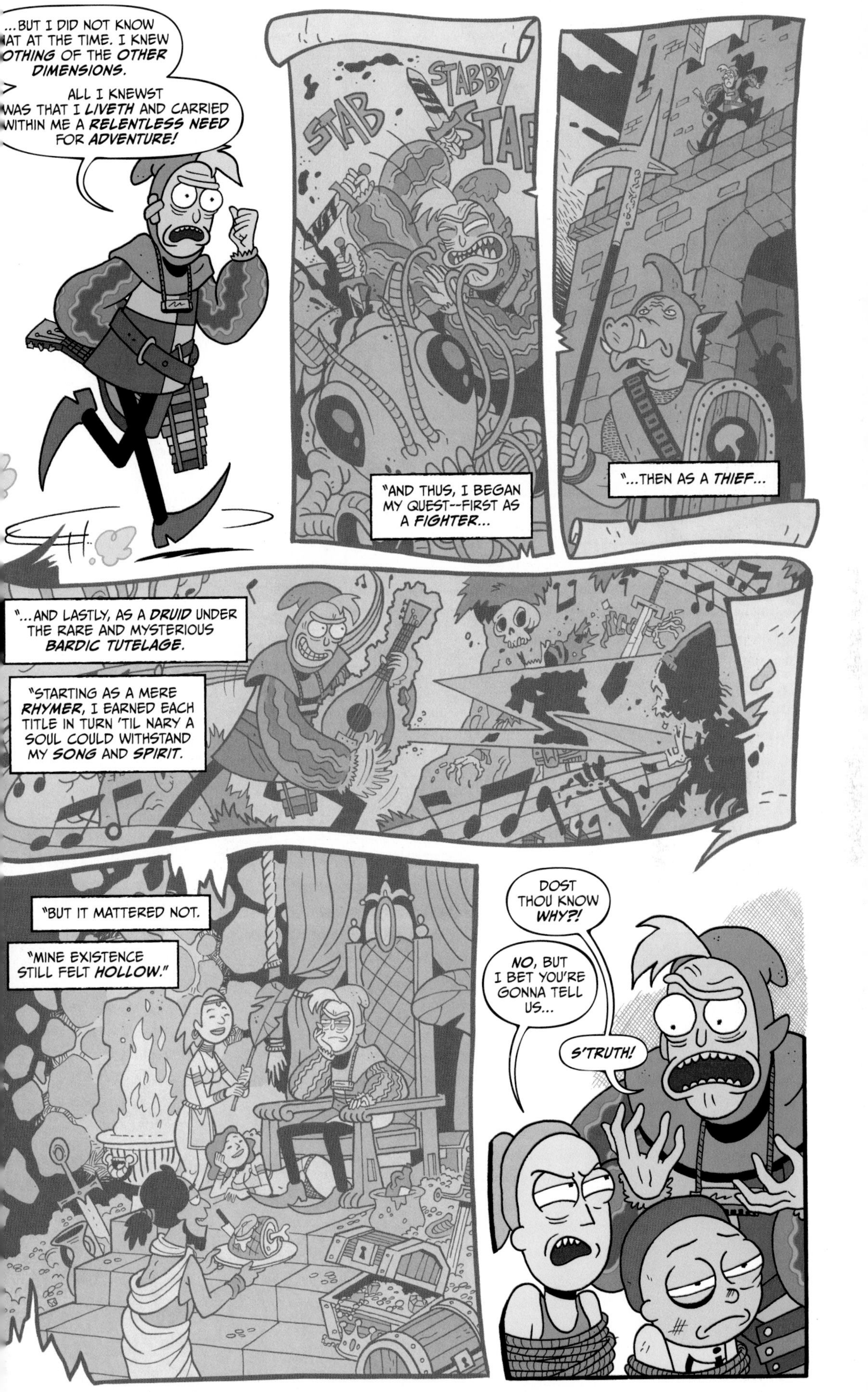

...BUT I DID NOT KNOW
IAT AT THE TIME. I KNEW
OTHING OF THE OTHER
DIMENSIONS.
ALL I KNEWST
WAS THAT I LIVETH AND CARRIED
WITHIN ME A RELENTLESS NEED
FOR ADVENTURE!
STAB
STABBY
STAB
"AND THUS, I BEGAN
MY QUEST--FIRST AS
A FIGHTER...
"...THEN AS A THIEF...
"...AND LASTLY, AS A DRUID UNDER
THE RARE AND MYSTERIOUS
BARDIC TUTELAGE.
"STARTING AS A MERE
RHYMER, I EARNED EACH
TITLE IN TURN 'TIL NARY A
SOUL COULD WITHSTAND
MY SONG AND SPIRIT.
"BUT IT MATTERED NOT.
"MINE EXISTENCE
STILL FELT HOLLOW."
DOST
THOU KNOW
WHY?!
NO, BUT
I BET YOU'RE
GONNA TELL
US...
S'TRUTH!

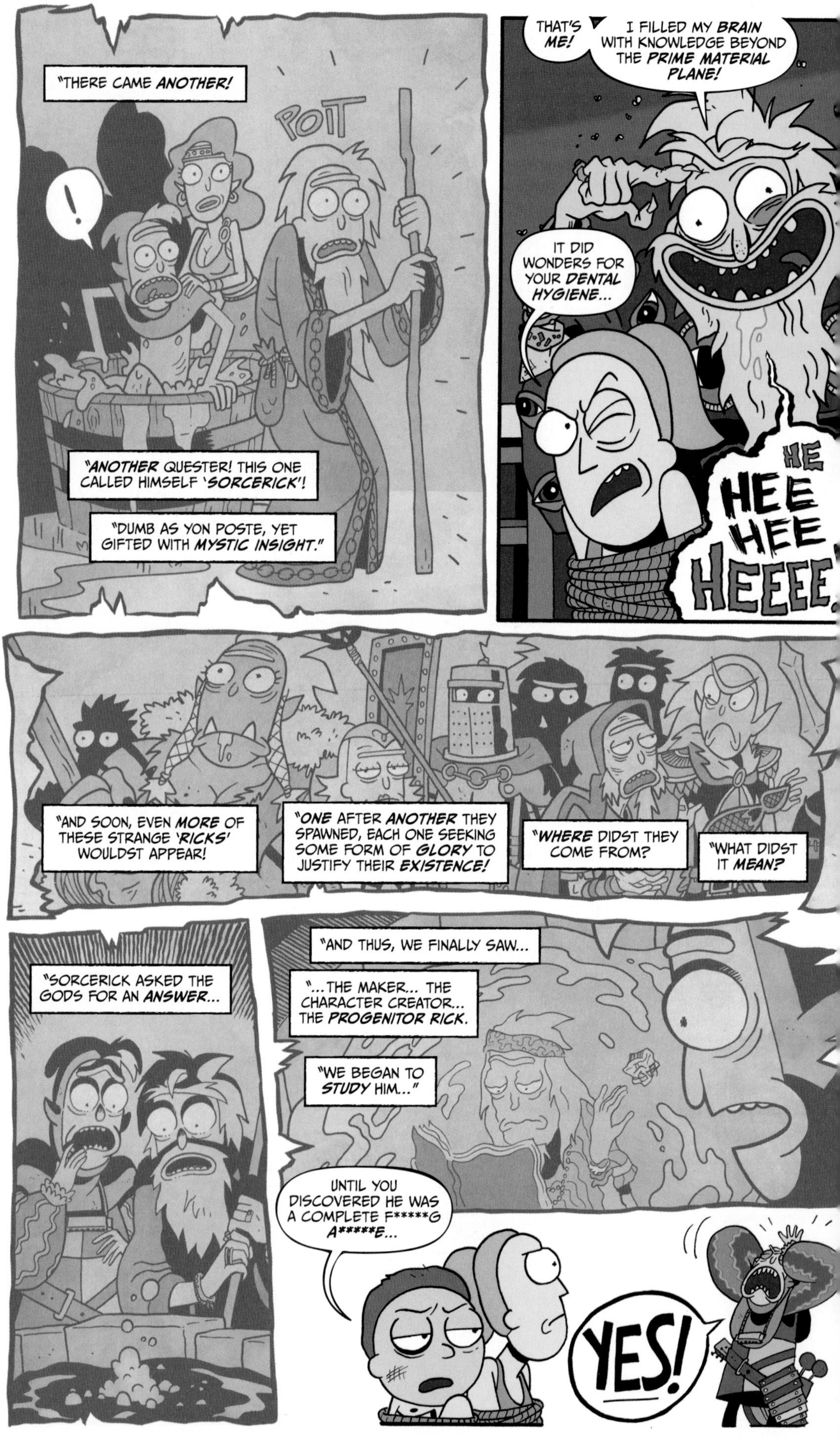
"THERE CAME ANOTHER!
!
POIT
"ANOTHER QUESTER! THIS ONE CALLED HIMSELF 'SORCERICK'!
"DUMB AS YON POSTE, YET GIFTED WITH MYSTIC INSIGHT."
THAT'S ME!
I FILLED MY BRAIN WITH KNOWLEDGE BEYOND THE PRIME MATERIAL PLANE!
IT DID WONDERS FOR YOUR DENTAL HYGIENE...
HE HEE HEE HEEEE
"AND SOON, EVEN MORE OF THESE STRANGE 'RICKS' WOULDST APPEAR!
"ONE AFTER ANOTHER THEY SPAWNED, EACH ONE SEEKING SOME FORM OF GLORY TO JUSTIFY THEIR EXISTENCE!
"WHERE DIDST THEY COME FROM?
"WHAT DIDST IT MEAN?
"SORCERICK ASKED THE GODS FOR AN ANSWER...
"AND THUS, WE FINALLY SAW...
"...THE MAKER... THE CHARACTER CREATOR... THE PROGENITOR RICK.
"WE BEGAN TO STUDY HIM..."
UNTIL YOU DISCOVERED HE WAS A COMPLETE F*****G A*****E...
YES!

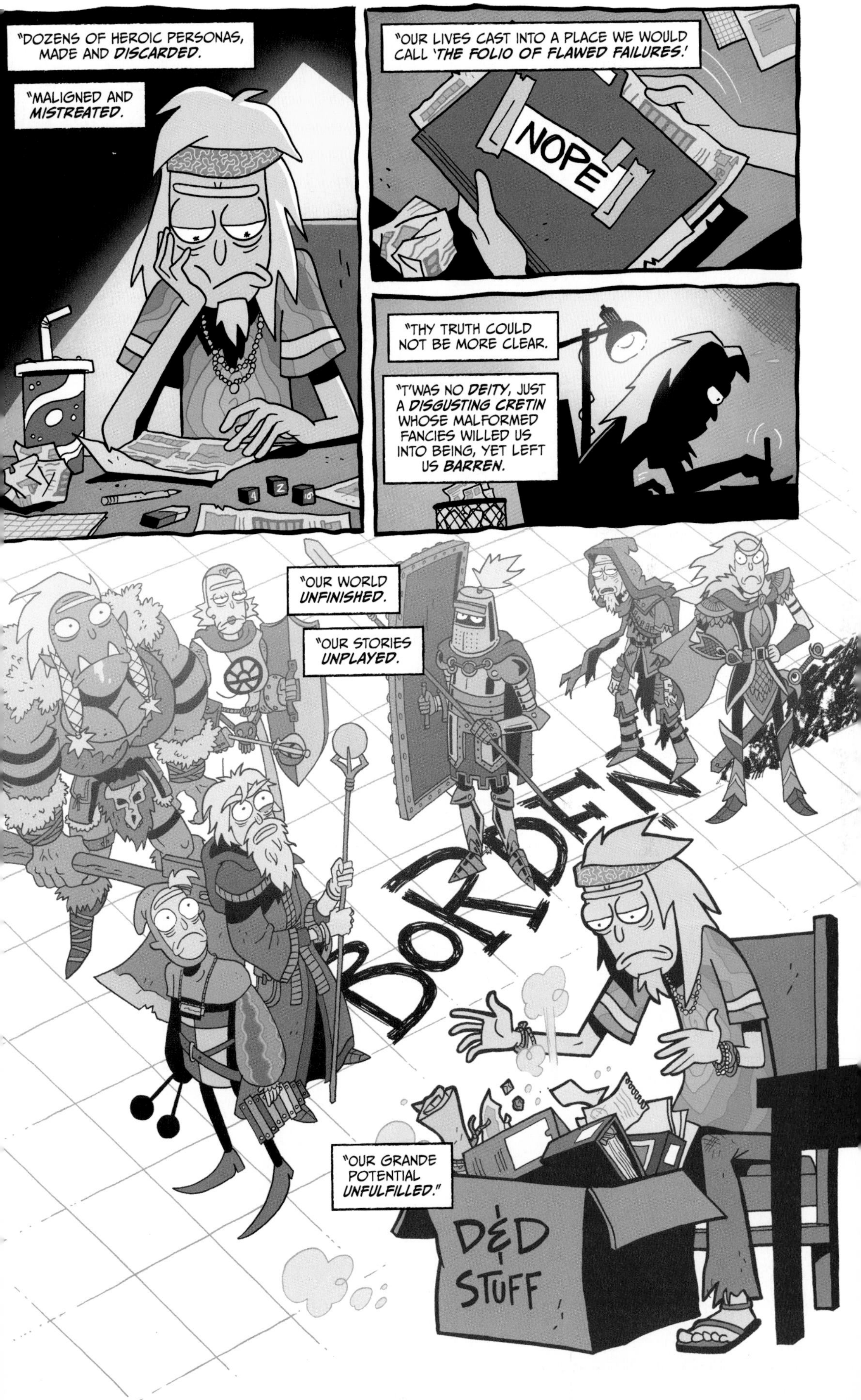
"DOZENS OF HEROIC PERSONAS, MADE AND *DISCARDED*.
"MALIGNED AND *MISTREATED*.
"OUR LIVES CAST INTO A PLACE WE WOULD CALL *'THE FOLIO OF FLAWED FAILURES.'*
NOPE
"THY TRUTH COULD NOT BE MORE CLEAR.
"T'WAS NO *DEITY*, JUST A *DISGUSTING CRETIN* WHOSE MALFORMED FANCIES WILLED US INTO BEING, YET LEFT US *BARREN*.
"OUR WORLD *UNFINISHED*.
"OUR STORIES *UNPLAYED*.
"OUR GRANDE POTENTIAL *UNFULFILLED*."
D&D STUFF

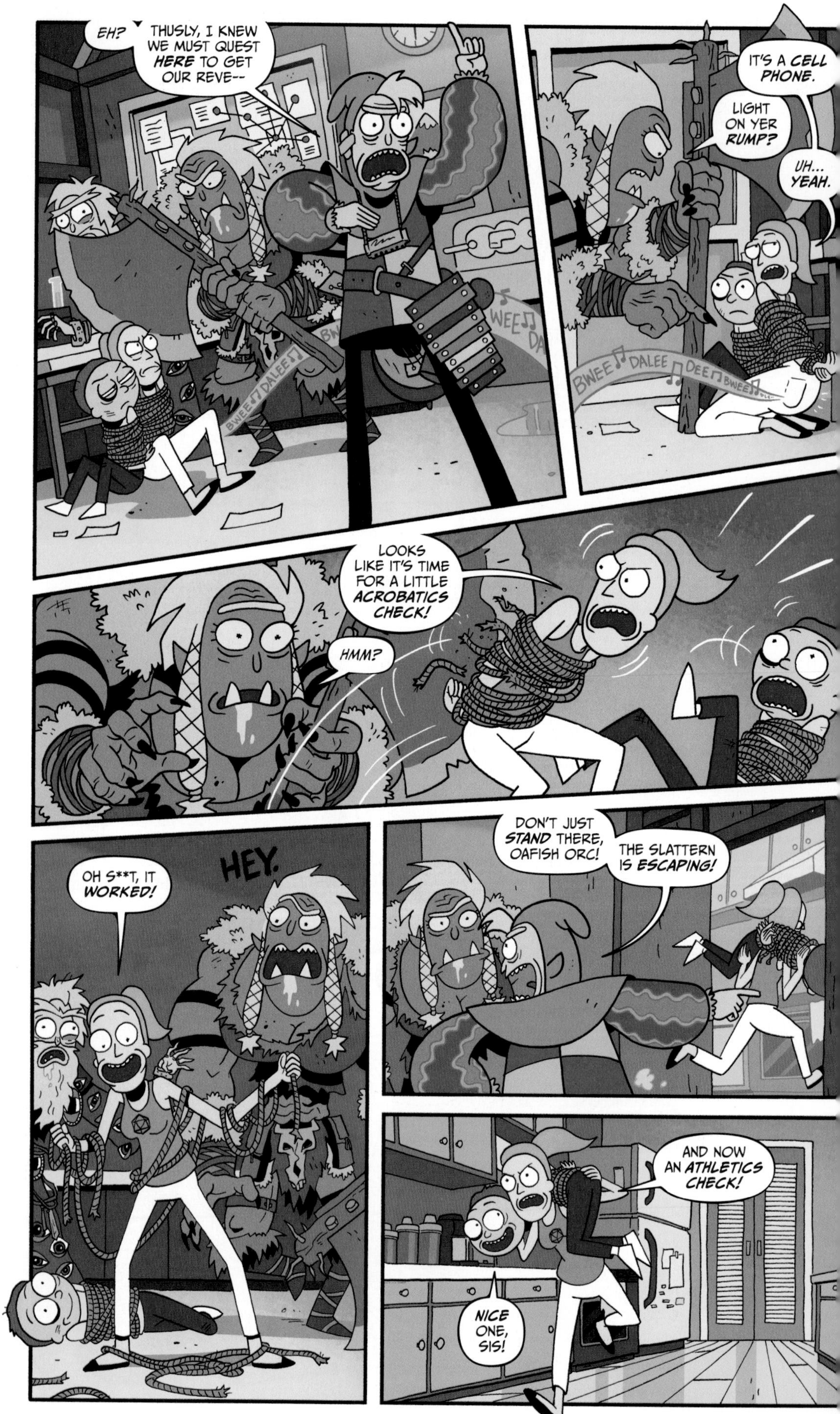
EH?
THUSLY, I KNEW WE MUST QUEST HERE TO GET OUR REVE--
BWEE♫ DALEE♫
WEE♫ DA
IT'S A CELL PHONE.
LIGHT ON YER RUMP?
UH... YEAH.
BWEE♫ DALEE♫ DEE♫ BWEE♫
LOOKS LIKE IT'S TIME FOR A LITTLE ACROBATICS CHECK!
HMM?
OH S**T, IT WORKED!
HEY.
DON'T JUST STAND THERE, OAFISH ORC!
THE SLATTERN IS ESCAPING!
AND NOW AN ATHLETICS CHECK!
NICE ONE, SIS!

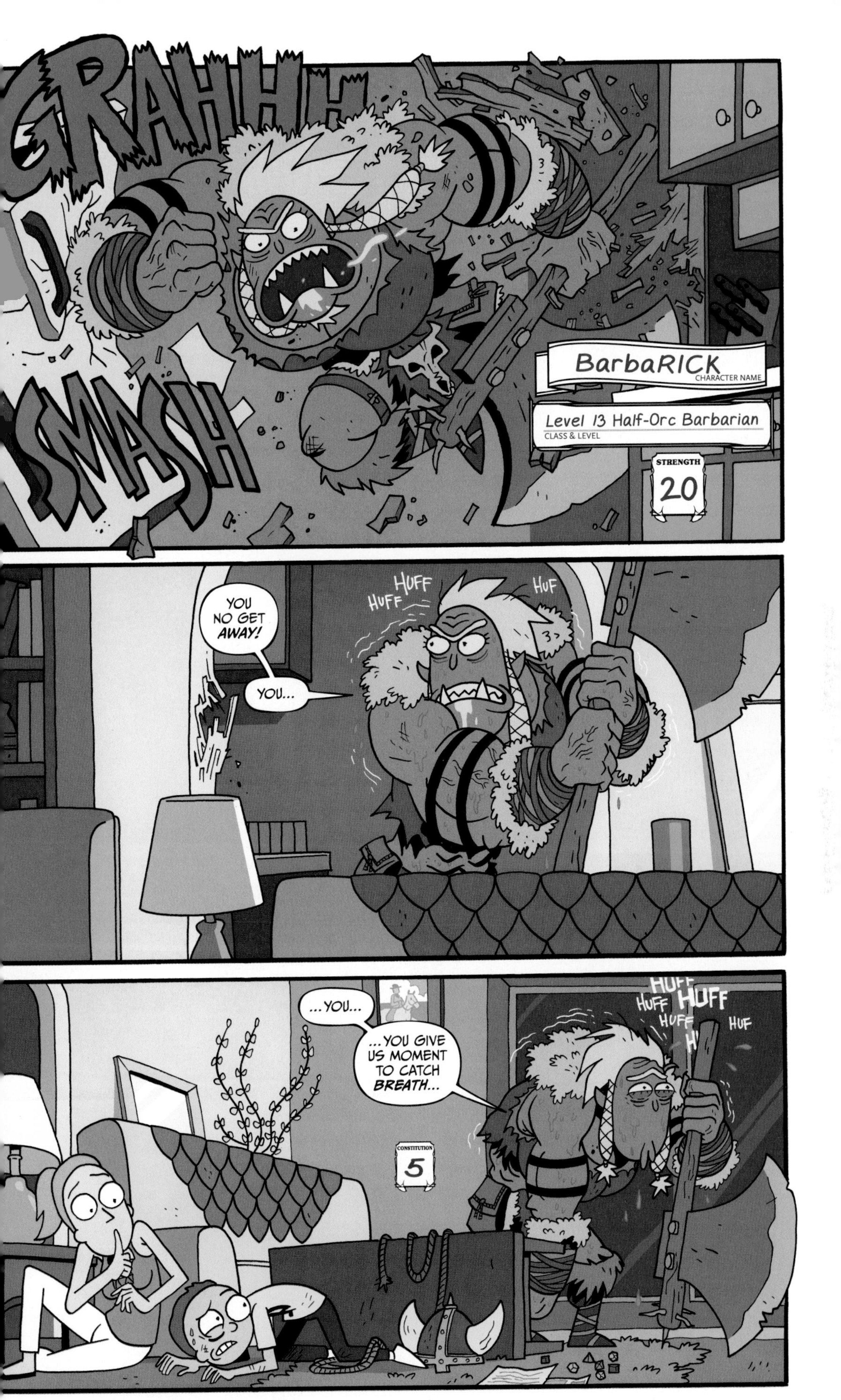
GRAHHHH
SMASH
BarbaRICK
CHARACTER NAME
Level 13 Half-Orc Barbarian
CLASS & LEVEL
STRENGTH
20
HUFF
HUFF
HUF
YOU NO GET AWAY!
YOU...
...YOU...
...YOU GIVE US MOMENT TO CATCH BREATH...
HUFF
HUFF HUFF
HUFF
HUF
CONSTITUTION
5

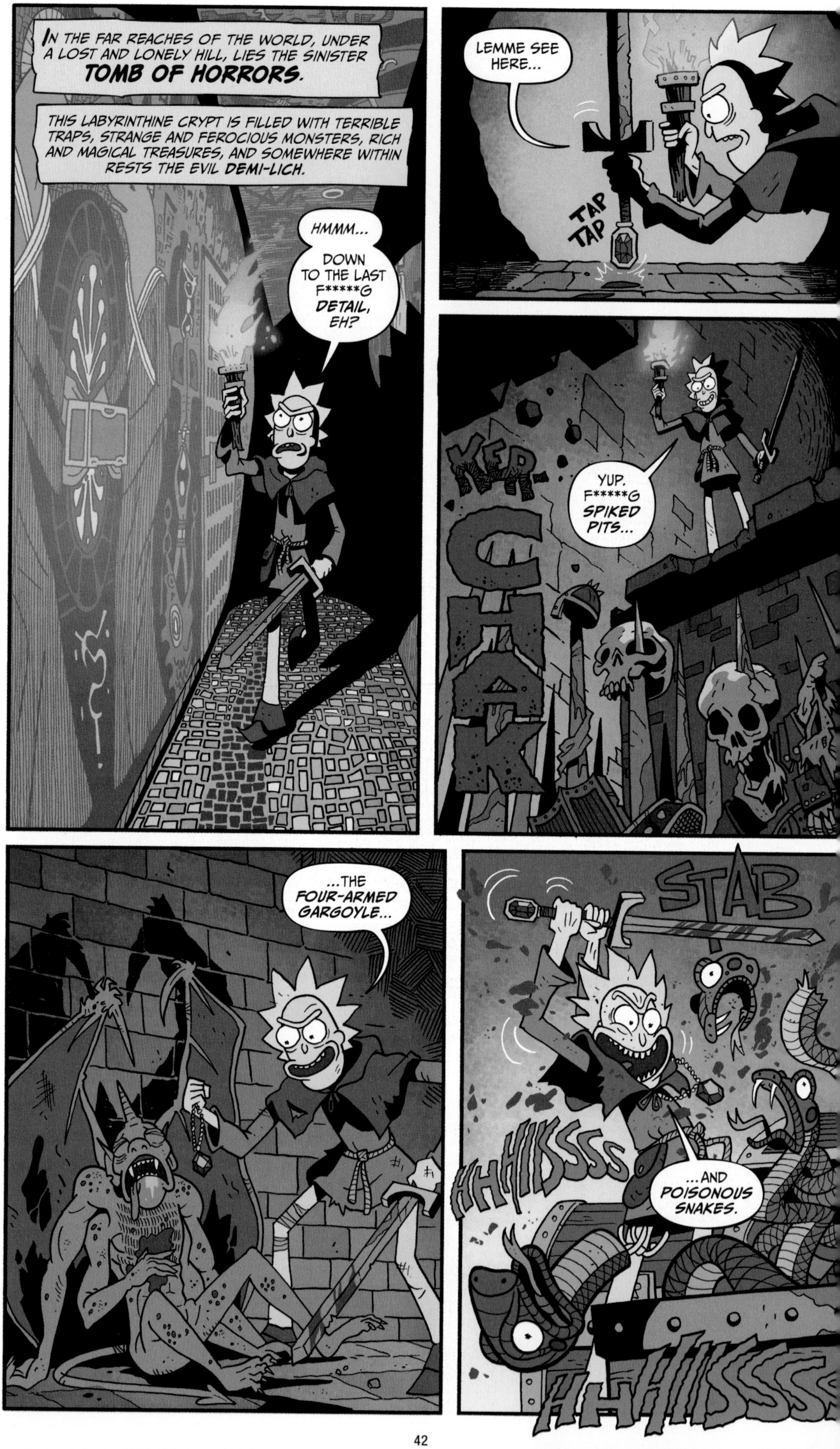

IN THE FAR REACHES OF THE WORLD, UNDER A LOST AND LONELY HILL, LIES THE SINISTER TOMB OF HORRORS.
THIS LABYRINTHINE CRYPT IS FILLED WITH TERRIBLE TRAPS, STRANGE AND FEROCIOUS MONSTERS, RICH AND MAGICAL TREASURES, AND SOMEWHERE WITHIN RESTS THE EVIL DEMI-LICH.
HMMM...
DOWN TO THE LAST F*****G DETAIL, EH?
LEMME SEE HERE...
TAP TAP
KER-
CHAK
YUP. F*****G SPIKED PITS...
...THE FOUR-ARMED GARGOYLE...
STAB
HHHISSSS
...AND POISONOUS SNAKES.
HHHISSSS

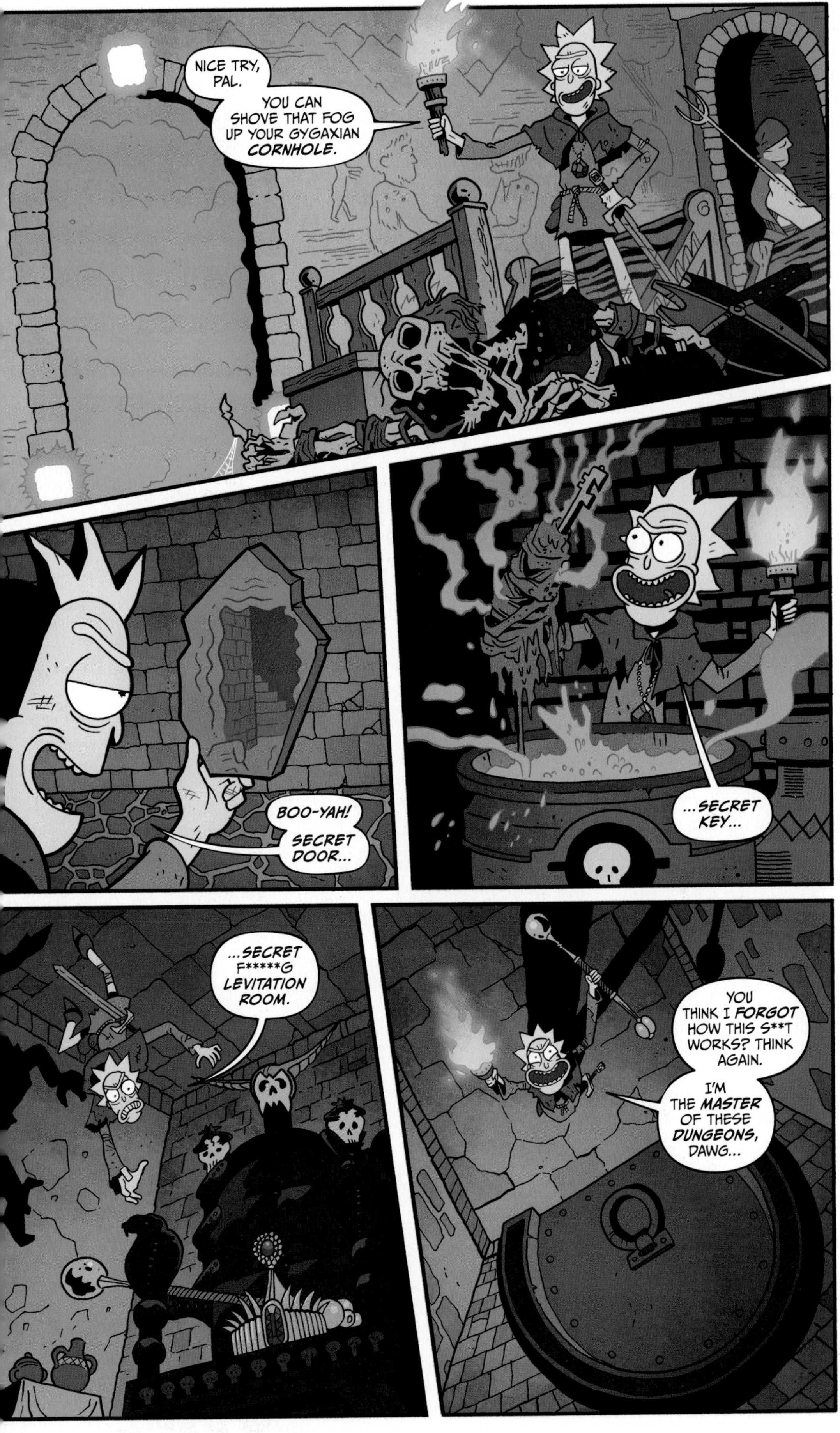
NICE TRY, PAL.
YOU CAN SHOVE THAT FOG UP YOUR GYGAXIAN CORNHOLE.
BOO-YAH! SECRET DOOR...
...SECRET KEY...
...SECRET F*****G LEVITATION ROOM.
YOU THINK I FORGOT HOW THIS S**T WORKS? THINK AGAIN.
I'M THE MASTER OF THESE DUNGEONS, DAWG...

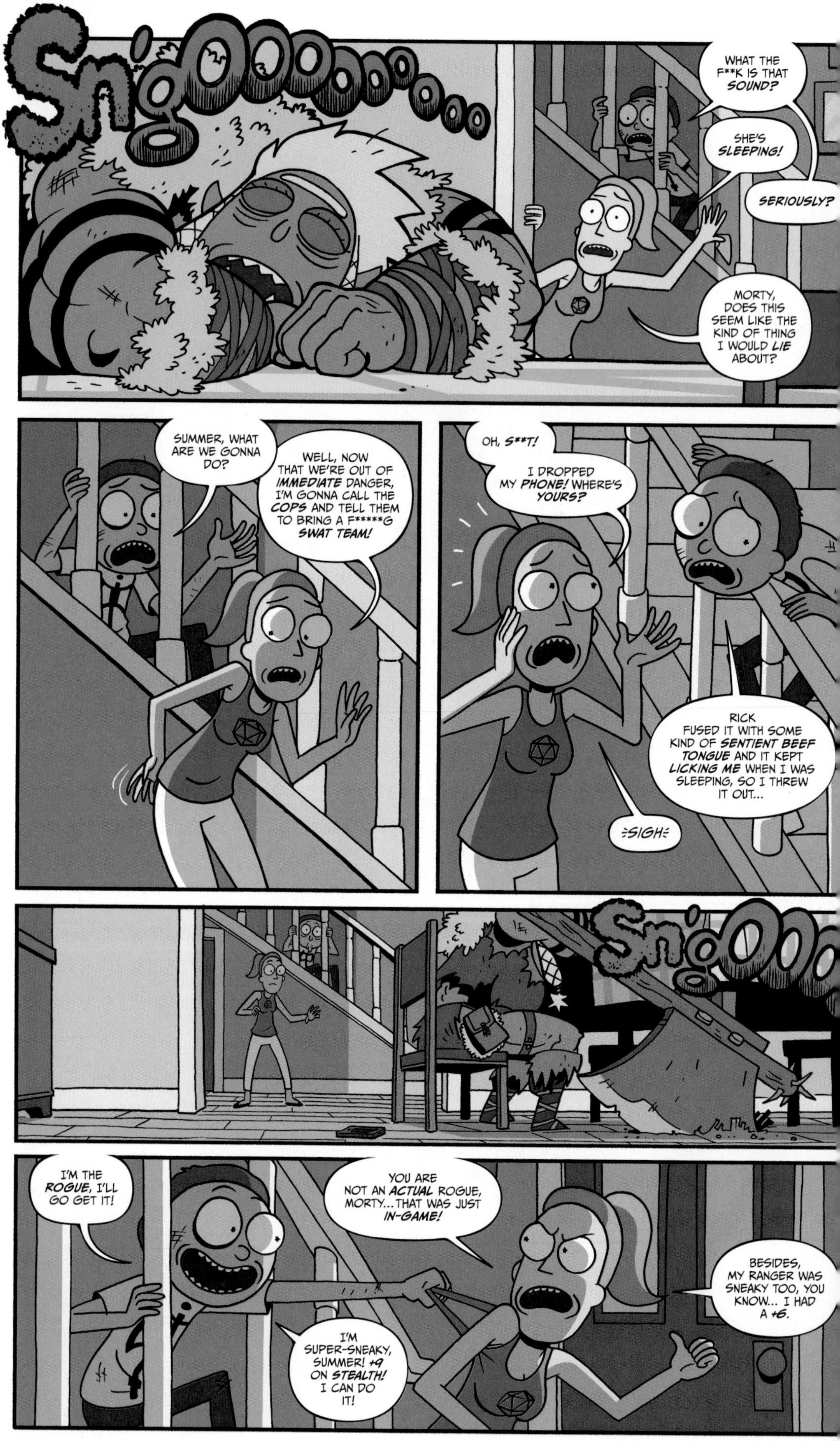
SNGOOOOOOOOOO
WHAT THE F**K IS THAT SOUND?
SHE'S SLEEPING!
SERIOUSLY?
MORTY, DOES THIS SEEM LIKE THE KIND OF THING I WOULD LIE ABOUT?
SUMMER, WHAT ARE WE GONNA DO?
WELL, NOW THAT WE'RE OUT OF IMMEDIATE DANGER, I'M GONNA CALL THE COPS AND TELL THEM TO BRING A F*****G SWAT TEAM!
OH, S**T!
I DROPPED MY PHONE! WHERE'S YOURS?
RICK FUSED IT WITH SOME KIND OF SENTIENT BEEF TONGUE AND IT KEPT LICKING ME WHEN I WAS SLEEPING, SO I THREW IT OUT...
SIGH
SNGOOO
I'M THE ROGUE, I'LL GO GET IT!
YOU ARE NOT AN ACTUAL ROGUE, MORTY... THAT WAS JUST IN-GAME!
I'M SUPER-SNEAKY, SUMMER! +9 ON STEALTH! I CAN DO IT!
BESIDES, MY RANGER WAS SNEAKY TOO, YOU KNOW... I HAD A +6.

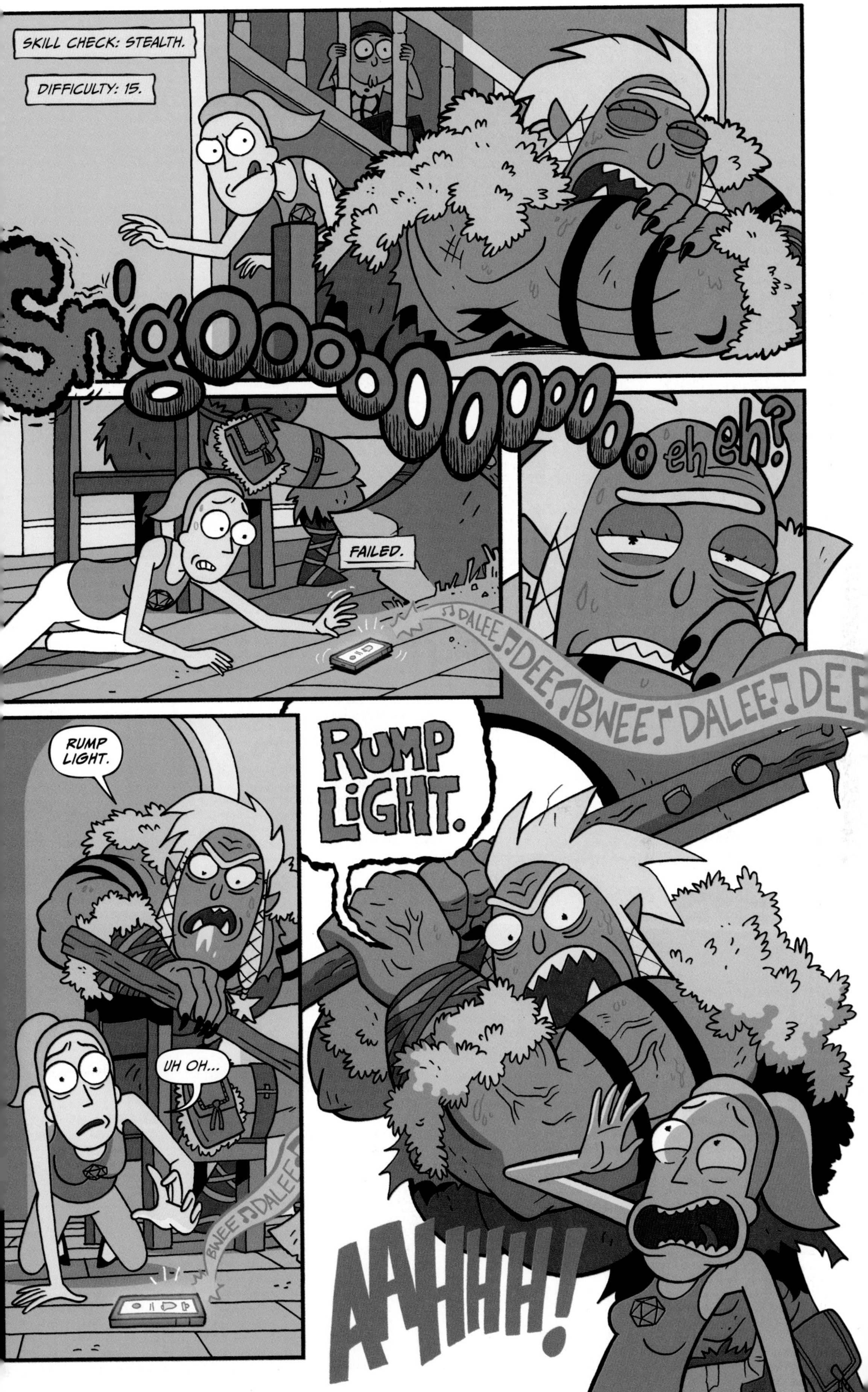

SKILL CHECK: STEALTH.
DIFFICULTY: 15.
SNGOOOOOOOOOOOOOOoeh eh?
FAILED.
DALEE DEE BWEE DALEE DE
RUMP LIGHT.
RUMP LIGHT.
UH OH...
BWEE DALEE
AAHHHH!

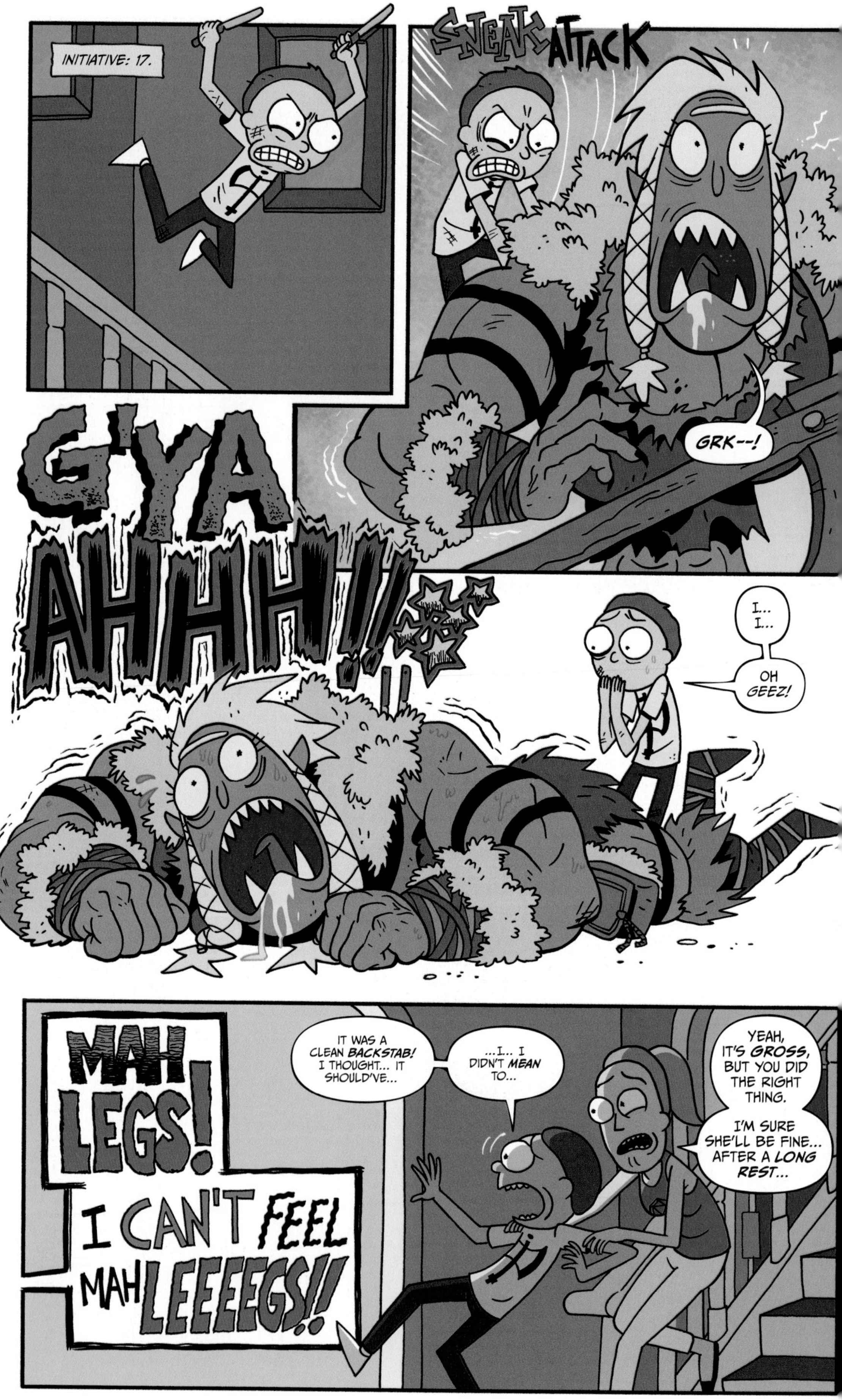
INITIATIVE: 17.
SNEAK ATTACK
GRK--!
G'YA AHHH!!
I... I...
OH GEEZ!
MAH LEGS!
I CAN'T FEEL MAH LEEEEGS!!
IT WAS A CLEAN BACKSTAB! I THOUGHT... IT SHOULD'VE...
...I... I DIDN'T MEAN TO...
YEAH, IT'S GROSS, BUT YOU DID THE RIGHT THING.
I'M SURE SHE'LL BE FINE... AFTER A LONG REST...

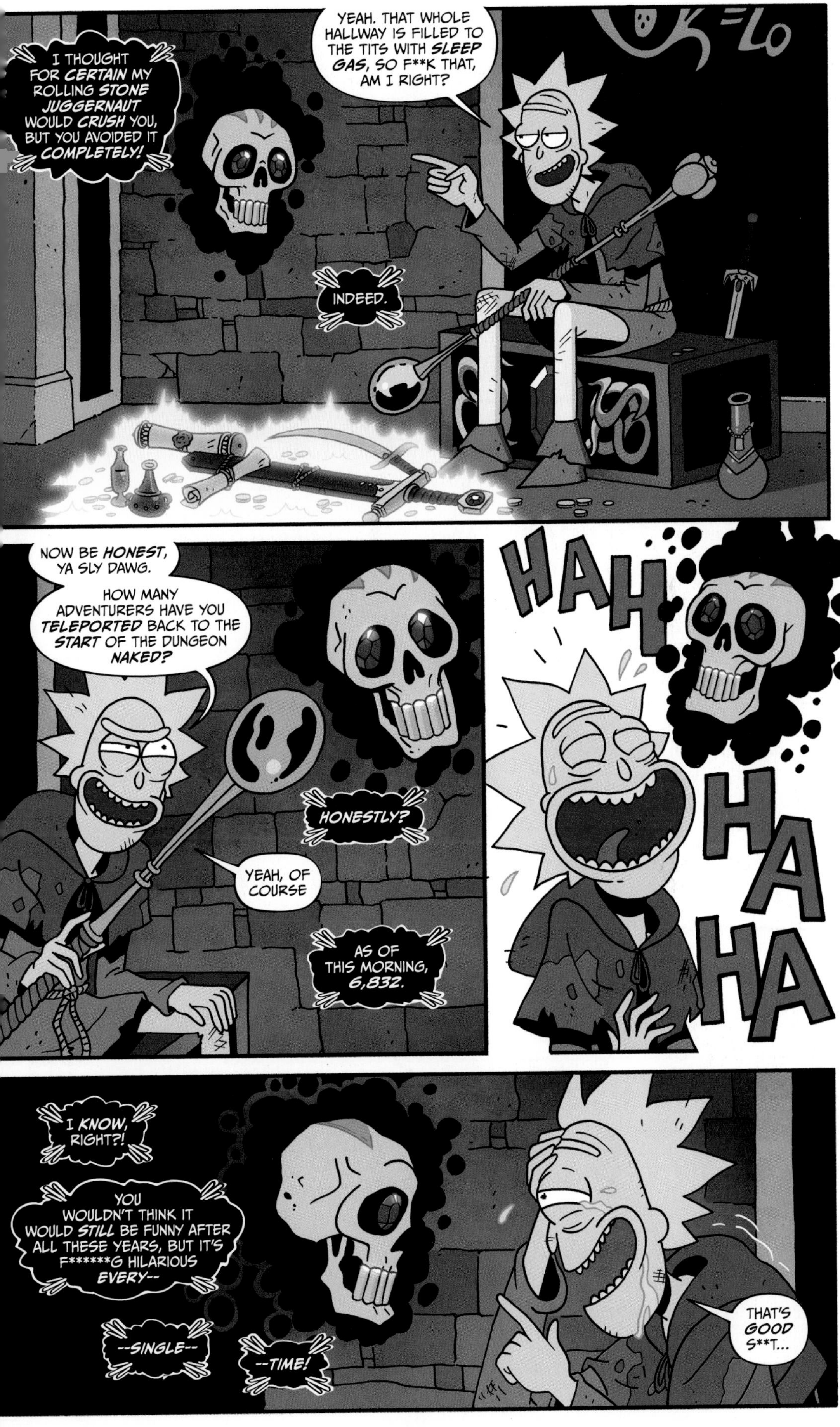
I THOUGHT FOR CERTAIN MY ROLLING STONE JUGGERNAUT WOULD CRUSH YOU, BUT YOU AVOIDED IT COMPLETELY!
YEAH. THAT WHOLE HALLWAY IS FILLED TO THE TITS WITH SLEEP GAS, SO F**K THAT, AM I RIGHT?
INDEED.
NOW BE HONEST, YA SLY DAWG.
HOW MANY ADVENTURERS HAVE YOU TELEPORTED BACK TO THE START OF THE DUNGEON NAKED?
HONESTLY?
YEAH, OF COURSE
AS OF THIS MORNING, 6,832.
HAH HAHAHA
I KNOW, RIGHT?!
YOU WOULDN'T THINK IT WOULD STILL BE FUNNY AFTER ALL THESE YEARS, BUT IT'S F******G HILARIOUS EVERY--
--SINGLE--
--TIME!
THAT'S GOOD S**T...

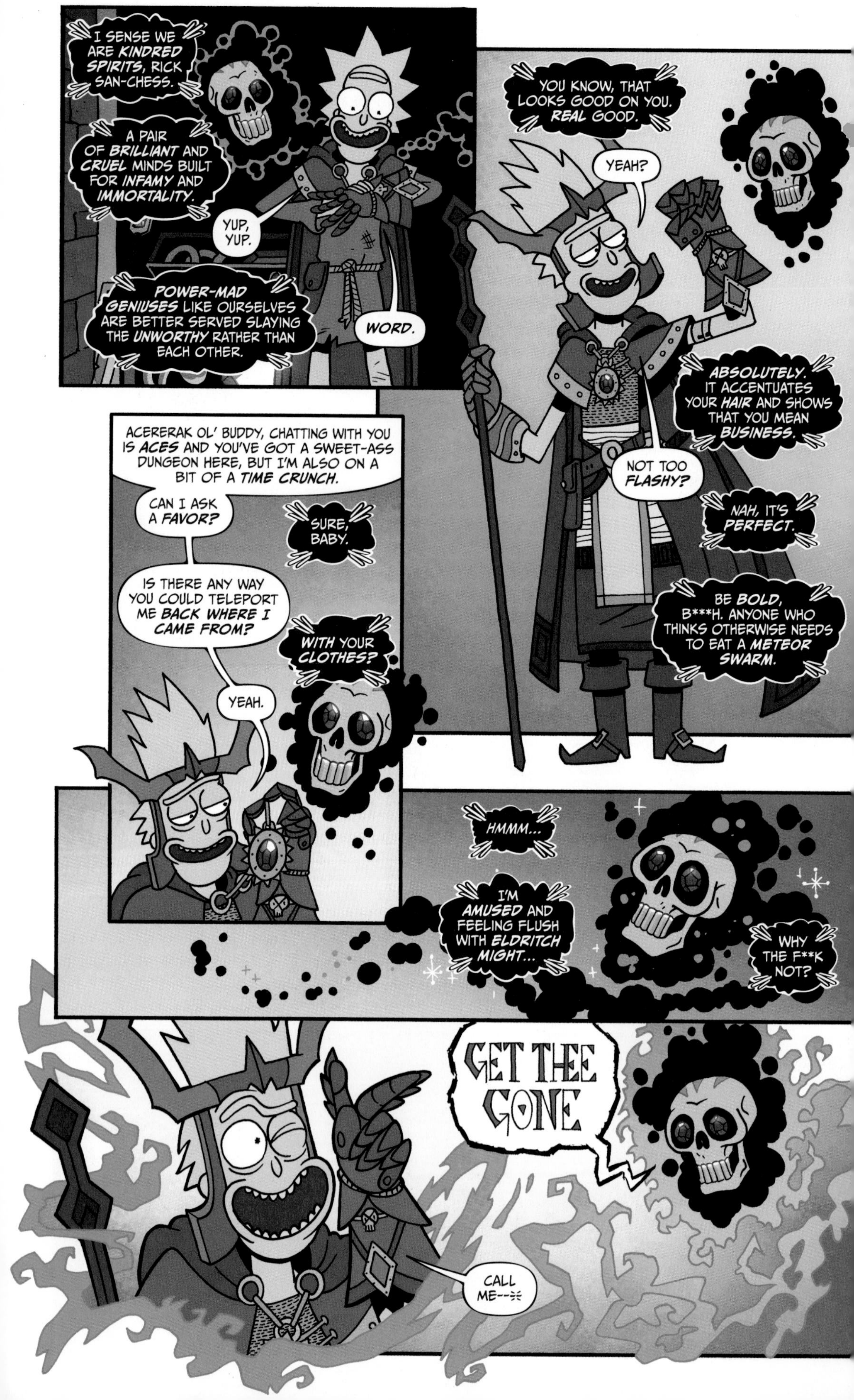
I SENSE WE ARE KINDRED SPIRITS, RICK SAN-CHESS.
A PAIR OF BRILLIANT AND CRUEL MINDS BUILT FOR INFAMY AND IMMORTALITY.
YUP, YUP.
POWER-MAD GENIUSES LIKE OURSELVES ARE BETTER SERVED SLAYING THE UNWORTHY RATHER THAN EACH OTHER.
WORD.
YOU KNOW, THAT LOOKS GOOD ON YOU. REAL GOOD.
YEAH?
ABSOLUTELY. IT ACCENTUATES YOUR HAIR AND SHOWS THAT YOU MEAN BUSINESS.
NOT TOO FLASHY?
NAH, IT'S PERFECT.
BE BOLD, B***H. ANYONE WHO THINKS OTHERWISE NEEDS TO EAT A METEOR SWARM.
ACERERAK OL' BUDDY, CHATTING WITH YOU IS ACES AND YOU'VE GOT A SWEET-ASS DUNGEON HERE, BUT I'M ALSO ON A BIT OF A TIME CRUNCH.
CAN I ASK A FAVOR?
SURE, BABY.
IS THERE ANY WAY YOU COULD TELEPORT ME BACK WHERE I CAME FROM?
WITH YOUR CLOTHES?
YEAH.
HMMM...
I'M AMUSED AND FEELING FLUSH WITH ELDRITCH MIGHT...
WHY THE F**K NOT?
GET THEE GONE
CALL ME--

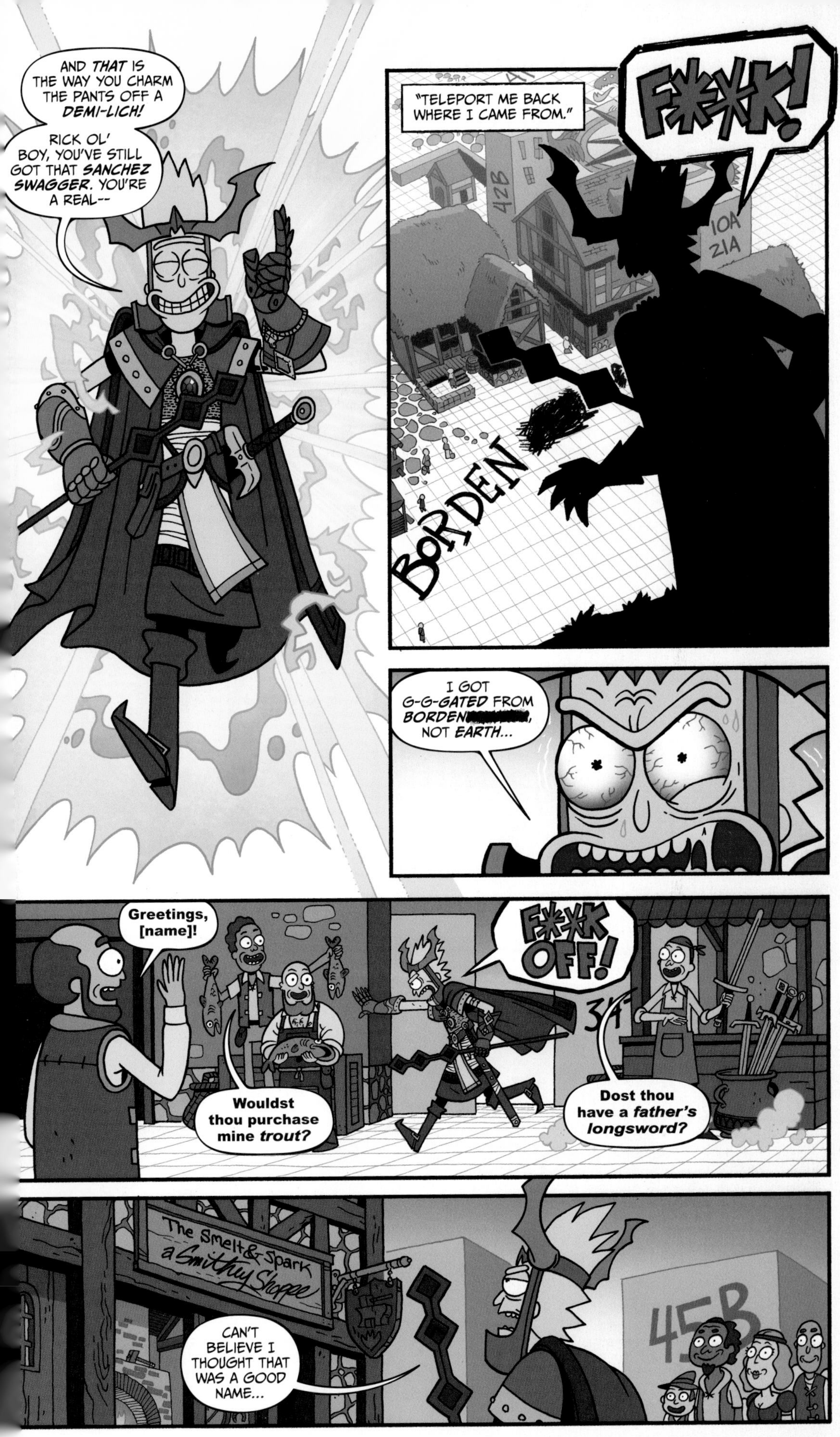
AND *THAT* IS THE WAY YOU CHARM THE PANTS OFF A *DEMI-LICH!*
RICK OL' BOY, YOU'VE STILL GOT THAT *SANCHEZ SWAGGER*. YOU'RE A REAL--
"TELEPORT ME BACK WHERE I CAME FROM."
F**K!
42B
10A 21A
BORDEN
I GOT G-G-*GATED* FROM *BORDEN*[redacted], NOT *EARTH*...
Greetings, [name]!
F**K OFF!
Wouldst thou purchase mine *trout?*
Dost thou have a *father's longsword?*
The Smelt & Spark a Smithy Shoppe
45B
CAN'T BELIEVE I THOUGHT THAT WAS A GOOD NAME...

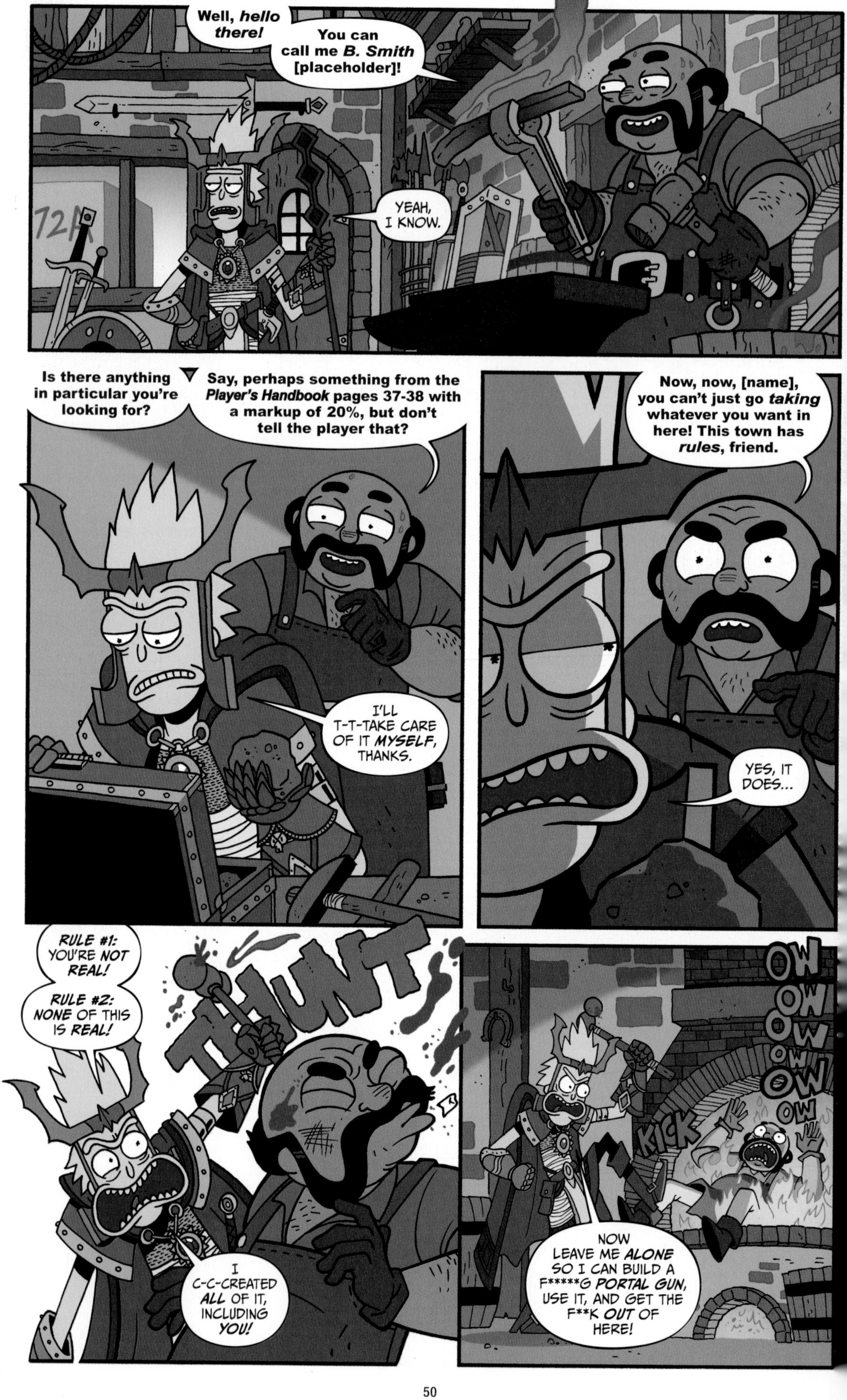
Well, *hello* there!
You can call me *B. Smith* [placeholder]!
YEAH, I KNOW.
Is there anything in particular you're looking for?
Say, perhaps something from the *Player's Handbook* pages 37-38 with a markup of 20%, but don't tell the player that?
I'LL T-T-TAKE CARE OF IT *MYSELF*, THANKS.
Now, now, [name], you can't just go *taking* whatever you want in here! This town has *rules*, friend.
YES, IT DOES...
RULE #1: YOU'RE *NOT REAL!*
RULE #2: NONE OF THIS IS *REAL!*
THUNT
I C-C-CREATED *ALL* OF IT, INCLUDING *YOU!*
KICK
OW OW OW OW OW OW OW
NOW LEAVE ME *ALONE* SO I CAN BUILD A F*****G *PORTAL GUN*, USE IT, AND GET THE F**K *OUT* OF HERE!

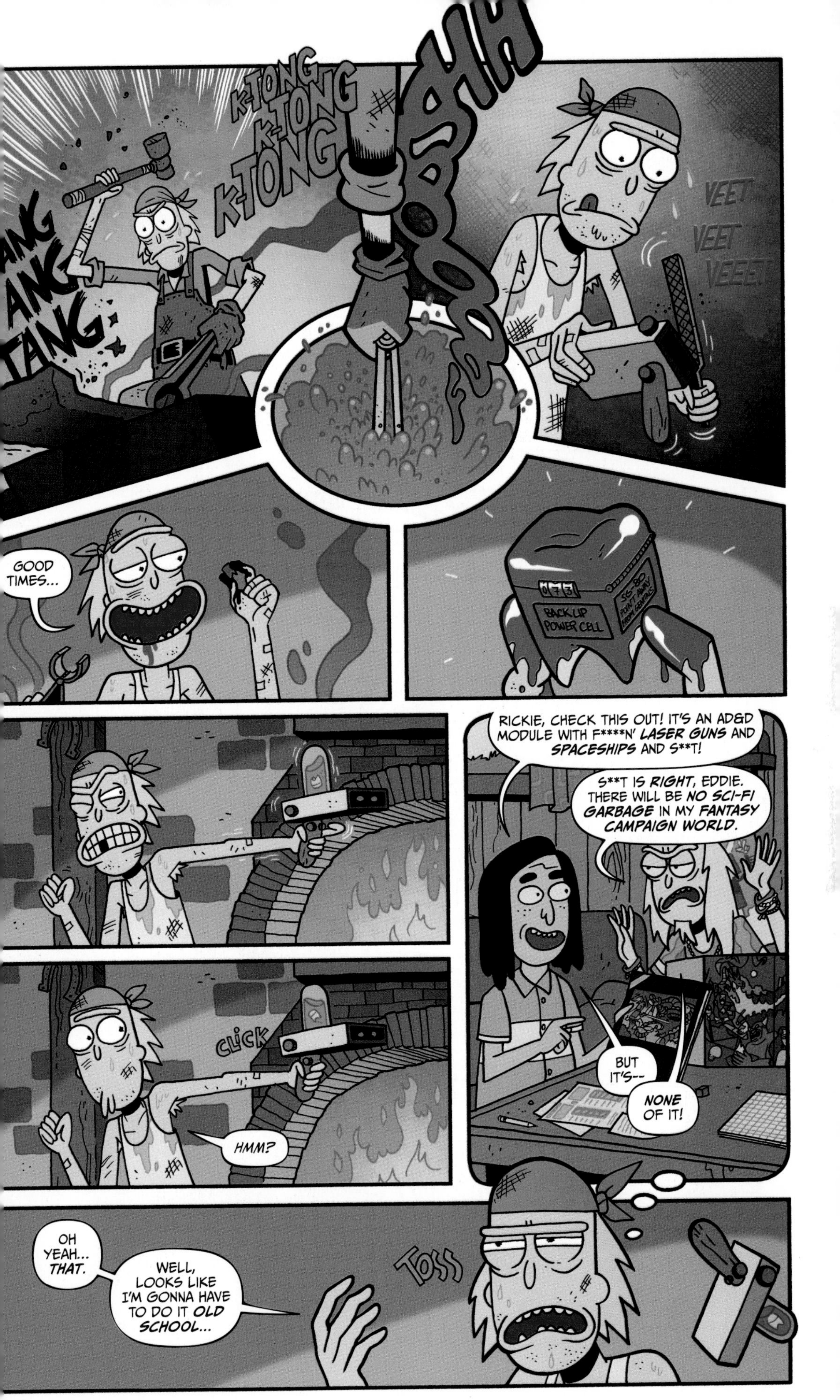
TANG
K-TONG K-TONG K-TONG
VEET VEET VEEET
GOOD TIMES...
BACK UP POWER CELL
SG-80
POINT AWAY FROM GENITALS
CLICK
HMM?
RICKIE, CHECK THIS OUT! IT'S AN AD&D MODULE WITH F****N' LASER GUNS AND SPACESHIPS AND S**T!
S**T IS RIGHT, EDDIE. THERE WILL BE NO SCI-FI GARBAGE IN MY FANTASY CAMPAIGN WORLD.
BUT IT'S--
NONE OF IT!
OH YEAH... THAT.
WELL, LOOKS LIKE I'M GONNA HAVE TO DO IT OLD SCHOOL...
TOSS

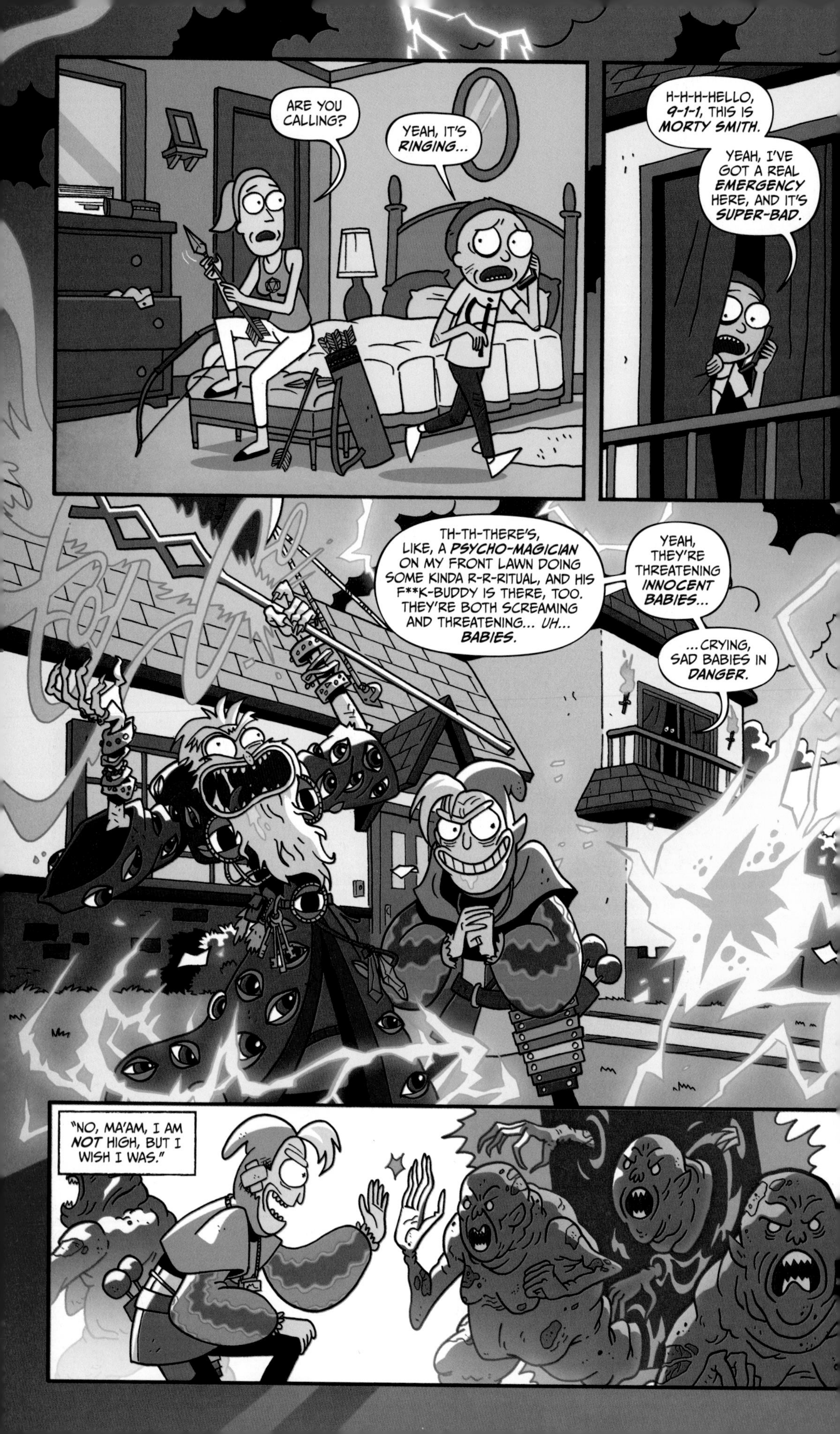
ARE YOU CALLING?
YEAH, IT'S RINGING...
H-H-H-HELLO, 9-1-1, THIS IS MORTY SMITH.
YEAH, I'VE GOT A REAL EMERGENCY HERE, AND IT'S SUPER-BAD.
TH-TH-THERE'S, LIKE, A PSYCHO-MAGICIAN ON MY FRONT LAWN DOING SOME KINDA R-R-RITUAL, AND HIS F**K-BUDDY IS THERE, TOO. THEY'RE BOTH SCREAMING AND THREATENING... UH... BABIES.
YEAH, THEY'RE THREATENING INNOCENT BABIES...
...CRYING, SAD BABIES IN DANGER.
"NO, MA'AM, I AM NOT HIGH, BUT I WISH I WAS."

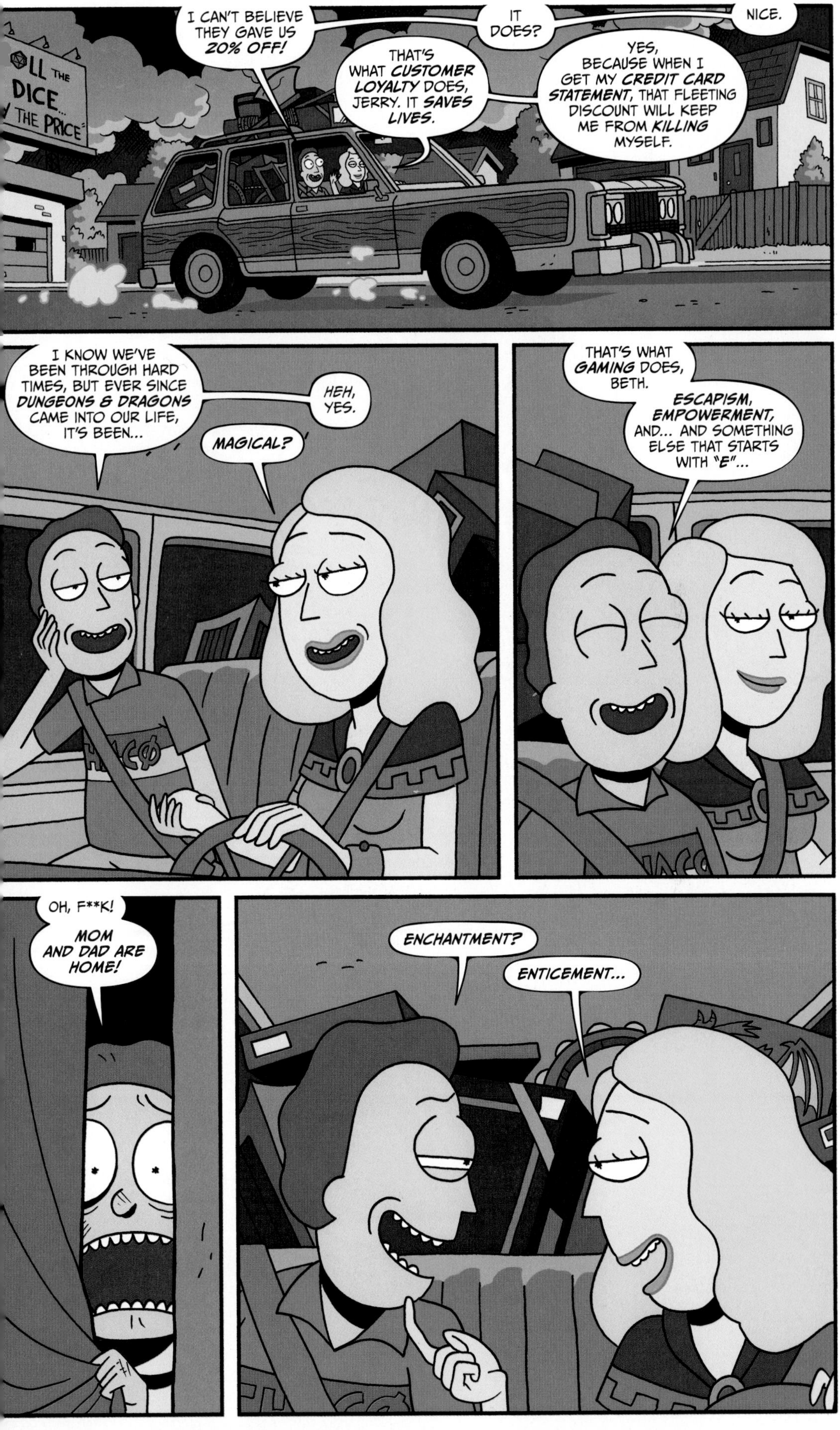
ROLL THE DICE... THE PRICE
I CAN'T BELIEVE THEY GAVE US 20% OFF!
IT DOES?
NICE.
THAT'S WHAT CUSTOMER LOYALTY DOES, JERRY. IT SAVES LIVES.
YES, BECAUSE WHEN I GET MY CREDIT CARD STATEMENT, THAT FLEETING DISCOUNT WILL KEEP ME FROM KILLING MYSELF.
I KNOW WE'VE BEEN THROUGH HARD TIMES, BUT EVER SINCE DUNGEONS & DRAGONS CAME INTO OUR LIFE, IT'S BEEN...
HEH, YES.
MAGICAL?
THAT'S WHAT GAMING DOES, BETH.
ESCAPISM, EMPOWERMENT, AND... AND SOMETHING ELSE THAT STARTS WITH "E"...
OH, F**K!
MOM AND DAD ARE HOME!
ENCHANTMENT?
ENTICEMENT...

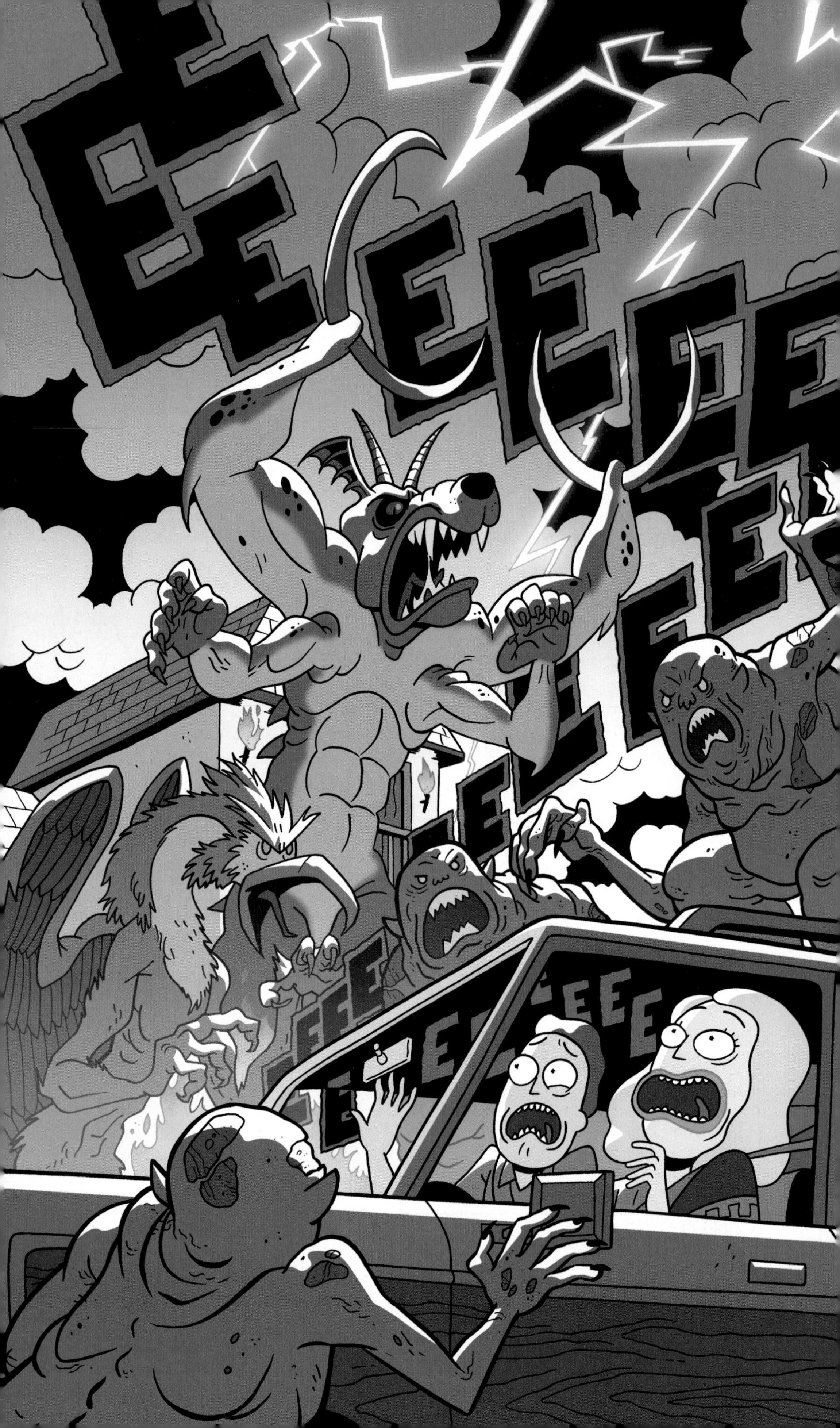

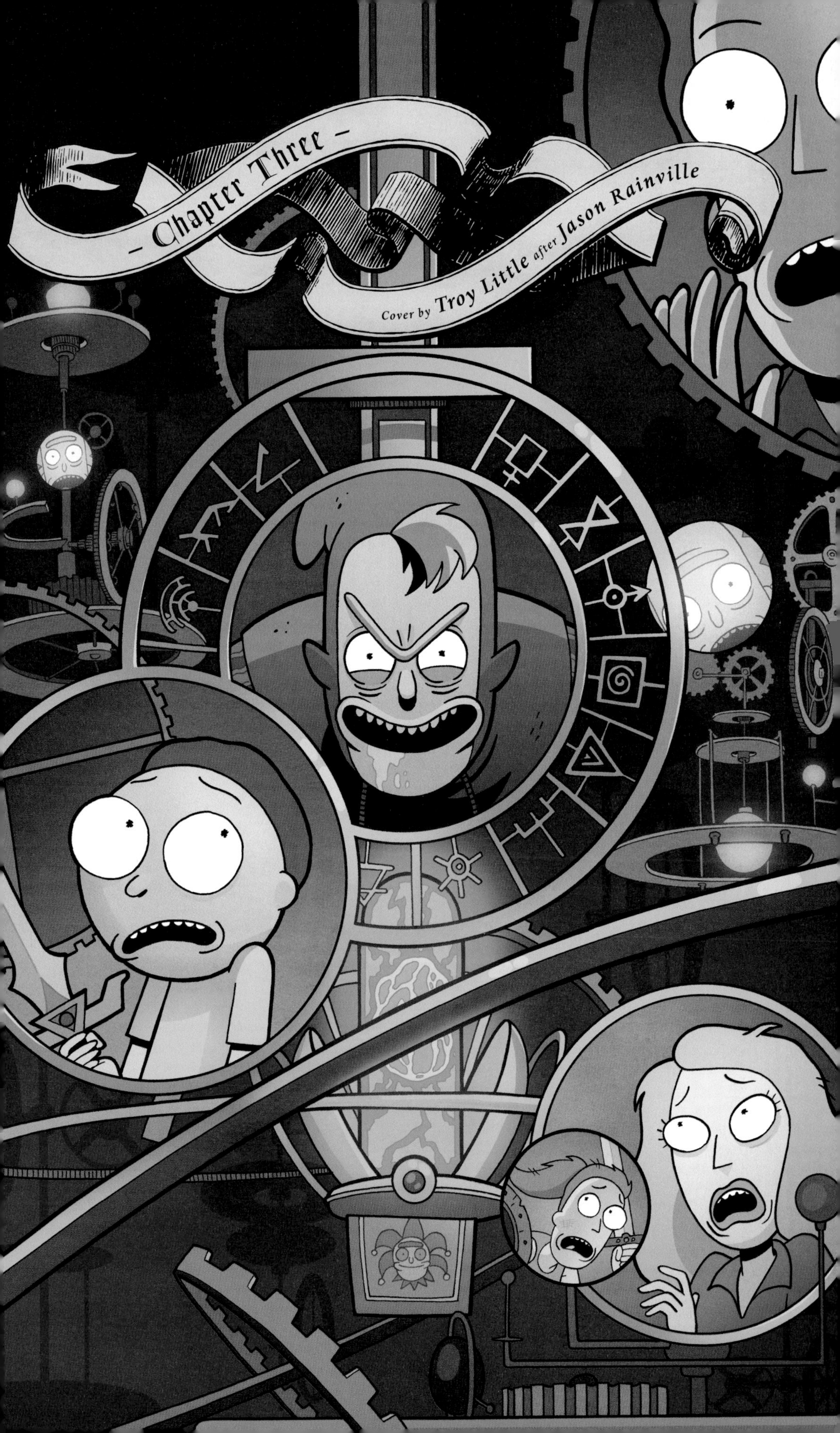
- Chapter Three -
Cover by Troy Little after Jason Rainville

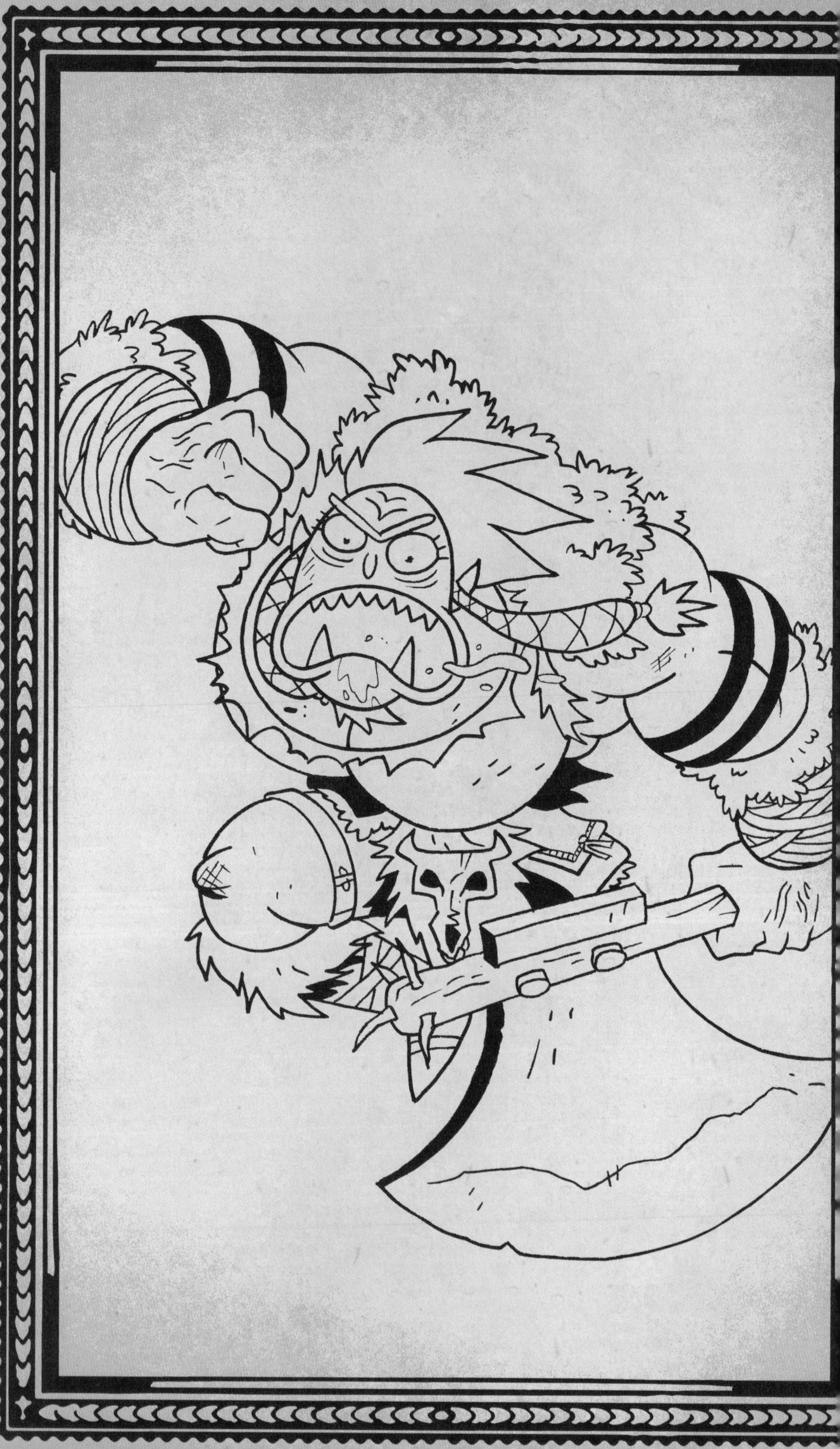

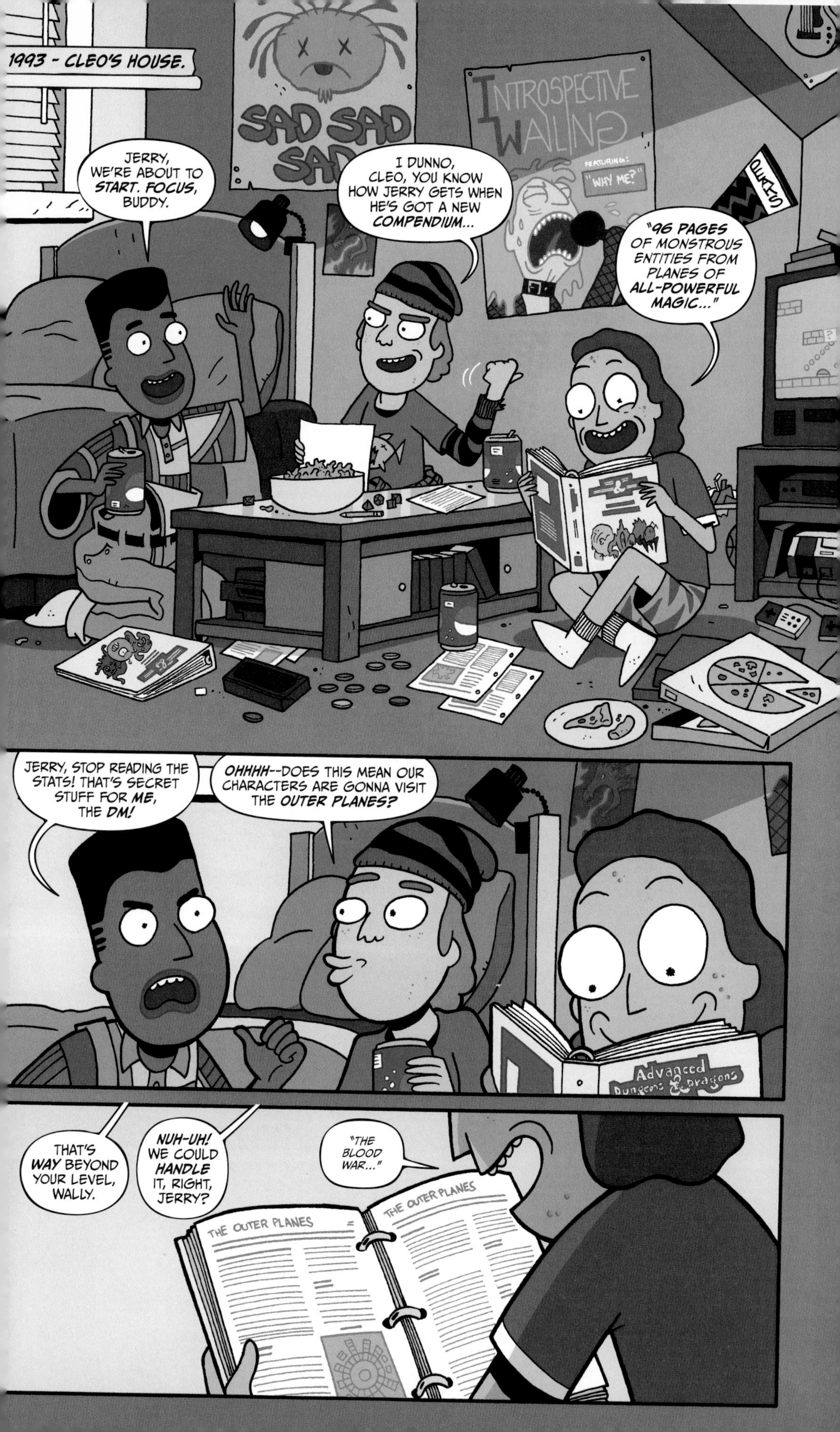

1993 - CLEO'S HOUSE.
SAD SAD SAD
INTROSPECTIVE WAILING
FEATURING: "WHY ME?"
JERRY, WE'RE ABOUT TO START. FOCUS, BUDDY.
I DUNNO, CLEO, YOU KNOW HOW JERRY GETS WHEN HE'S GOT A NEW COMPENDIUM...
"96 PAGES OF MONSTROUS ENTITIES FROM PLANES OF ALL-POWERFUL MAGIC..."
JERRY, STOP READING THE STATS! THAT'S SECRET STUFF FOR ME, THE DM!
OHHHH--DOES THIS MEAN OUR CHARACTERS ARE GONNA VISIT THE OUTER PLANES?
Advanced Dungeons & Dragons
THAT'S WAY BEYOND YOUR LEVEL, WALLY.
NUH-UH! WE COULD HANDLE IT, RIGHT, JERRY?
"THE BLOOD WAR..."
THE OUTER PLANES
THE OUTER PLANES

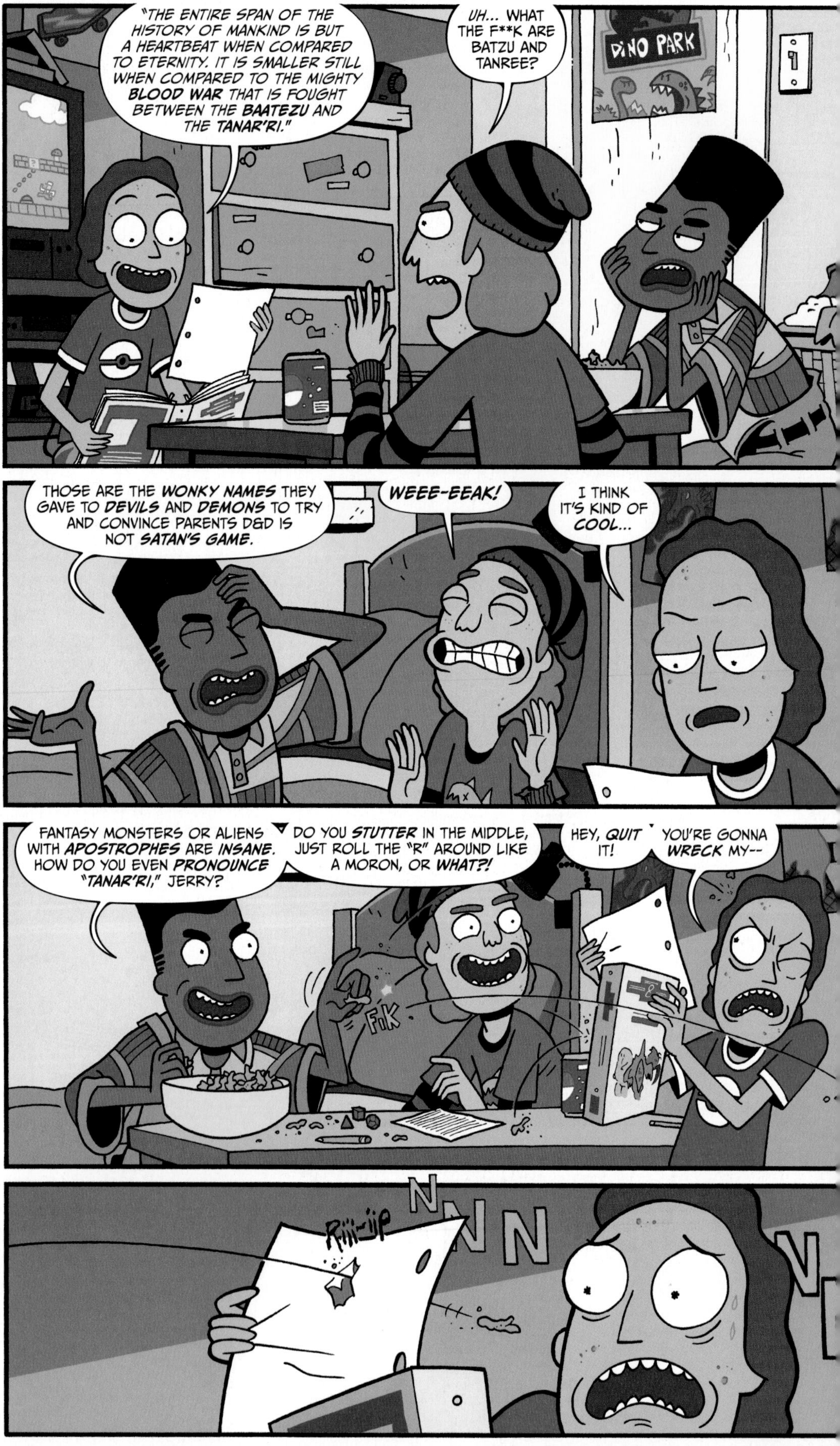
"THE ENTIRE SPAN OF THE HISTORY OF MANKIND IS BUT A HEARTBEAT WHEN COMPARED TO ETERNITY. IT IS SMALLER STILL WHEN COMPARED TO THE MIGHTY BLOOD WAR THAT IS FOUGHT BETWEEN THE BAATEZU AND THE TANAR'RI."
UH... WHAT THE F**K ARE BATZU AND TANREE?
DINO PARK
THOSE ARE THE WONKY NAMES THEY GAVE TO DEVILS AND DEMONS TO TRY AND CONVINCE PARENTS D&D IS NOT SATAN'S GAME.
WEEE-EEAK!
I THINK IT'S KIND OF COOL...
FANTASY MONSTERS OR ALIENS WITH APOSTROPHES ARE INSANE. HOW DO YOU EVEN PRONOUNCE "TANAR'RI," JERRY?
DO YOU STUTTER IN THE MIDDLE, JUST ROLL THE "R" AROUND LIKE A MORON, OR WHAT?!
HEY, QUIT IT!
YOU'RE GONNA WRECK MY--
FlK
Riiii-iip
NNNN

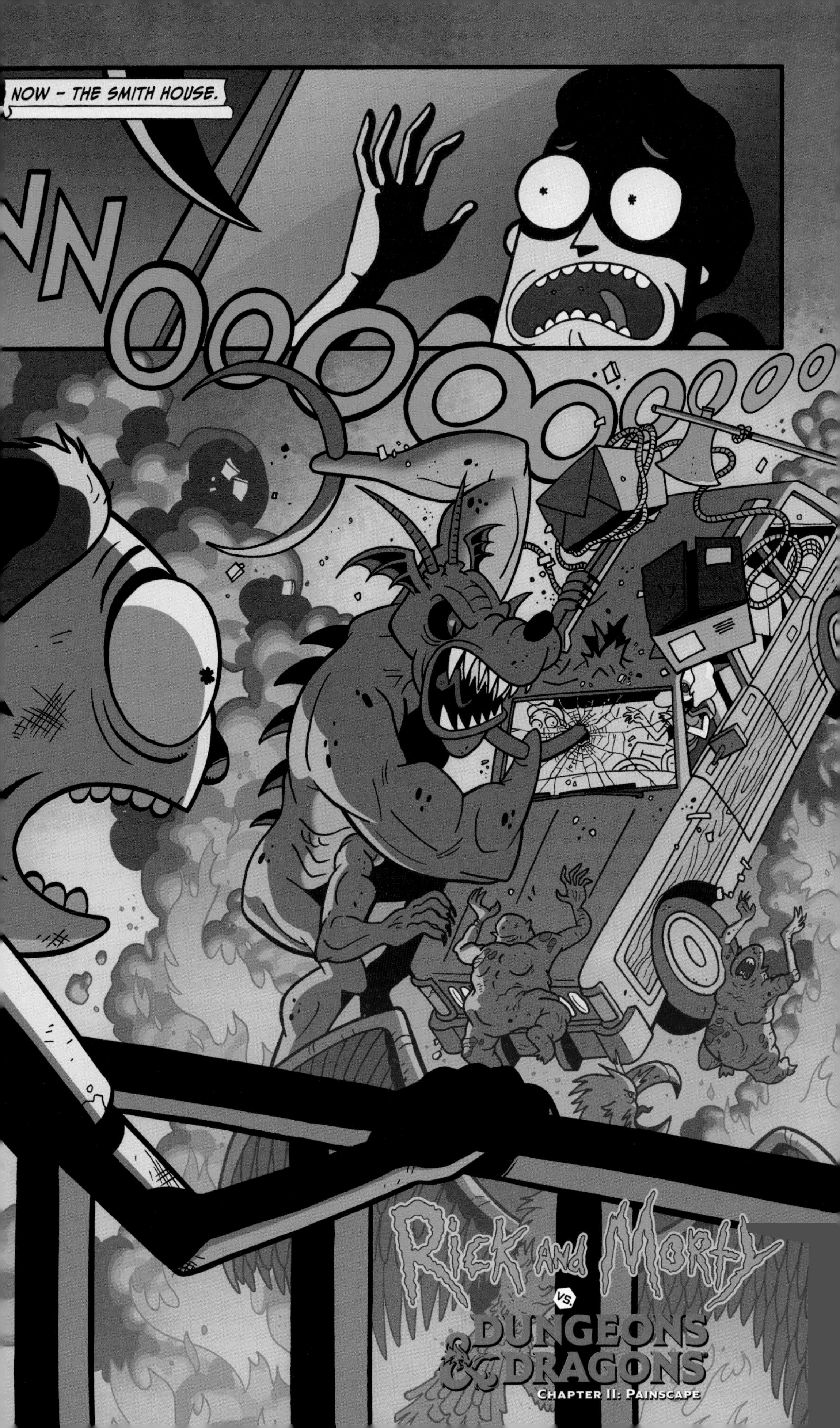
NOW – THE SMITH HOUSE.
NNOOOOOOOOOOOO
RICK AND MORTY VS. DUNGEONS & DRAGONS
CHAPTER II: PAINSCAPE

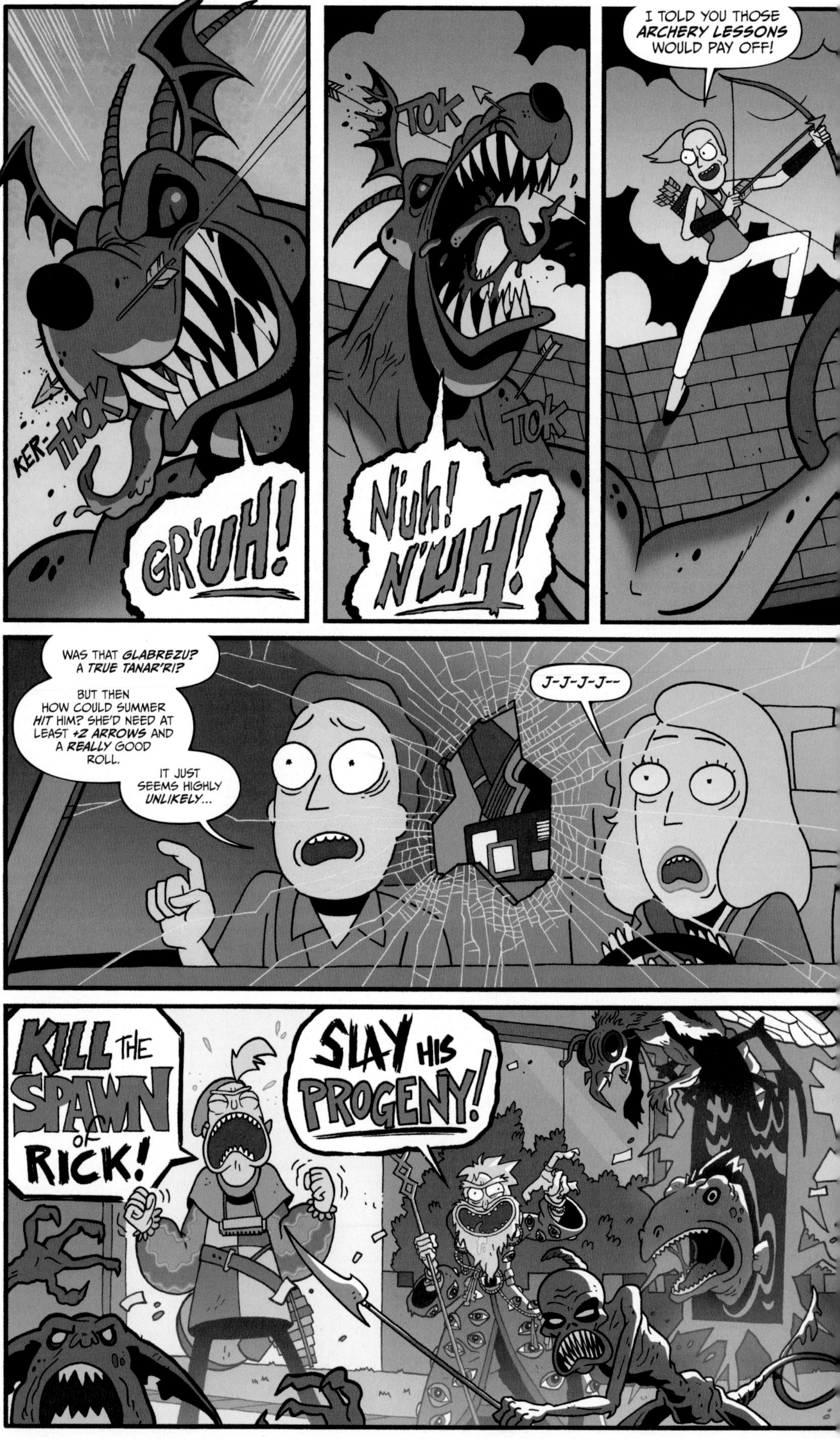
KER-THOK
GR'UH!
TOK
TOK
N'uh! N'UH!
I TOLD YOU THOSE ARCHERY LESSONS WOULD PAY OFF!
WAS THAT GLABREZU? A TRUE TANAR'RI?
BUT THEN HOW COULD SUMMER HIT HIM? SHE'D NEED AT LEAST +2 ARROWS AND A REALLY GOOD ROLL.
IT JUST SEEMS HIGHLY UNLIKELY...
J-J-J-J--
KILL THE SPAWN of RICK!
SLAY HIS PROGENY!

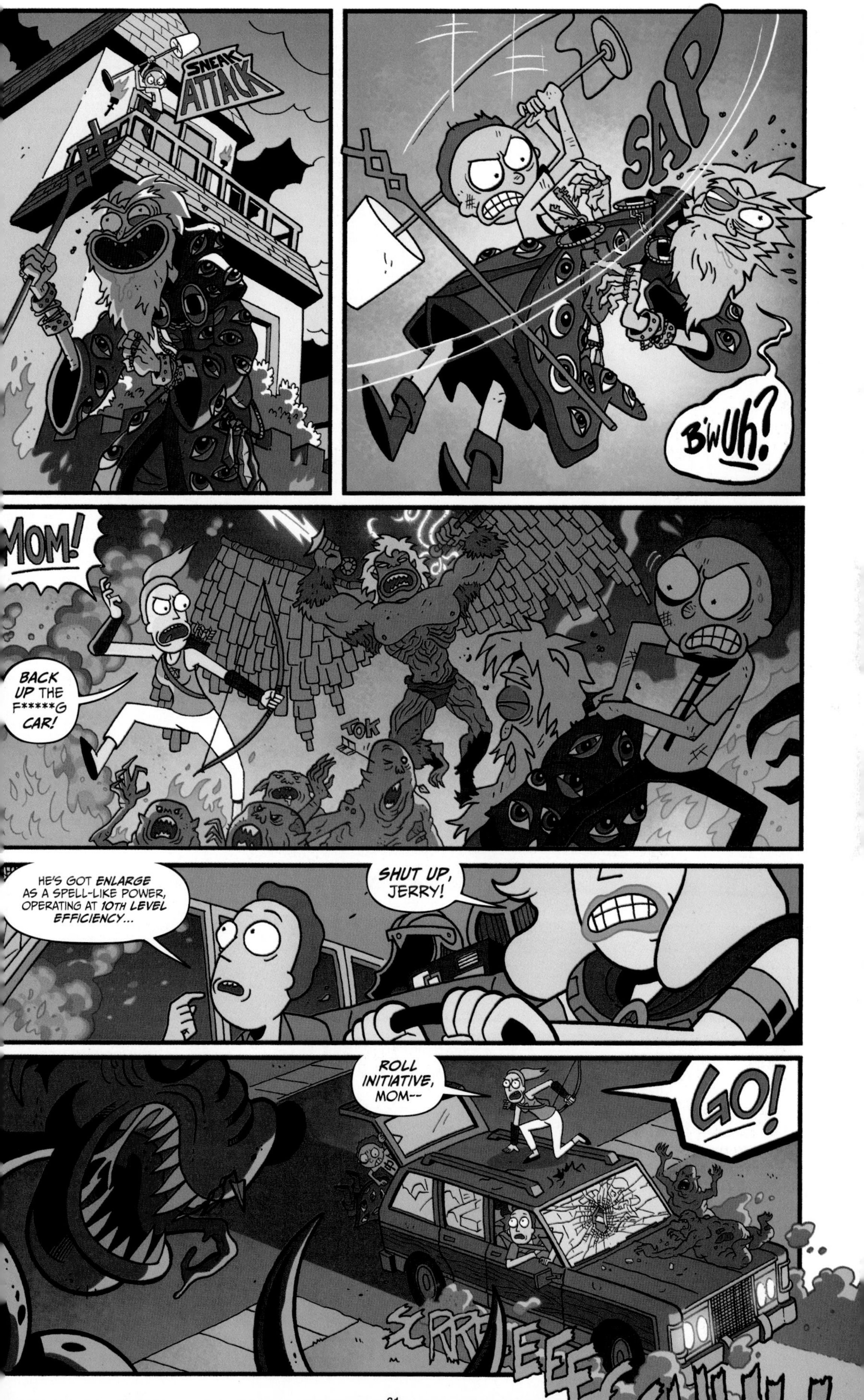

SNEAK ATTACK
SAP
B'WUH?
MOM!
BACK UP THE F*****G CAR!
TOK
HE'S GOT ENLARGE AS A SPELL-LIKE POWER, OPERATING AT 10TH LEVEL EFFICIENCY...
SHUT UP, JERRY!
ROLL INITIATIVE, MOM--
GO!

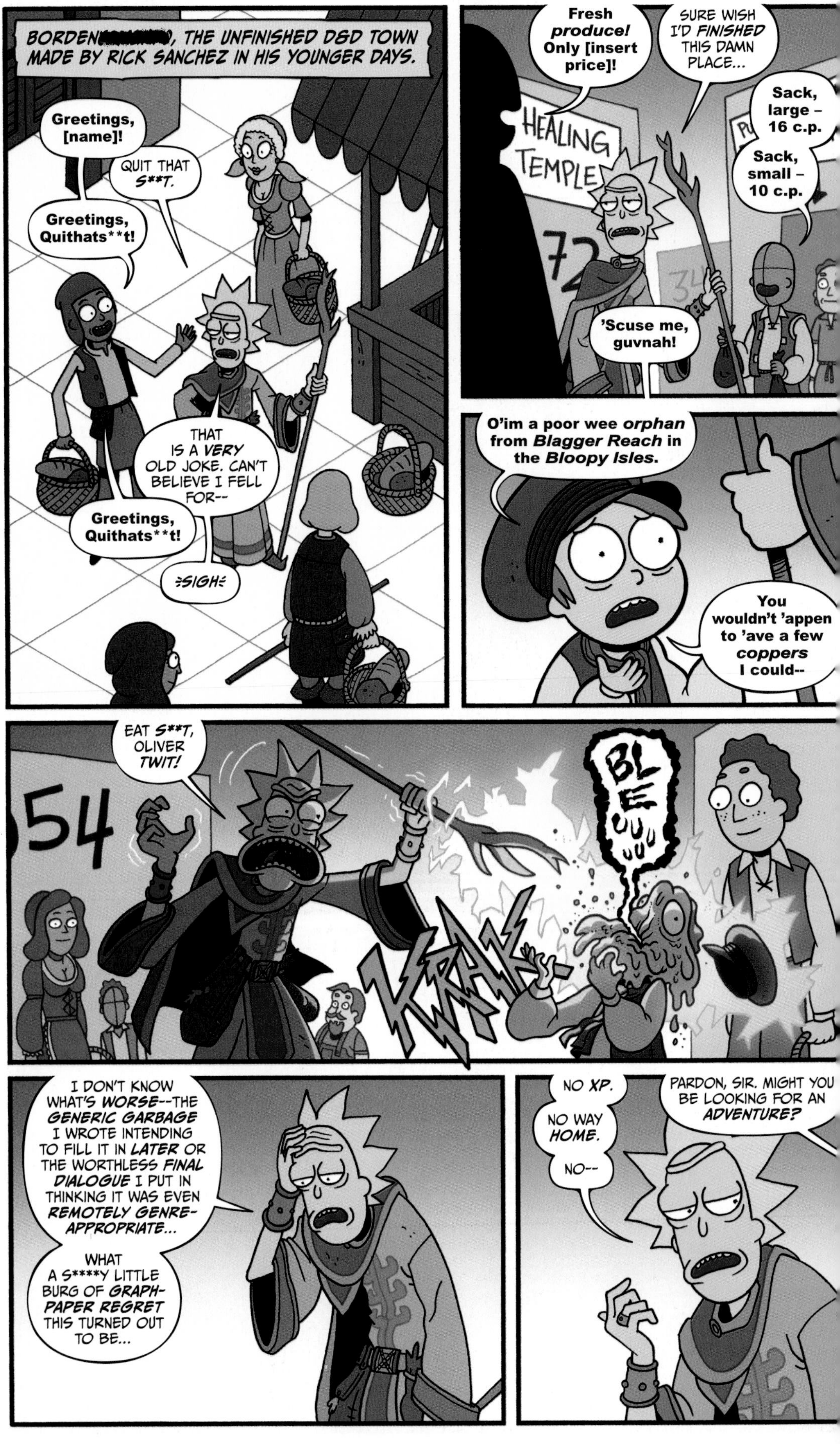
BORDEN[redacted], THE UNFINISHED D&D TOWN MADE BY RICK SANCHEZ IN HIS YOUNGER DAYS.
Greetings, [name]!
QUIT THAT S**T.
Greetings, Quithats**t!
THAT IS A VERY OLD JOKE. CAN'T BELIEVE I FELL FOR--
Greetings, Quithats**t!
SIGH
Fresh produce! Only [insert price]!
SURE WISH I'D FINISHED THIS DAMN PLACE...
HEALING TEMPLE
Sack, large – 16 c.p.
Sack, small – 10 c.p.
72
'Scuse me, guvnah!
O'im a poor wee orphan from Blagger Reach in the Bloopy Isles.
You wouldn't 'appen to 'ave a few coppers I could--
EAT S**T, OLIVER TWIT!
54
BLEUUUU
KRAK
I DON'T KNOW WHAT'S WORSE--THE GENERIC GARBAGE I WROTE INTENDING TO FILL IT IN LATER OR THE WORTHLESS FINAL DIALOGUE I PUT IN THINKING IT WAS EVEN REMOTELY GENRE-APPROPRIATE...
WHAT A S****Y LITTLE BURG OF GRAPH-PAPER REGRET THIS TURNED OUT TO BE...
NO XP.
NO WAY HOME.
NO--
PARDON, SIR. MIGHT YOU BE LOOKING FOR AN ADVENTURE?

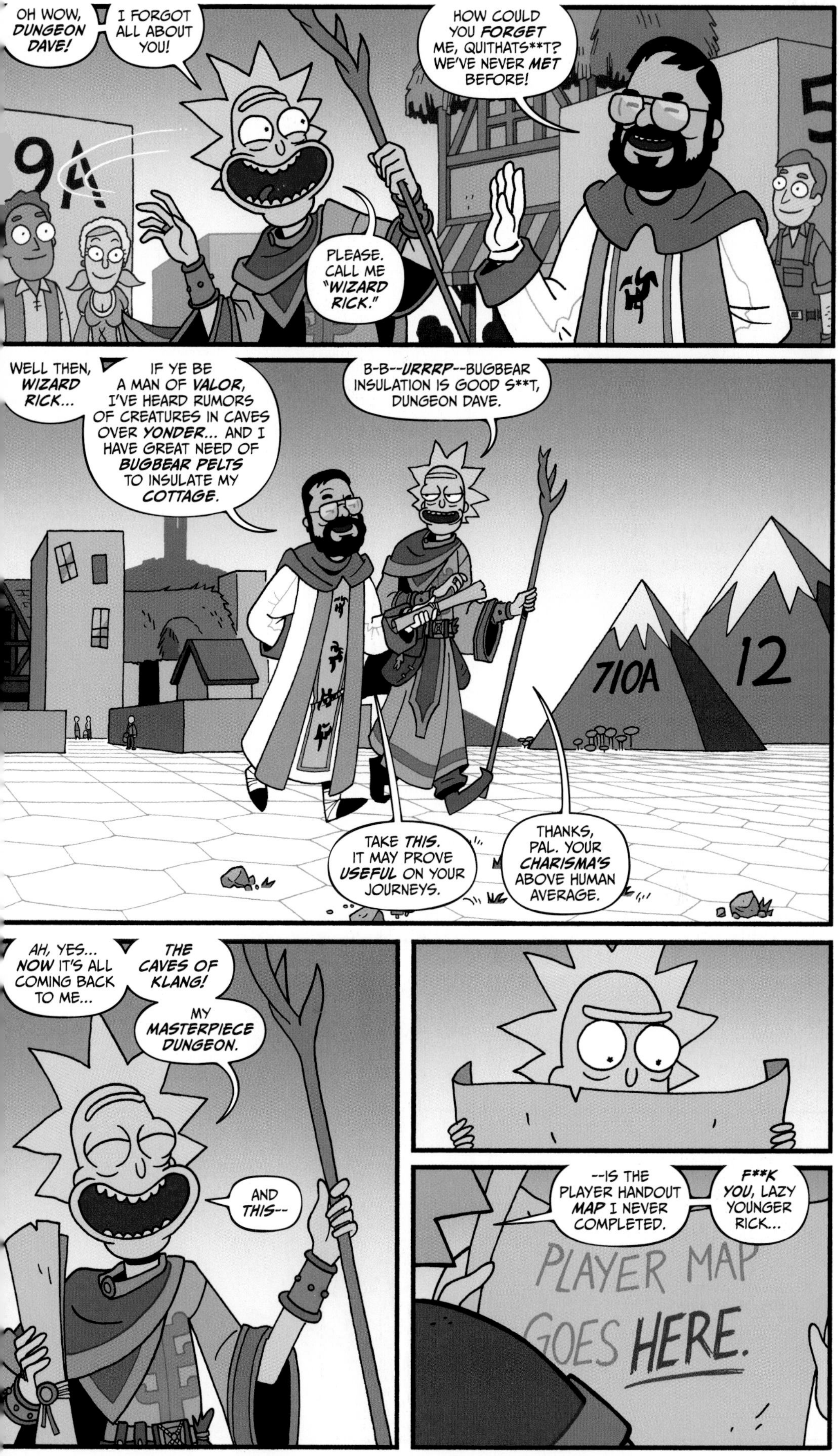
OH WOW, DUNGEON DAVE!
I FORGOT ALL ABOUT YOU!
HOW COULD YOU FORGET ME, QUITHATS**T? WE'VE NEVER MET BEFORE!
PLEASE. CALL ME "WIZARD RICK."
9A
5
WELL THEN, WIZARD RICK...
IF YE BE A MAN OF VALOR, I'VE HEARD RUMORS OF CREATURES IN CAVES OVER YONDER... AND I HAVE GREAT NEED OF BUGBEAR PELTS TO INSULATE MY COTTAGE.
B-B--URRRP--BUGBEAR INSULATION IS GOOD S**T, DUNGEON DAVE.
TAKE THIS. IT MAY PROVE USEFUL ON YOUR JOURNEYS.
THANKS, PAL. YOUR CHARISMA'S ABOVE HUMAN AVERAGE.
710A
12
AH, YES... NOW IT'S ALL COMING BACK TO ME...
THE CAVES OF KLANG!
MY MASTERPIECE DUNGEON.
AND THIS--
--IS THE PLAYER HANDOUT MAP I NEVER COMPLETED.
F**K YOU, LAZY YOUNGER RICK...
PLAYER MAP GOES HERE.

WELL, THERE IT IS!

KIND OF ON THE *NOSE*, BUT HEY, THAT'S WHAT *BEGINNER DUNGEONS* ARE ALL ABOUT.

THE CAVES OF KLANG

AN ADVENTURE FOR CHARACTERS LEVELS 1-4

(LIGHT.)

HA! I'M A *FIRST-LEVEL WIZARD* WITH THAT "NEW ADVENTURER SMELL."

OF COURSE, IT'D FEEL A LOT MORE *NOSTALGIC* IF I HAD SOMETHING BETTER THAN *ITCHY LINEN* PROTECTING MY *JANGLIES* AND DIDN'T HAVE *HIT POINTS* SO LOW A *PREGNANT MUSKRAT* COULD K.O. MY ASS...

WAIT A SEC...

KLANG

...*LAZY YOUNGER RICK* WAS ALSO "F**K YOUR *PLAYERS* OVER JUST *BECAUSE YOU CAN*" DUNGEON MASTER RICK...

I REMEMBER EVERY 10X10 SQUARE OF THE *TOMB OF HORRORS* LIKE IT WAS MY FIRST *ORGASM*, BUT FOR THE LIFE OF ME I CAN'T REMEMBER THE S**T I PUT IN *HERE*...

KLANG

BbbBURP BLAH!! HEHE HEHE HEH

KLANG KLANG KLANG KLANG FOOK! KLANG

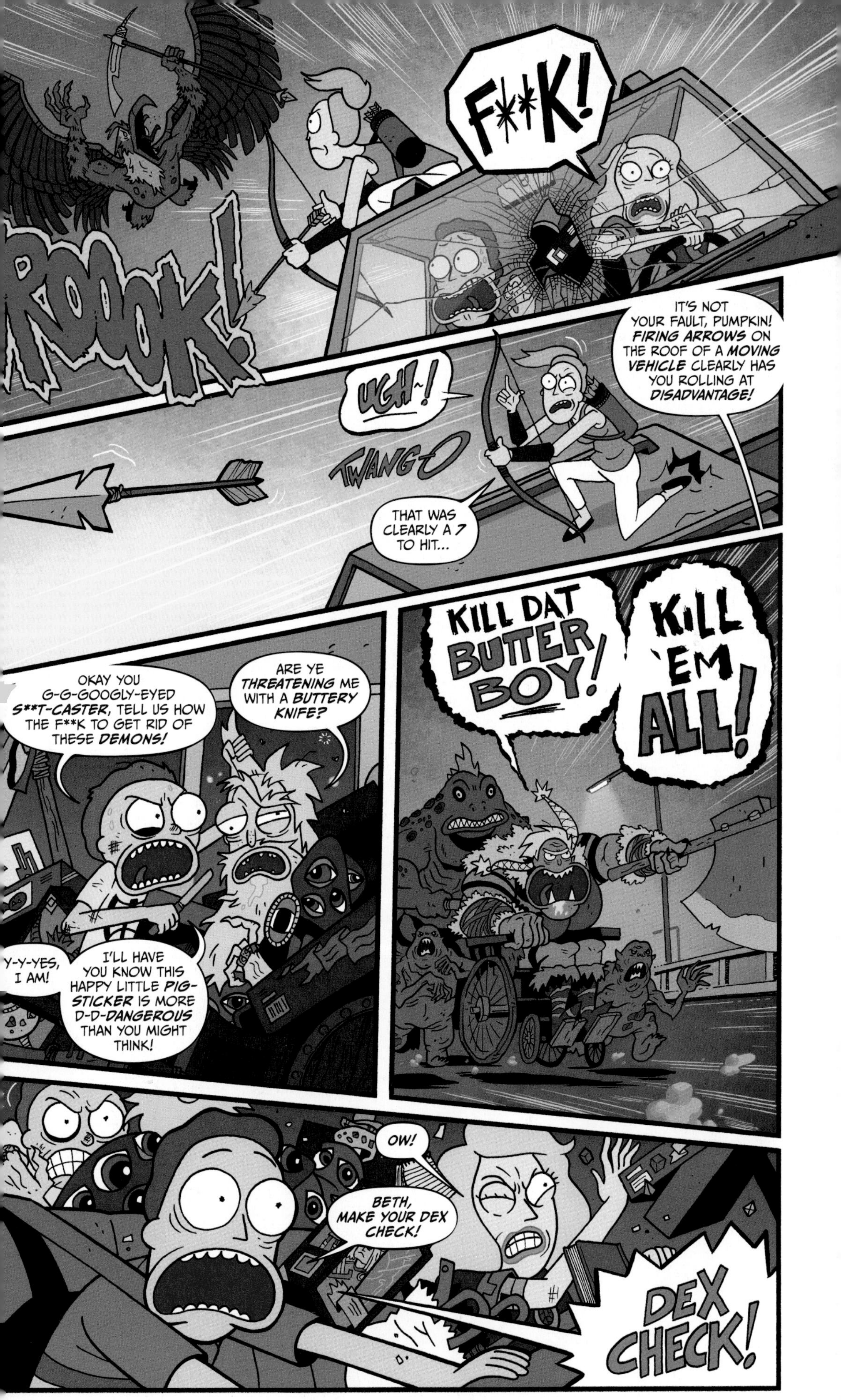
F**K!
ROOOK!
UGH~!
TWANG-O
IT'S NOT YOUR FAULT, PUMPKIN! FIRING ARROWS ON THE ROOF OF A MOVING VEHICLE CLEARLY HAS YOU ROLLING AT DISADVANTAGE!
THAT WAS CLEARLY A 7 TO HIT...
OKAY YOU G-G-GOOGLY-EYED S**T-CASTER, TELL US HOW THE F**K TO GET RID OF THESE DEMONS!
ARE YE THREATENING ME WITH A BUTTERY KNIFE?
Y-Y-YES, I AM!
I'LL HAVE YOU KNOW THIS HAPPY LITTLE PIG-STICKER IS MORE D-D-DANGEROUS THAN YOU MIGHT THINK!
KILL DAT BUTTER BOY!
KILL 'EM ALL!
OW!
BETH, MAKE YOUR DEX CHECK!
DEX CHECK!

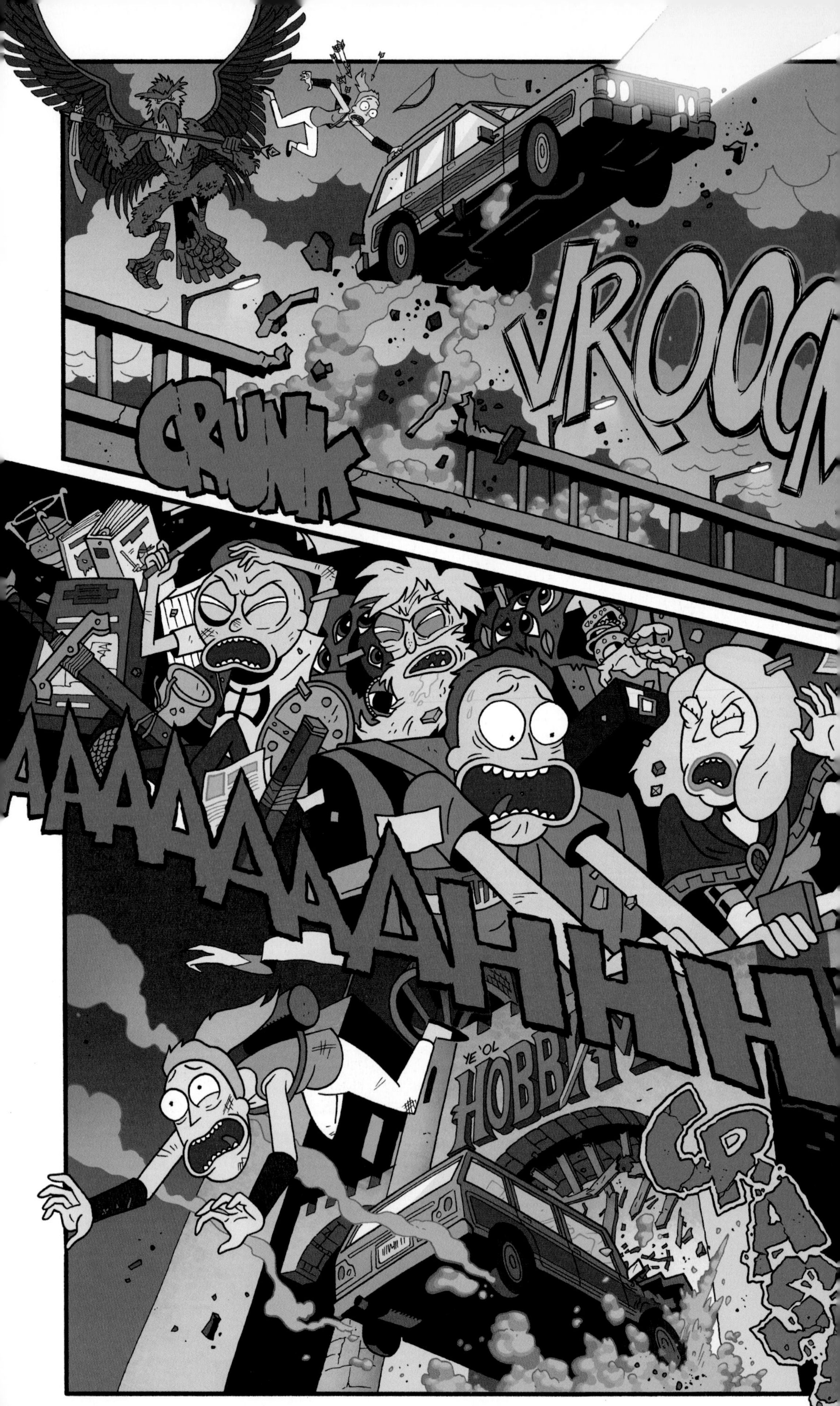
CRUNK
YE 'OL

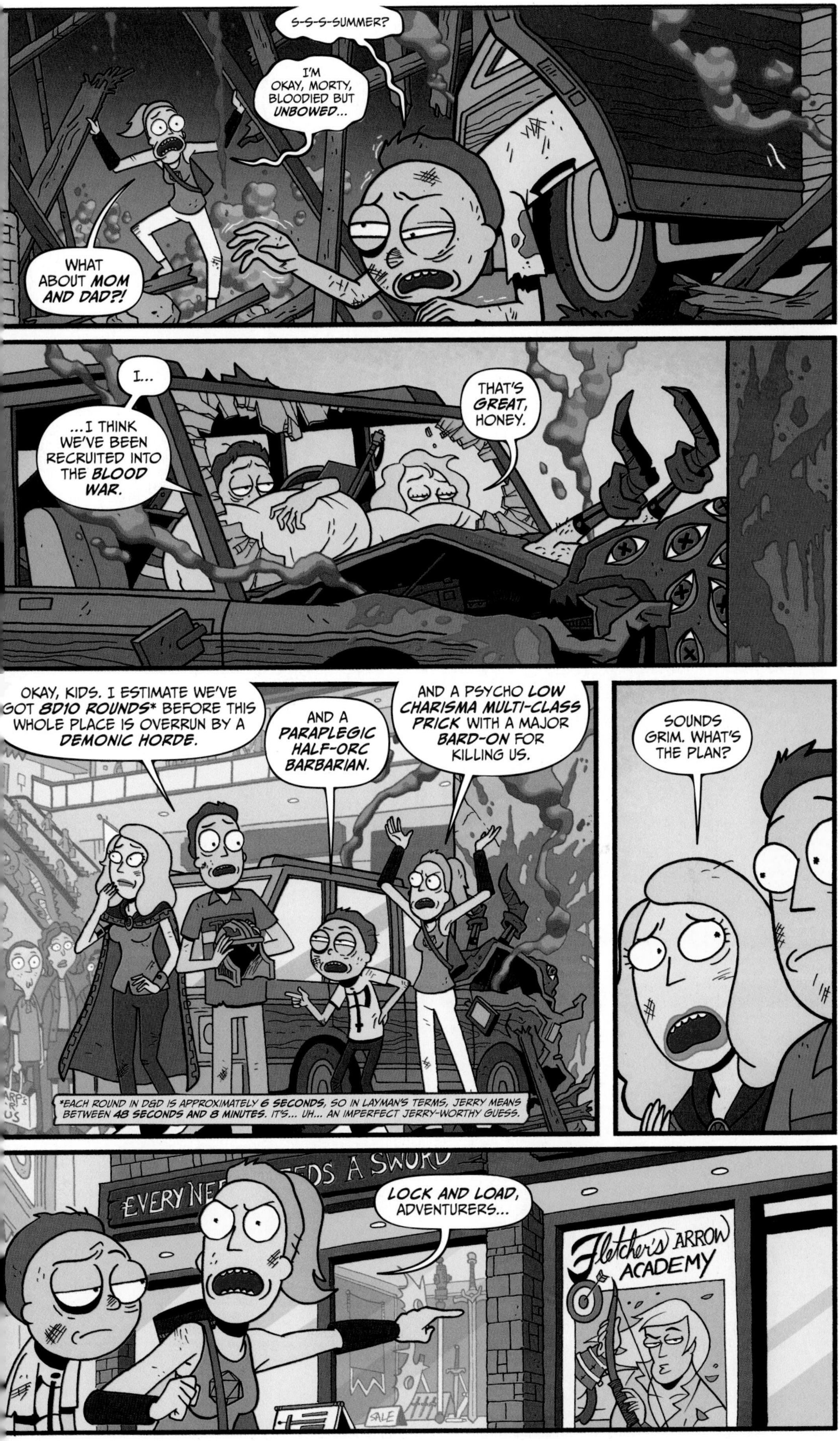
S-S-S-SUMMER?
I'M OKAY, MORTY, BLOODIED BUT UNBOWED...
WHAT ABOUT MOM AND DAD?!
I...
...I THINK WE'VE BEEN RECRUITED INTO THE BLOOD WAR.
THAT'S GREAT, HONEY.
OKAY, KIDS. I ESTIMATE WE'VE GOT 8D10 ROUNDS* BEFORE THIS WHOLE PLACE IS OVERRUN BY A DEMONIC HORDE.
AND A PARAPLEGIC HALF-ORC BARBARIAN.
AND A PSYCHO LOW CHARISMA MULTI-CLASS PRICK WITH A MAJOR BARD-ON FOR KILLING US.
*EACH ROUND IN D&D IS APPROXIMATELY 6 SECONDS, SO IN LAYMAN'S TERMS, JERRY MEANS BETWEEN 48 SECONDS AND 8 MINUTES. IT'S... UH... AN IMPERFECT JERRY-WORTHY GUESS.
SOUNDS GRIM. WHAT'S THE PLAN?
EVERY NE EDS A SWORD
LOCK AND LOAD, ADVENTURERS...
Fletcher's ARROW ACADEMY
SALE

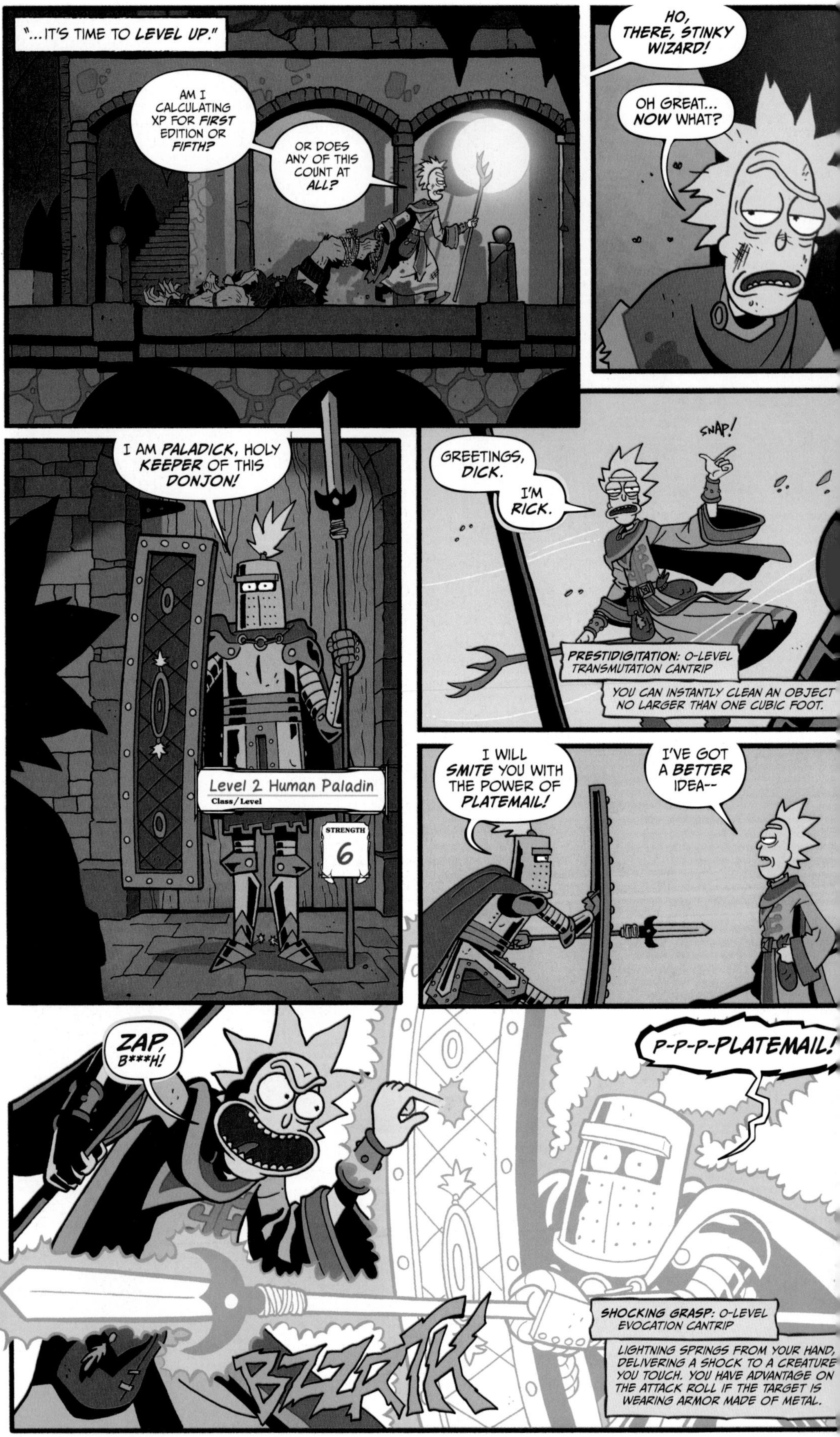

"...IT'S TIME TO LEVEL UP."
AM I CALCULATING XP FOR FIRST EDITION OR FIFTH?
OR DOES ANY OF THIS COUNT AT ALL?
HO, THERE, STINKY WIZARD!
OH GREAT... NOW WHAT?
I AM PALADICK, HOLY KEEPER OF THIS DONJON!
Level 2 Human Paladin
Class/Level
STRENGTH
6
SNAP!
GREETINGS, DICK.
I'M RICK.
PRESTIDIGITATION: O-LEVEL TRANSMUTATION CANTRIP
YOU CAN INSTANTLY CLEAN AN OBJECT NO LARGER THAN ONE CUBIC FOOT.
I WILL SMITE YOU WITH THE POWER OF PLATEMAIL!
I'VE GOT A BETTER IDEA--
ZAP, B***H!
P-P-P-PLATEMAIL!
BZZRTK
SHOCKING GRASP: O-LEVEL EVOCATION CANTRIP
LIGHTNING SPRINGS FROM YOUR HAND, DELIVERING A SHOCK TO A CREATURE YOU TOUCH. YOU HAVE ADVANTAGE ON THE ATTACK ROLL IF THE TARGET IS WEARING ARMOR MADE OF METAL.

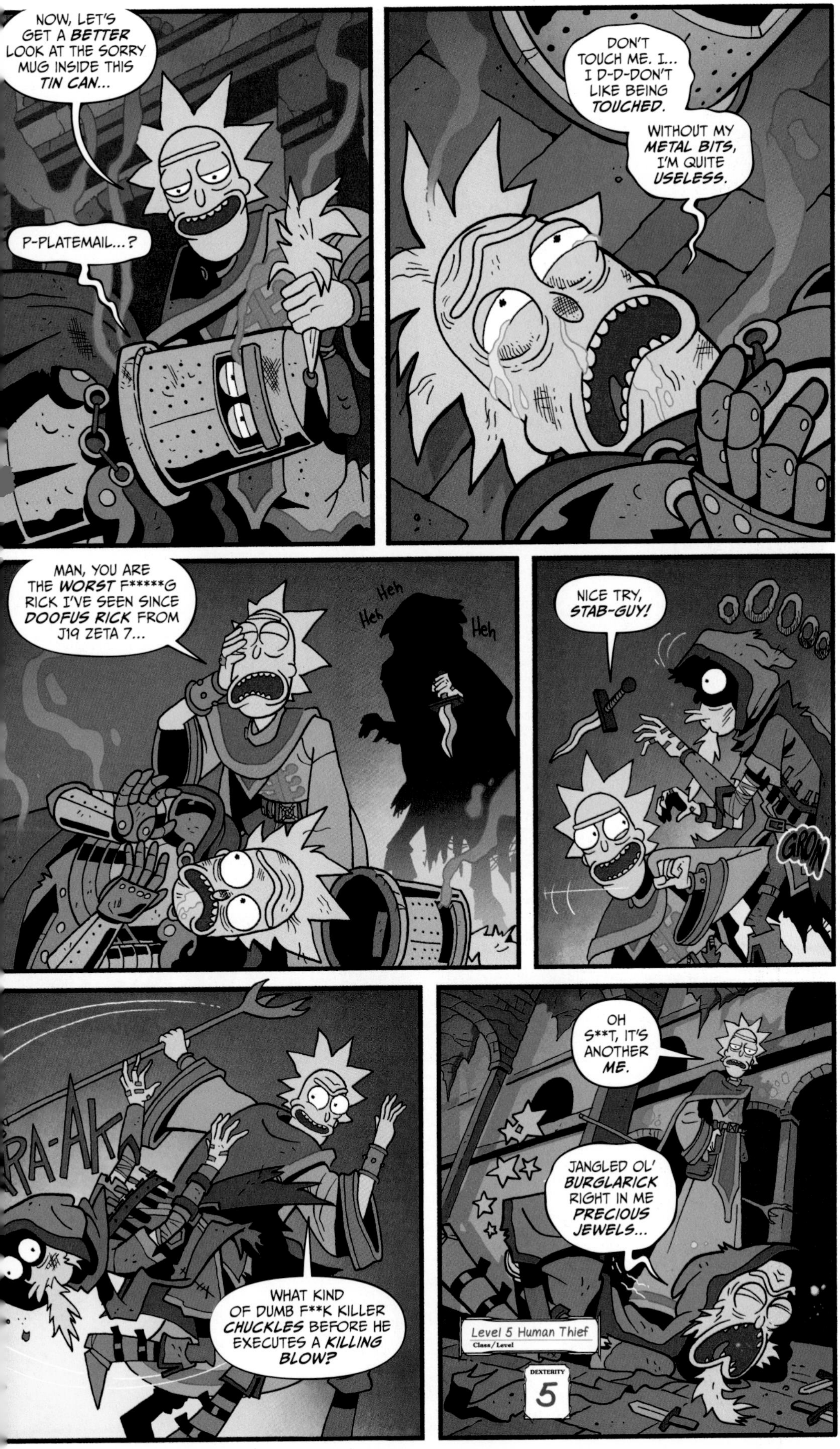
NOW, LET'S GET A BETTER LOOK AT THE SORRY MUG INSIDE THIS TIN CAN...
P-PLATEMAIL...?
DON'T TOUCH ME. I... I D-D-DON'T LIKE BEING TOUCHED.
WITHOUT MY METAL BITS, I'M QUITE USELESS.
MAN, YOU ARE THE WORST F*****G RICK I'VE SEEN SINCE DOOFUS RICK FROM J19 ZETA 7...
Heh Heh Heh
NICE TRY, STAB-GUY!
GRON
RA-AK
WHAT KIND OF DUMB F**K KILLER CHUCKLES BEFORE HE EXECUTES A KILLING BLOW?
OH S**T, IT'S ANOTHER ME.
JANGLED OL' BURGLARICK RIGHT IN ME PRECIOUS JEWELS...
Level 5 Human Thief
Class/Level
DEXTERITY
5

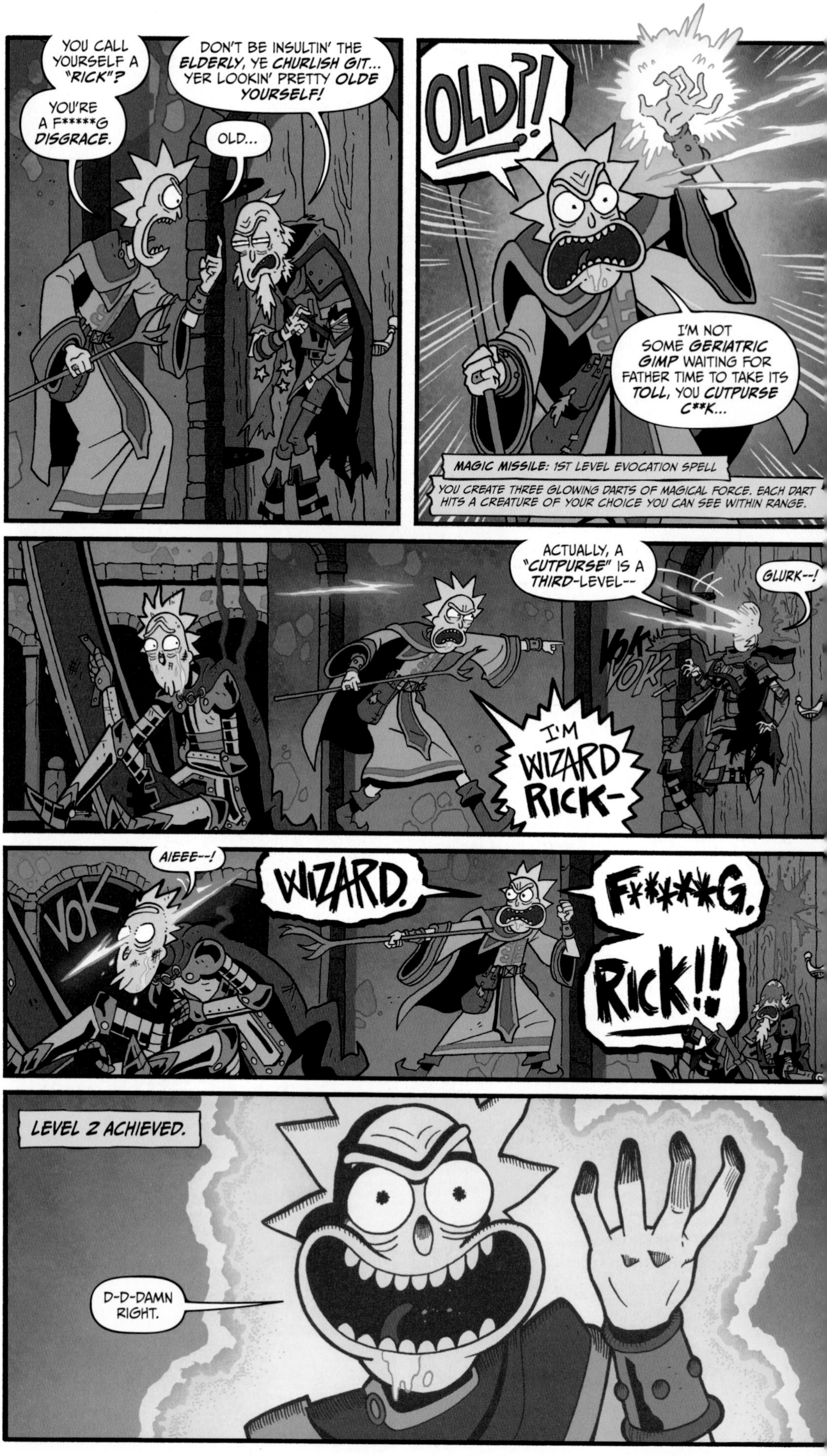

YOU CALL YOURSELF A "RICK"?
YOU'RE A F*****G DISGRACE.
DON'T BE INSULTIN' THE ELDERLY, YE CHURLISH GIT... YER LOOKIN' PRETTY OLDE YOURSELF!
OLD...
OLD?!
I'M NOT SOME GERIATRIC GIMP WAITING FOR FATHER TIME TO TAKE ITS TOLL, YOU CUTPURSE C**K...
MAGIC MISSILE: 1ST LEVEL EVOCATION SPELL
YOU CREATE THREE GLOWING DARTS OF MAGICAL FORCE. EACH DART HITS A CREATURE OF YOUR CHOICE YOU CAN SEE WITHIN RANGE.
ACTUALLY, A "CUTPURSE" IS A THIRD-LEVEL--
GLURK--!
VOK
VOK
I'M WIZARD RICK-
AIEEE--!
VOK
WIZARD.
F*****G.
RICK!!
LEVEL 2 ACHIEVED.
D-D-DAMN RIGHT.

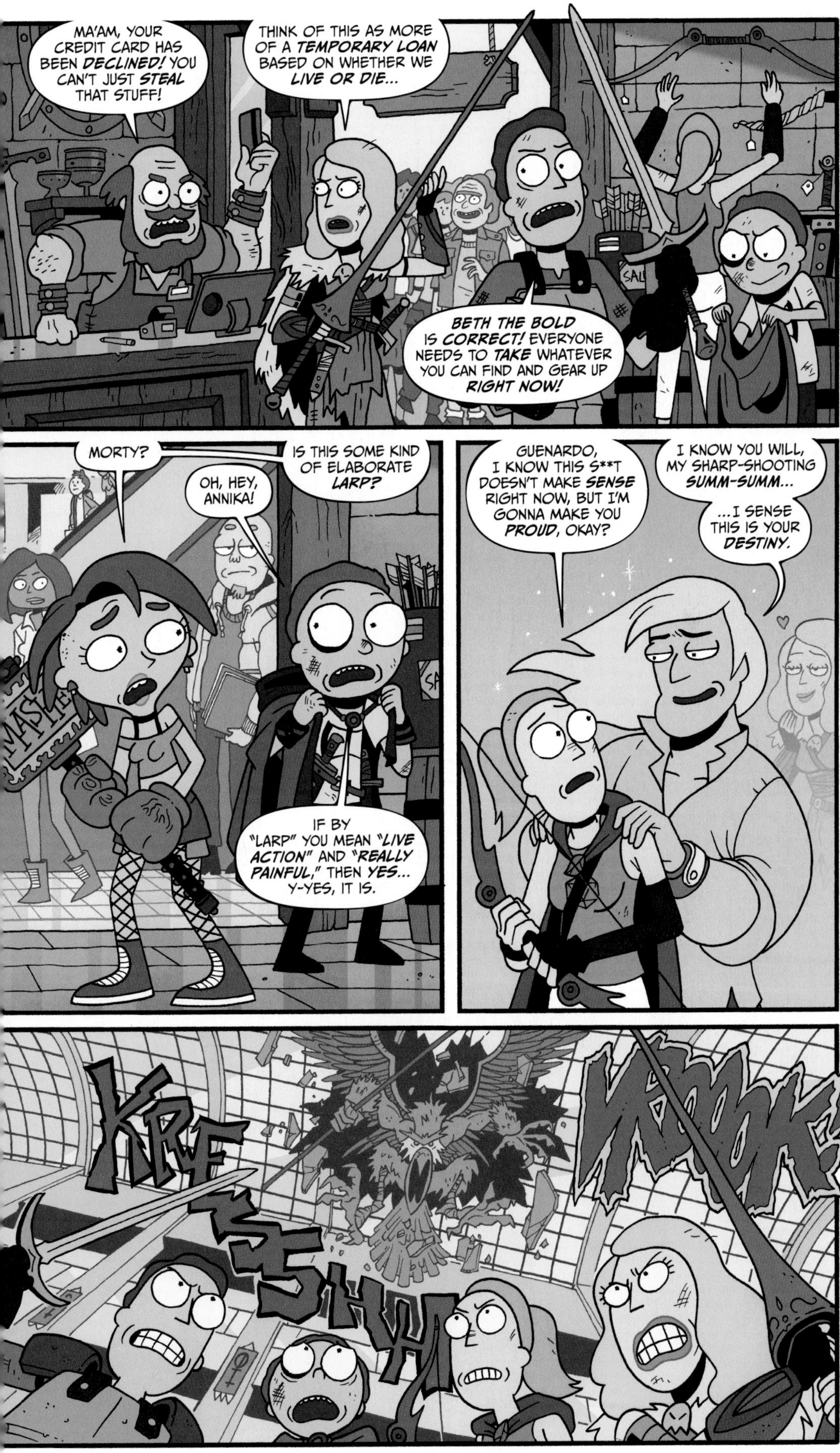

MA'AM, YOUR CREDIT CARD HAS BEEN DECLINED! YOU CAN'T JUST STEAL THAT STUFF!
THINK OF THIS AS MORE OF A TEMPORARY LOAN BASED ON WHETHER WE LIVE OR DIE...
BETH THE BOLD IS CORRECT! EVERYONE NEEDS TO TAKE WHATEVER YOU CAN FIND AND GEAR UP RIGHT NOW!
MORTY?
OH, HEY, ANNIKA!
IS THIS SOME KIND OF ELABORATE LARP?
IF BY "LARP" YOU MEAN "LIVE ACTION" AND "REALLY PAINFUL," THEN YES... Y-YES, IT IS.
GUENARDO, I KNOW THIS S**T DOESN'T MAKE SENSE RIGHT NOW, BUT I'M GONNA MAKE YOU PROUD, OKAY?
I KNOW YOU WILL, MY SHARP-SHOOTING SUMM-SUMM...
...I SENSE THIS IS YOUR DESTINY.
KRF
VROOOK!
SSHH

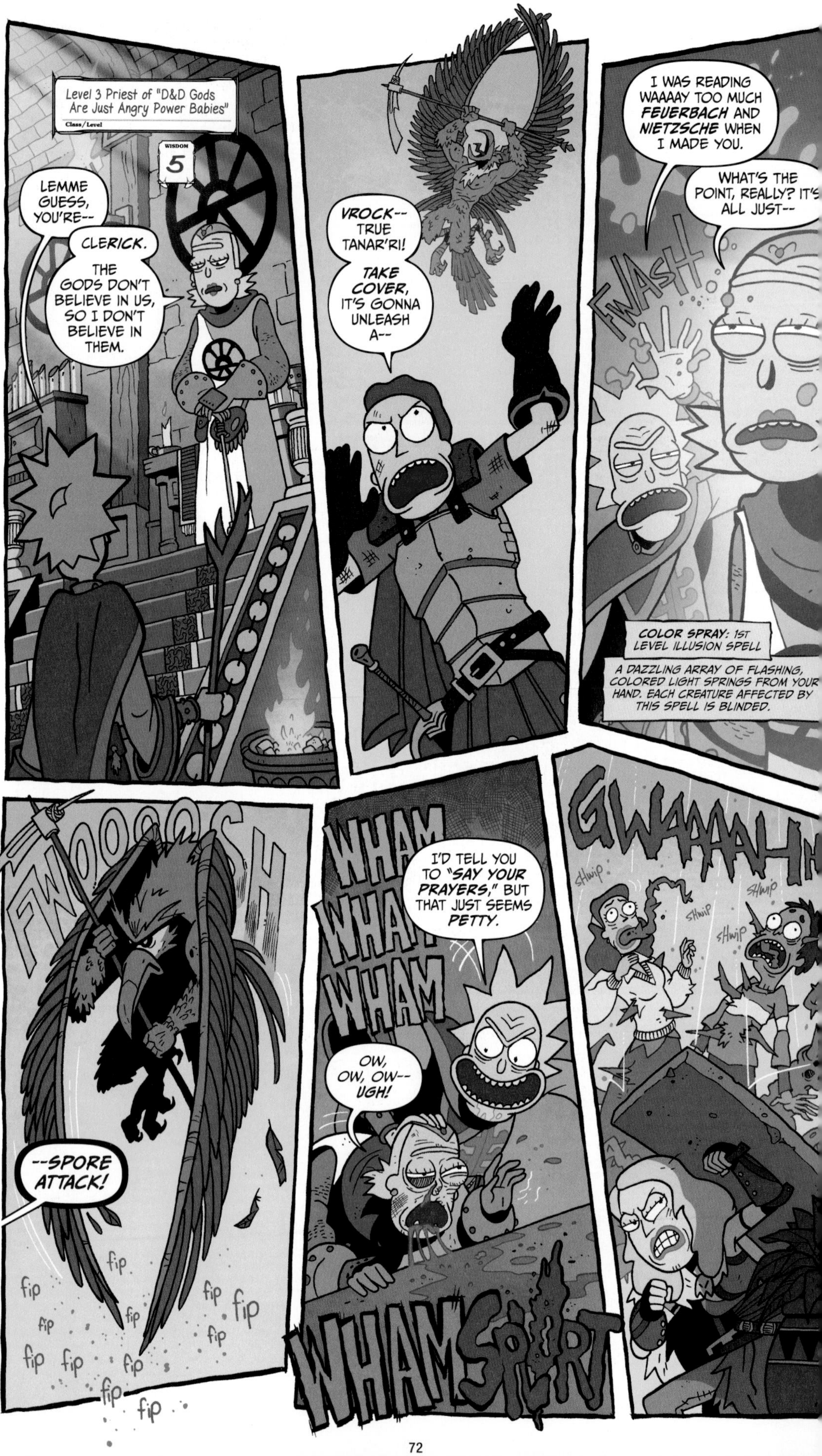

Level 3 Priest of "D&D Gods Are Just Angry Power Babies"
Class/Level
WISDOM
5
LEMME GUESS, YOU'RE--
CLERICK.
THE GODS DON'T BELIEVE IN US, SO I DON'T BELIEVE IN THEM.
VROCK-- TRUE TANAR'RI!
TAKE COVER, IT'S GONNA UNLEASH A--
I WAS READING WAAAAY TOO MUCH FEUERBACH AND NIETZSCHE WHEN I MADE YOU.
WHAT'S THE POINT, REALLY? IT'S ALL JUST--
FWASH
COLOR SPRAY: 1ST LEVEL ILLUSION SPELL
A DAZZLING ARRAY OF FLASHING, COLORED LIGHT SPRINGS FROM YOUR HAND. EACH CREATURE AFFECTED BY THIS SPELL IS BLINDED.
FWOOOOSH
--SPORE ATTACK!
fip fip fip fip fip fip fip fip fip fip fip fip
WHAM WHAM WHAM
I'D TELL YOU TO "SAY YOUR PRAYERS," BUT THAT JUST SEEMS PETTY.
OW, OW, OW-- UGH!
WHAM SPLURT
GWAAAAHH
SHWIP SHWIP SHWIP SHWIP

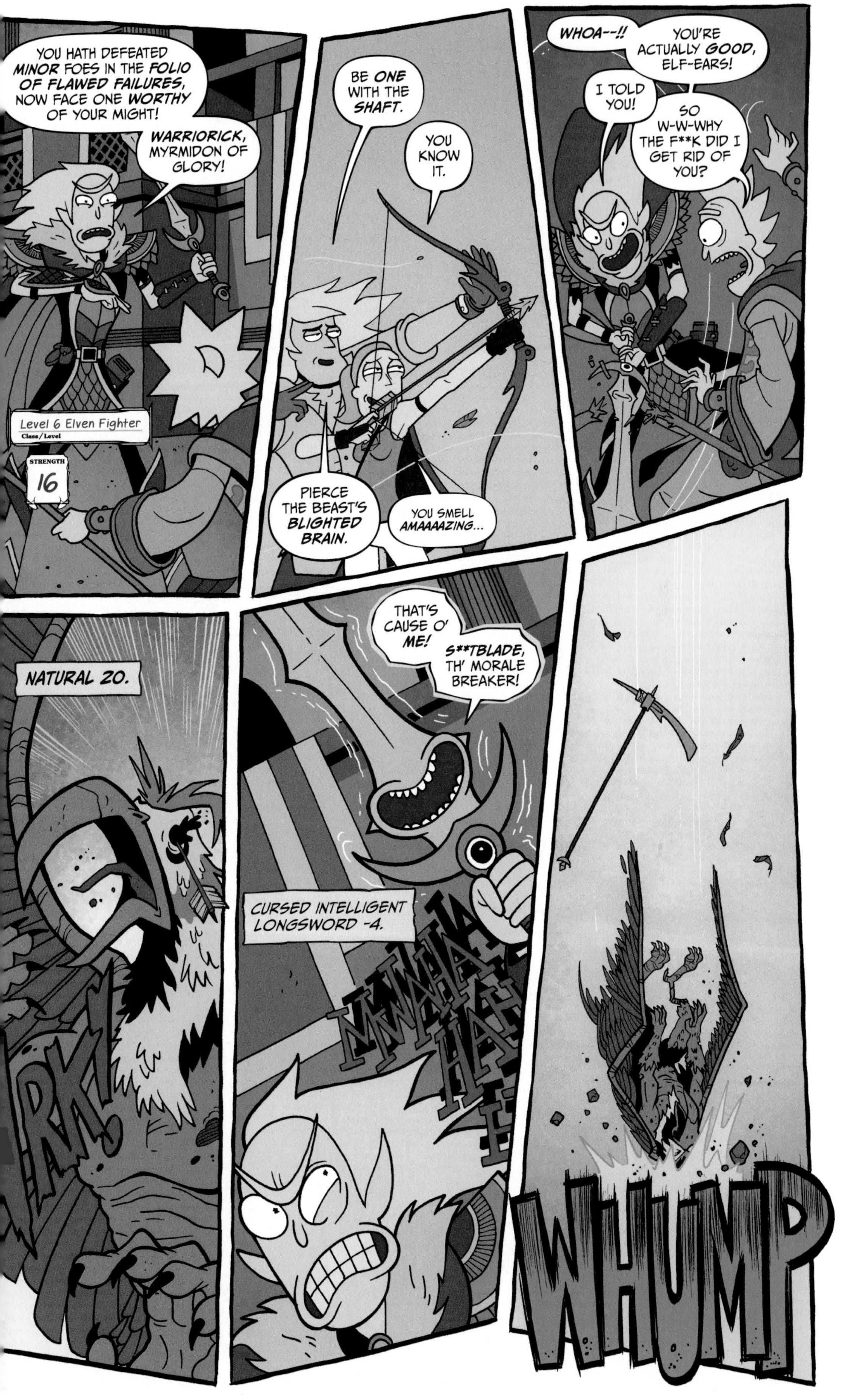

YOU HATH DEFEATED MINOR FOES IN THE FOLIO OF FLAWED FAILURES, NOW FACE ONE WORTHY OF YOUR MIGHT!
WARRIORICK, MYRMIDON OF GLORY!
Level 6 Elven Fighter
Class/Level
STRENGTH
16
BE ONE WITH THE SHAFT.
YOU KNOW IT.
PIERCE THE BEAST'S BLIGHTED BRAIN.
YOU SMELL AMAAAAZING...
WHOA--!!
YOU'RE ACTUALLY GOOD, ELF-EARS!
I TOLD YOU!
SO W-W-WHY THE F**K DID I GET RID OF YOU?
NATURAL 20.
RK!
THAT'S CAUSE O' ME!
S**TBLADE, TH' MORALE BREAKER!
CURSED INTELLIGENT LONGSWORD -4.
WHUMP

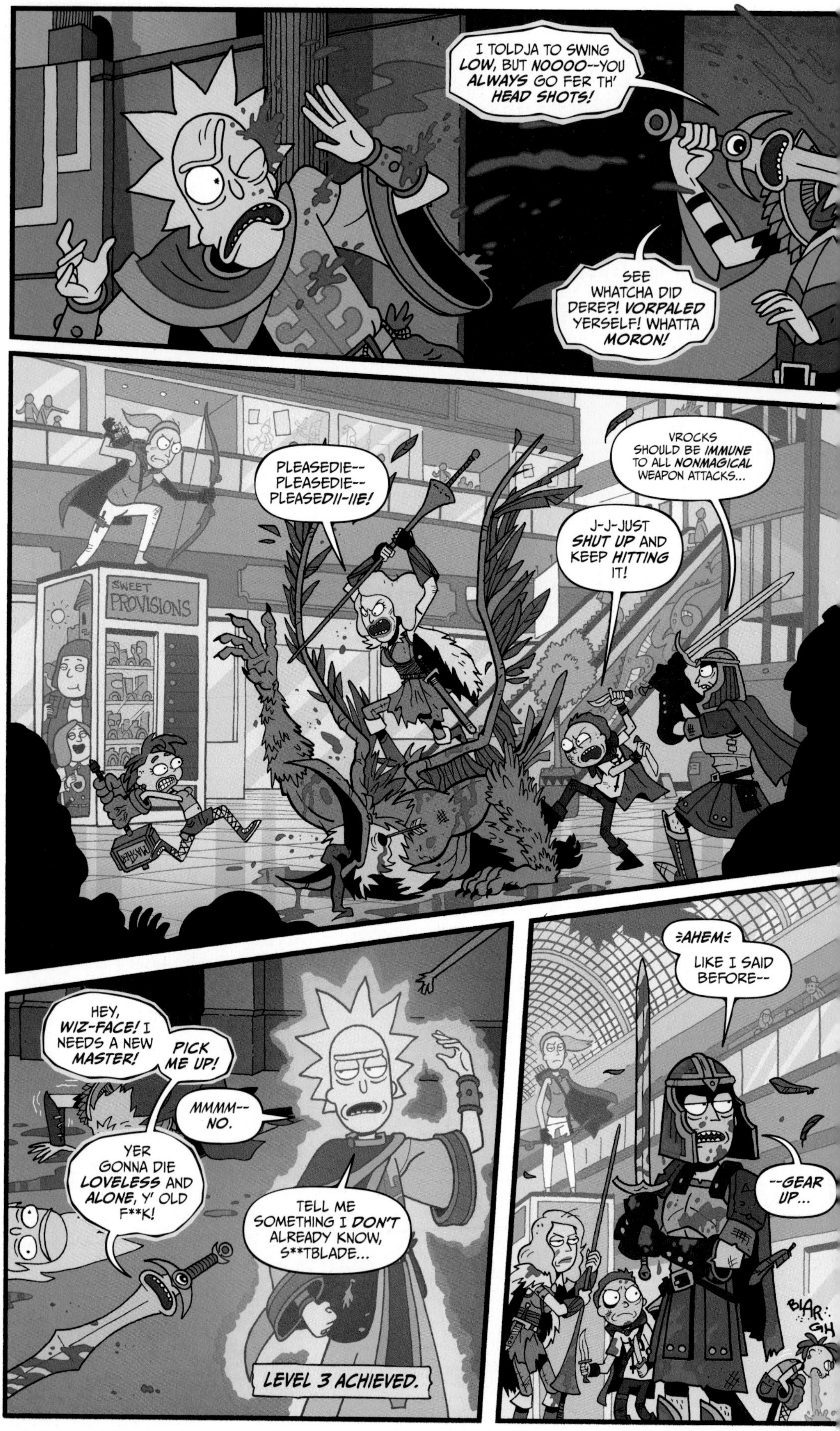
I TOLDJA TO SWING LOW, BUT NOOOO--YOU ALWAYS GO FER TH' HEAD SHOTS!
SEE WHATCHA DID DERE?! VORPALED YERSELF! WHATTA MORON!
SWEET PROVISIONS
PLEASEDIE--PLEASEDIE--PLEASEDII-IIE!
VROCKS SHOULD BE IMMUNE TO ALL NONMAGICAL WEAPON ATTACKS...
J-J-JUST SHUT UP AND KEEP HITTING IT!
HEY, WIZ-FACE! I NEEDS A NEW MASTER!
PICK ME UP!
MMMM--NO.
YER GONNA DIE LOVELESS AND ALONE, Y' OLD F**K!
TELL ME SOMETHING I DON'T ALREADY KNOW, S**TBLADE...
LEVEL 3 ACHIEVED.
AHEM
LIKE I SAID BEFORE--
--GEAR UP...
BLARGH

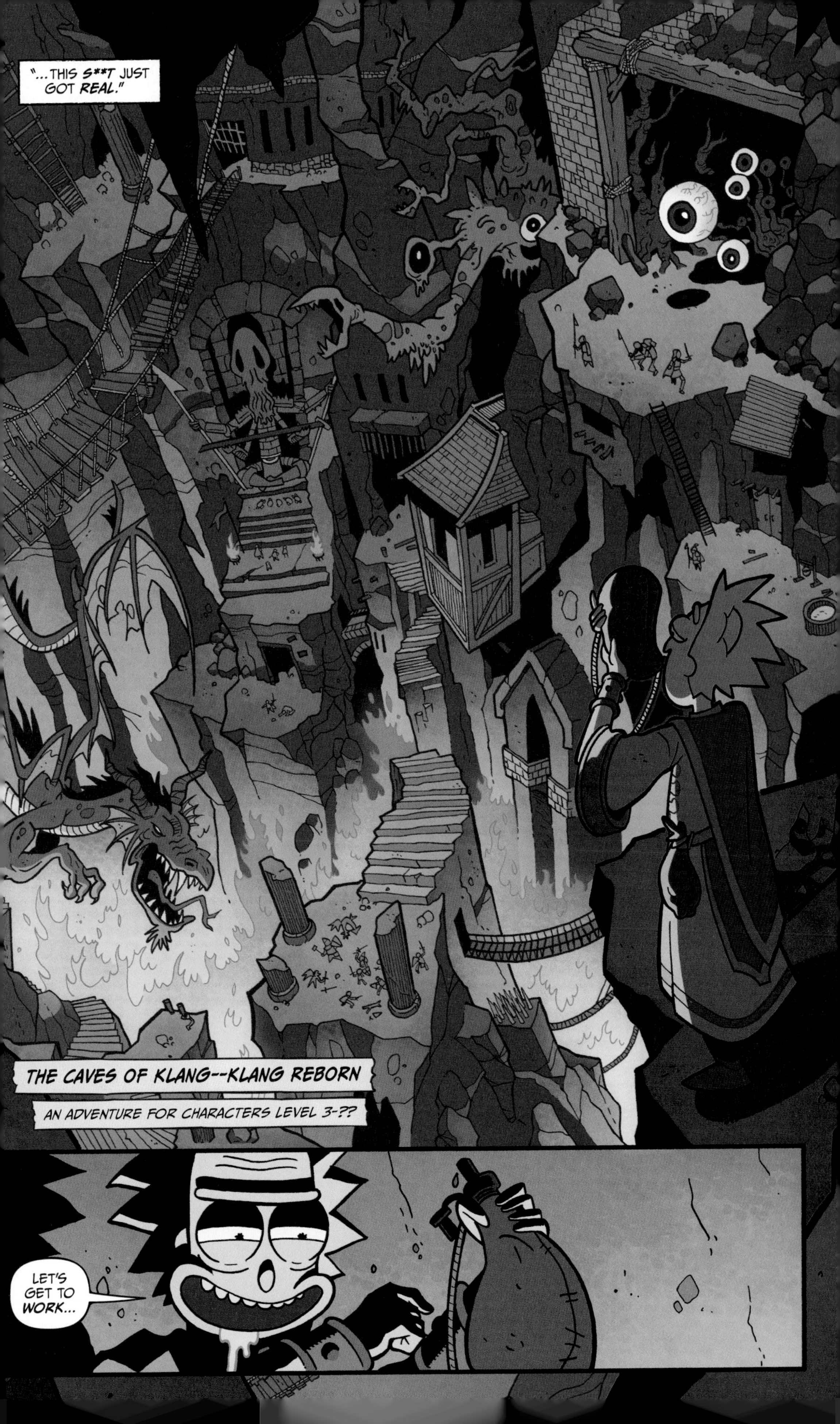
"...THIS S**T JUST GOT REAL."
THE CAVES OF KLANG--KLANG REBORN
AN ADVENTURE FOR CHARACTERS LEVEL 3-??
LET'S GET TO WORK...

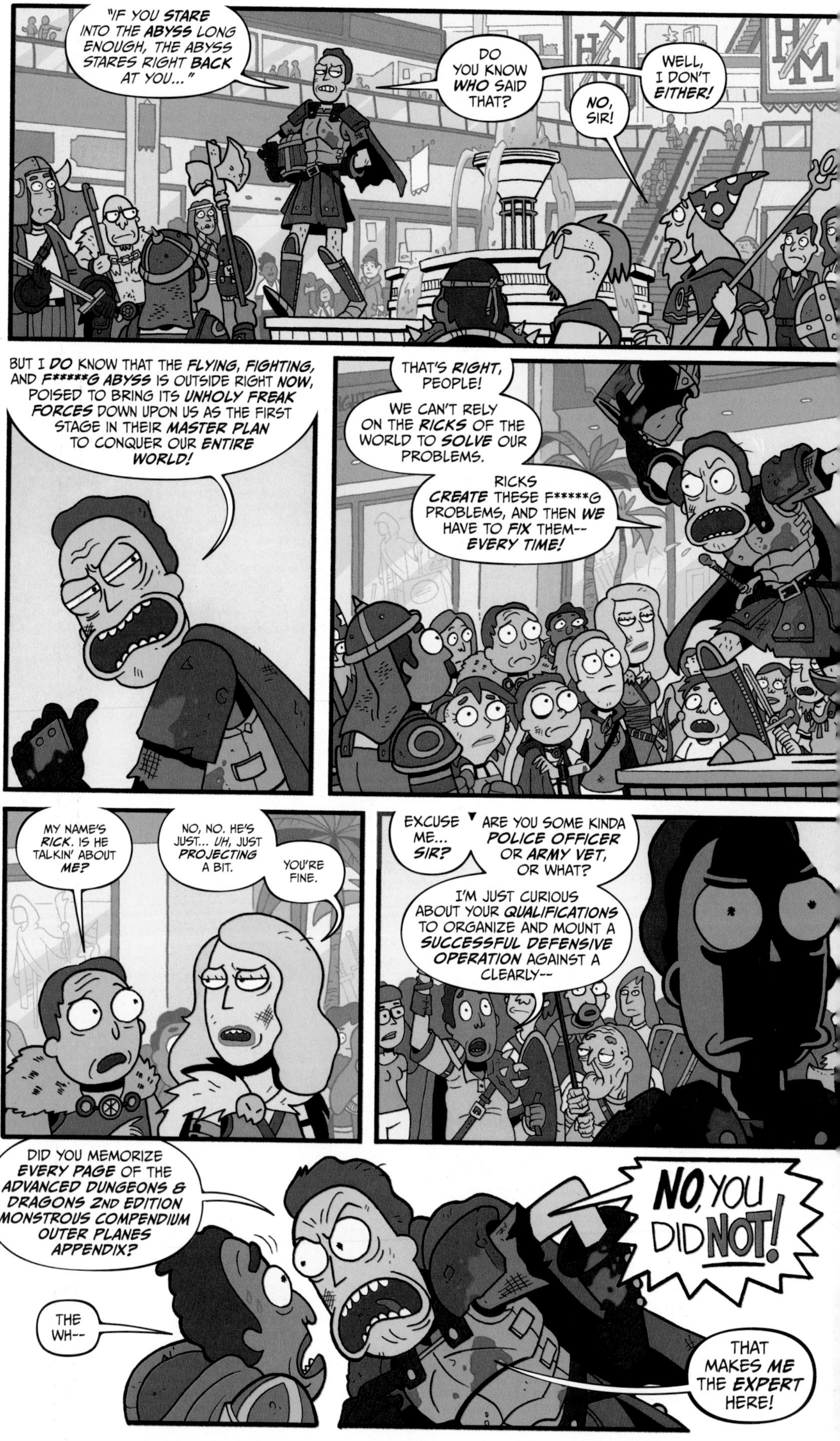
"IF YOU STARE INTO THE ABYSS LONG ENOUGH, THE ABYSS STARES RIGHT BACK AT YOU..."
DO YOU KNOW WHO SAID THAT?
NO, SIR!
WELL, I DON'T EITHER!
BUT I DO KNOW THAT THE FLYING, FIGHTING, AND F*****G ABYSS IS OUTSIDE RIGHT NOW, POISED TO BRING ITS UNHOLY FREAK FORCES DOWN UPON US AS THE FIRST STAGE IN THEIR MASTER PLAN TO CONQUER OUR ENTIRE WORLD!
THAT'S RIGHT, PEOPLE!
WE CAN'T RELY ON THE RICKS OF THE WORLD TO SOLVE OUR PROBLEMS.
RICKS CREATE THESE F*****G PROBLEMS, AND THEN WE HAVE TO FIX THEM-- EVERY TIME!
MY NAME'S RICK. IS HE TALKIN' ABOUT ME?
NO, NO. HE'S JUST... UH, JUST PROJECTING A BIT.
YOU'RE FINE.
EXCUSE ME... SIR?
ARE YOU SOME KINDA POLICE OFFICER OR ARMY VET, OR WHAT?
I'M JUST CURIOUS ABOUT YOUR QUALIFICATIONS TO ORGANIZE AND MOUNT A SUCCESSFUL DEFENSIVE OPERATION AGAINST A CLEARLY--
DID YOU MEMORIZE EVERY PAGE OF THE ADVANCED DUNGEONS & DRAGONS 2ND EDITION MONSTROUS COMPENDIUM OUTER PLANES APPENDIX?
THE WH--
NO, YOU DID NOT!
THAT MAKES ME THE EXPERT HERE!

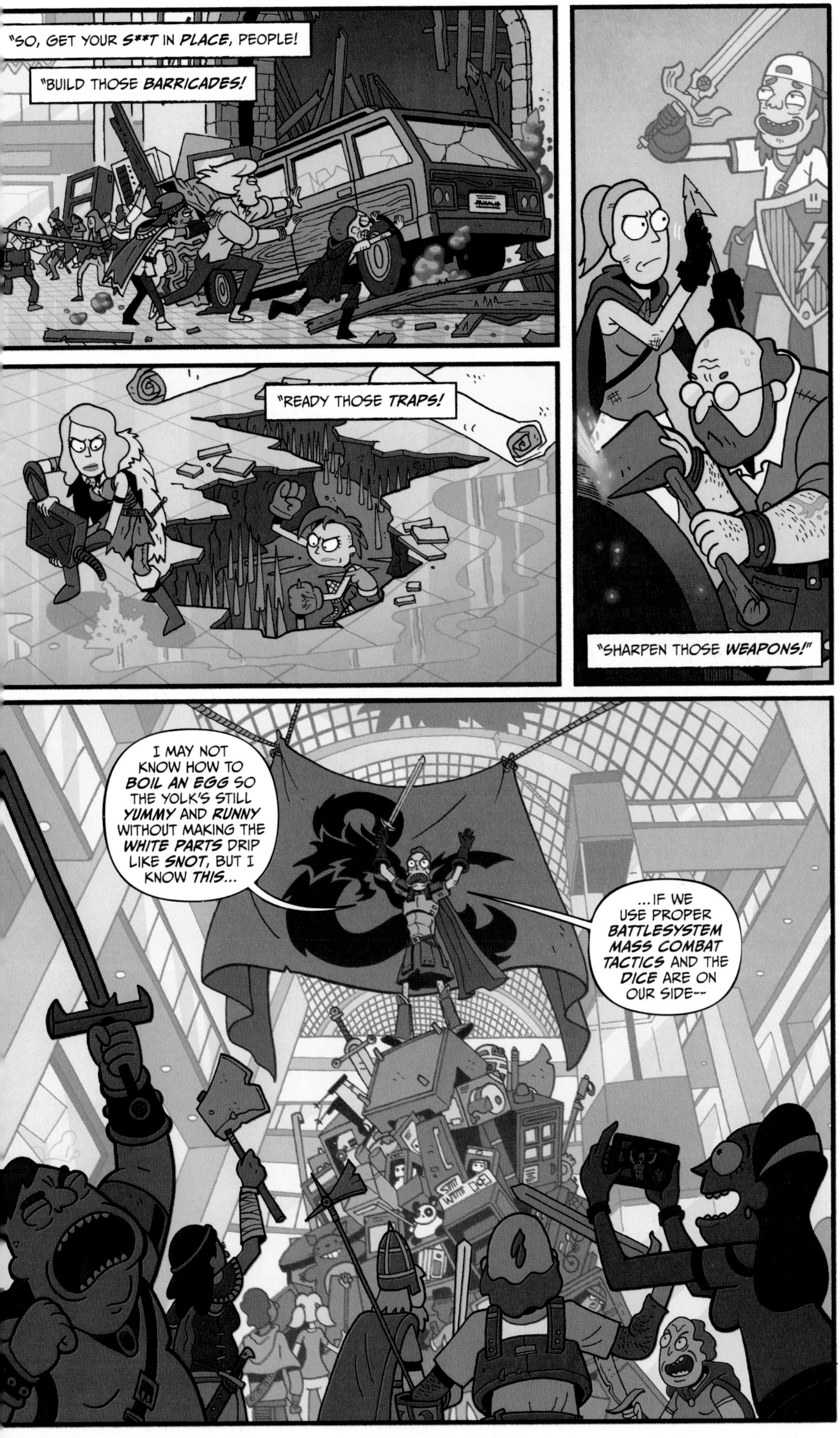
"SO, GET YOUR S**T IN PLACE, PEOPLE!
"BUILD THOSE BARRICADES!
"READY THOSE TRAPS!
"SHARPEN THOSE WEAPONS!"
I MAY NOT KNOW HOW TO BOIL AN EGG SO THE YOLK'S STILL YUMMY AND RUNNY WITHOUT MAKING THE WHITE PARTS DRIP LIKE SNOT, BUT I KNOW THIS...
...IF WE USE PROPER BATTLESYSTEM MASS COMBAT TACTICS AND THE DICE ARE ON OUR SIDE--

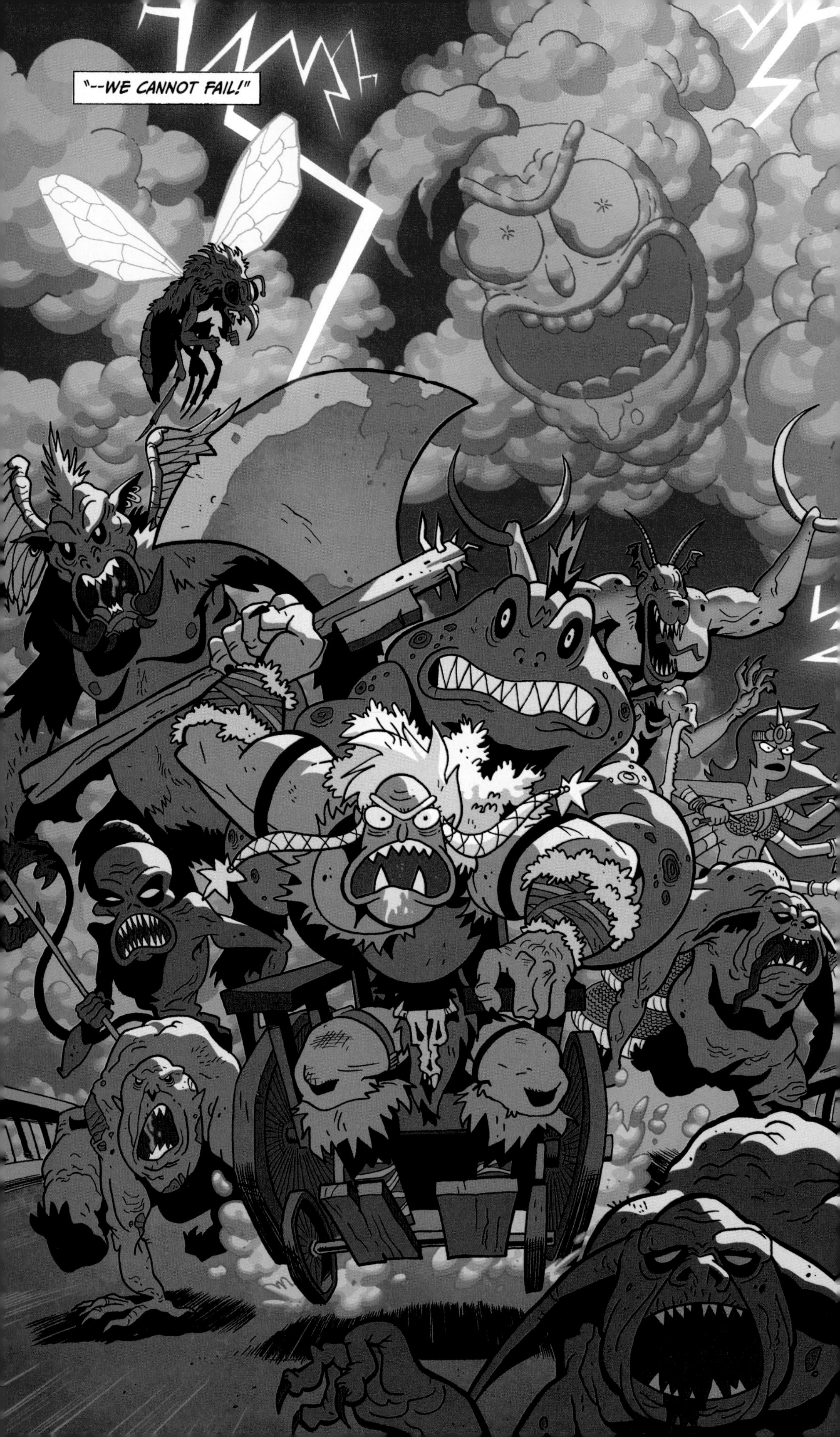
"--WE CANNOT FAIL!"

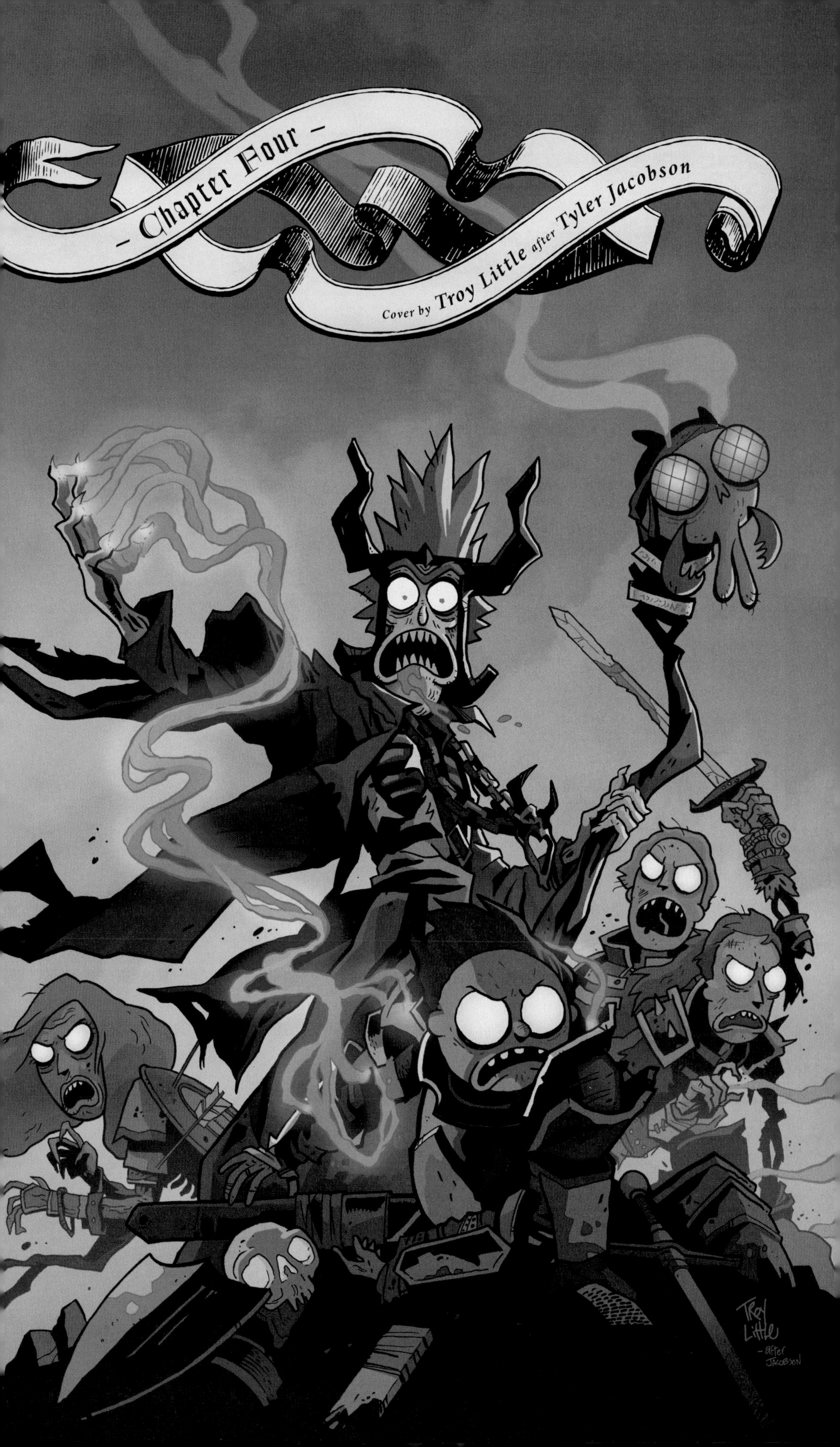
– Chapter Four –
Cover by Troy Little after Tyler Jacobson
TROY LITTLE
- after JACOBSON

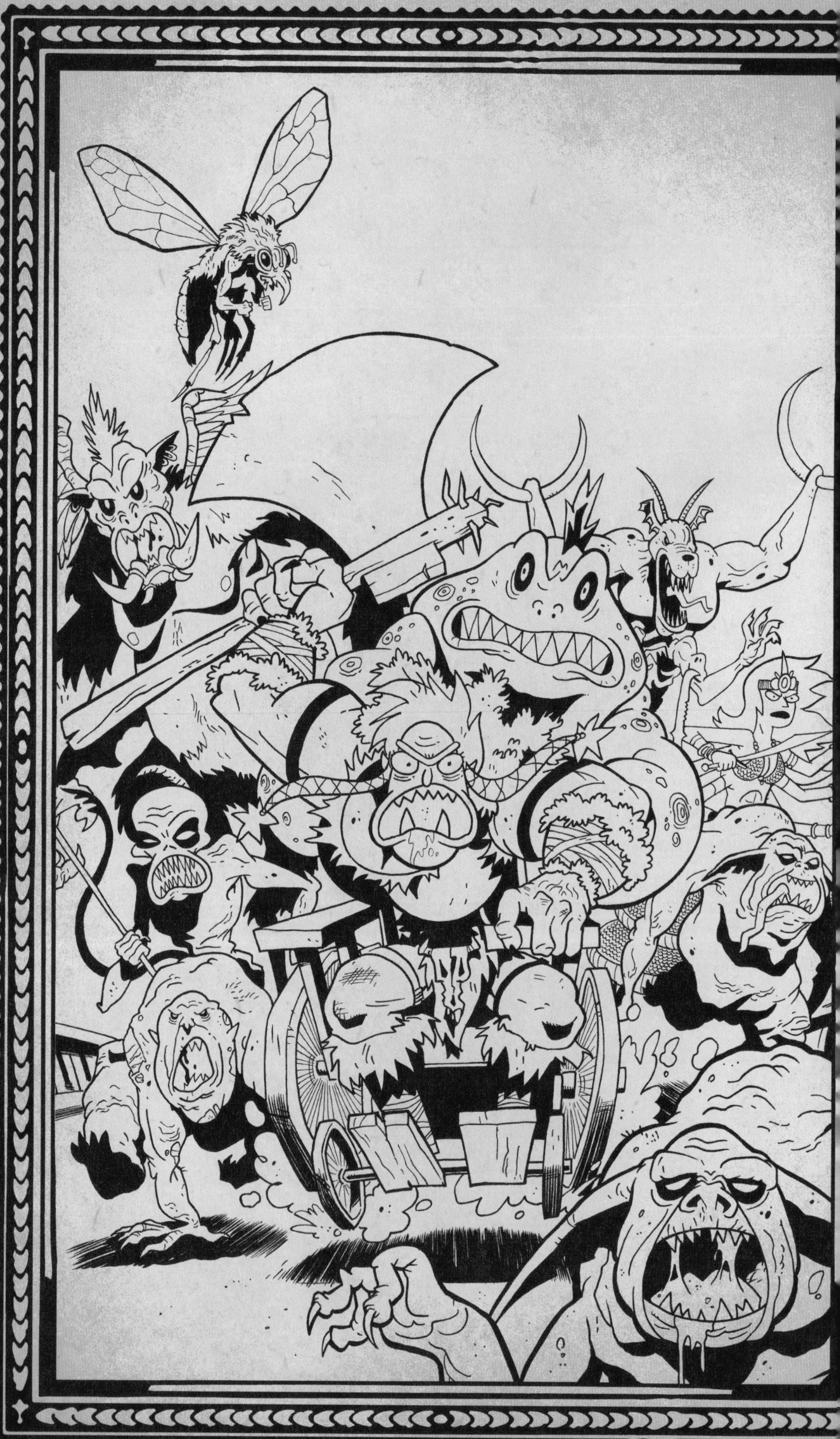

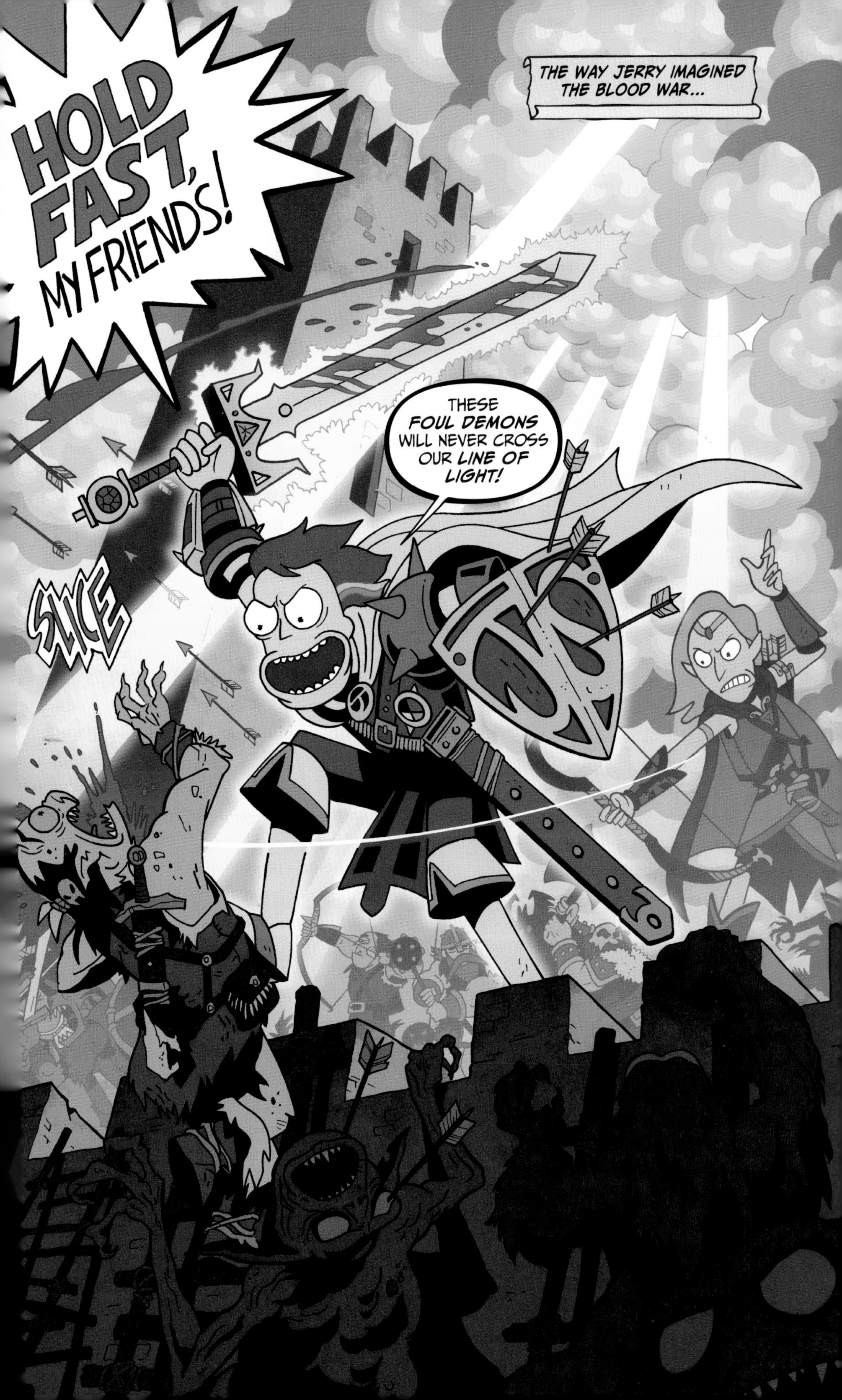
THE WAY JERRY IMAGINED THE BLOOD WAR...
HOLD FAST, MY FRIENDS!
THESE FOUL DEMONS WILL NEVER CROSS OUR LINE OF LIGHT!
SLICE

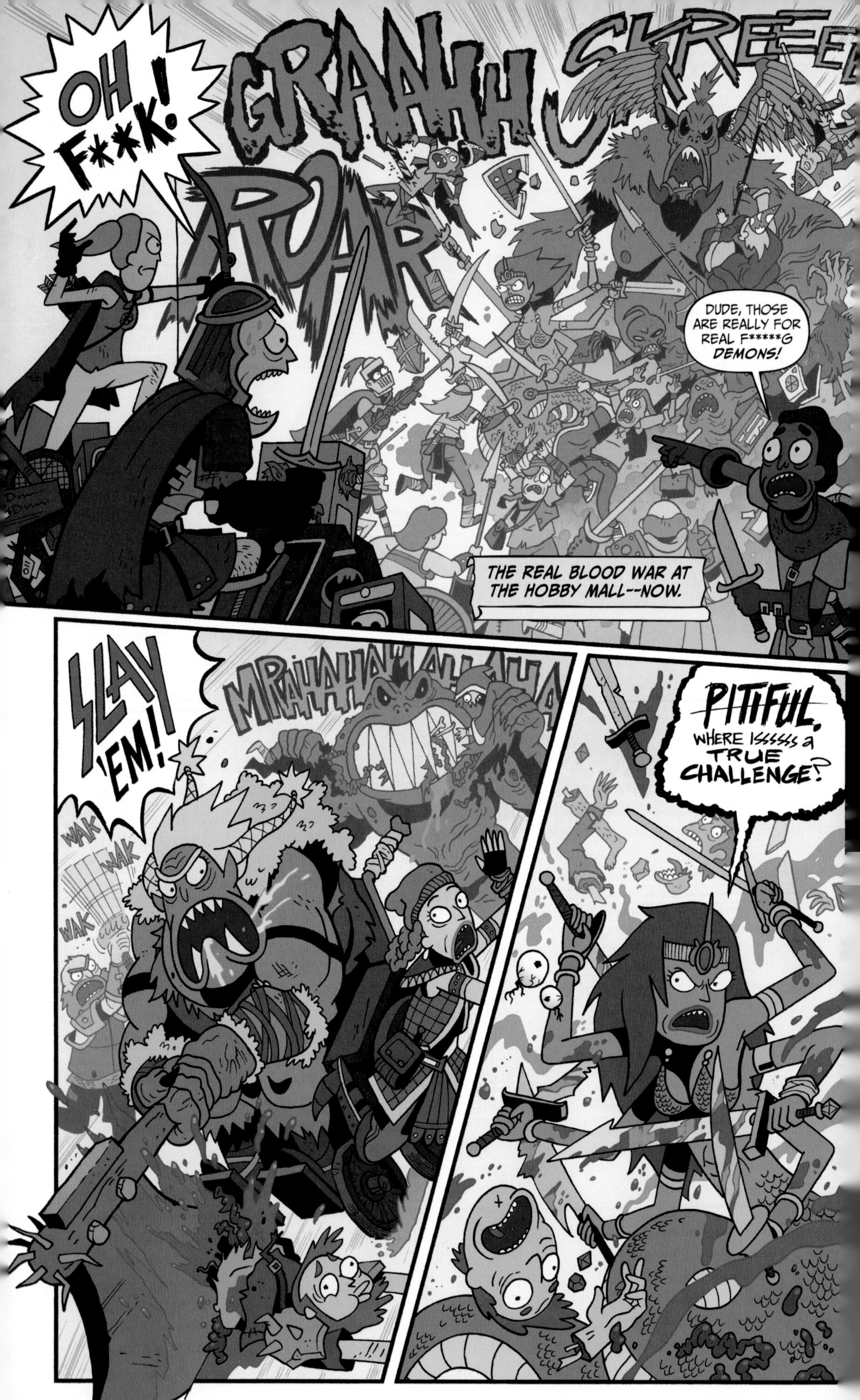

OH F**K!
GRAAHH
SKREEE
ROAR
DUDE, THOSE ARE REALLY FOR REAL F*****G DEMONS!
THE REAL BLOOD WAR AT THE HOBBY MALL--NOW.
SLAY 'EM!
MRAHAHAHAHAHA
WAK
WAK
WAK
PITIFUL. WHERE ISSSSSS a TRUE CHALLENGE?

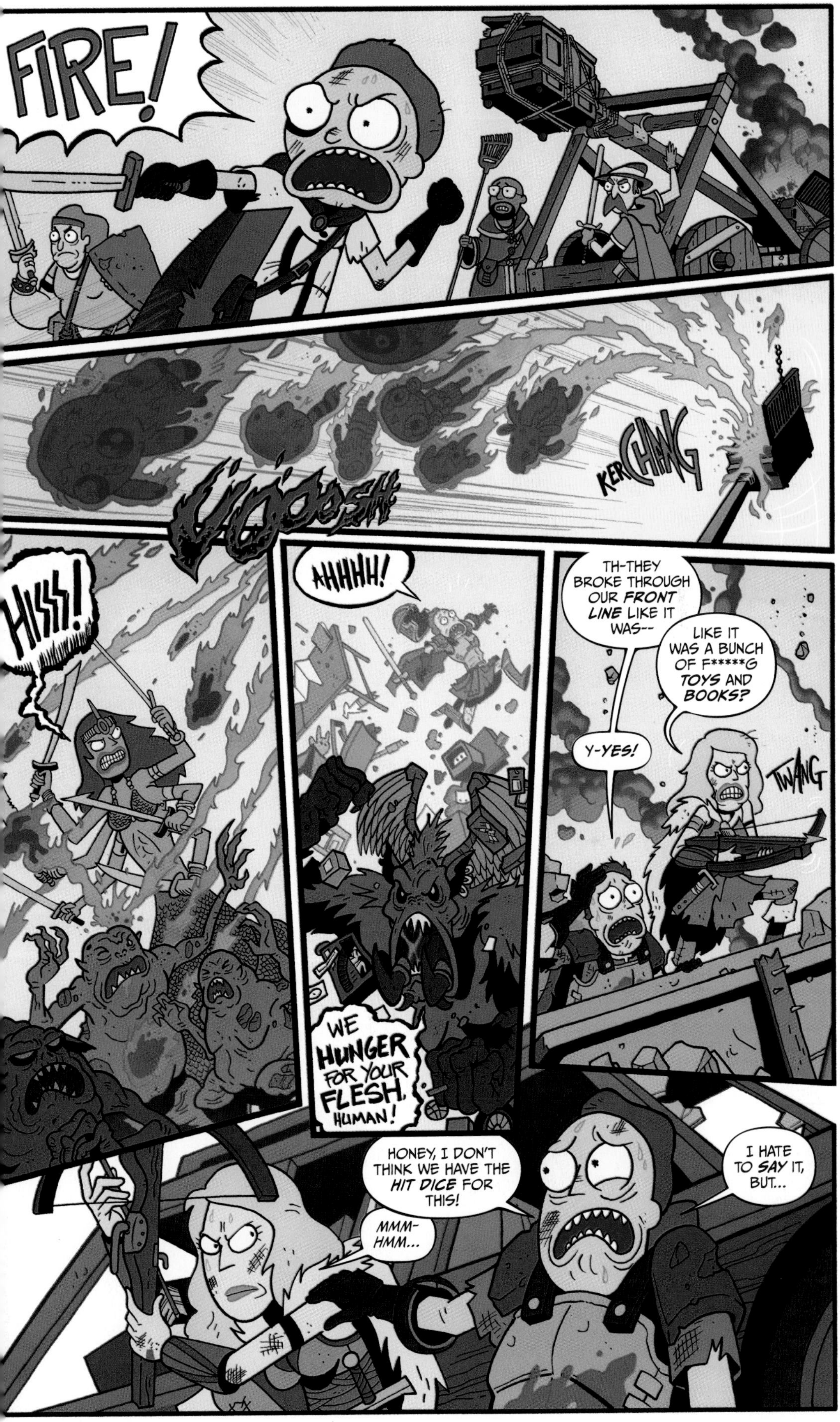
FIRE!
VOOOSH
KERCHANG
HISSSS!
AHHHH!
WE HUNGER FOR YOUR FLESH, HUMAN!
TH-THEY BROKE THROUGH OUR *FRONT LINE* LIKE IT WAS--
LIKE IT WAS A BUNCH OF F*****G *TOYS* AND *BOOKS?*
Y-*YES!*
TWANG
HONEY, I DON'T THINK WE HAVE THE *HIT DICE* FOR THIS!
MMM-HMM...
I HATE TO *SAY* IT, BUT...

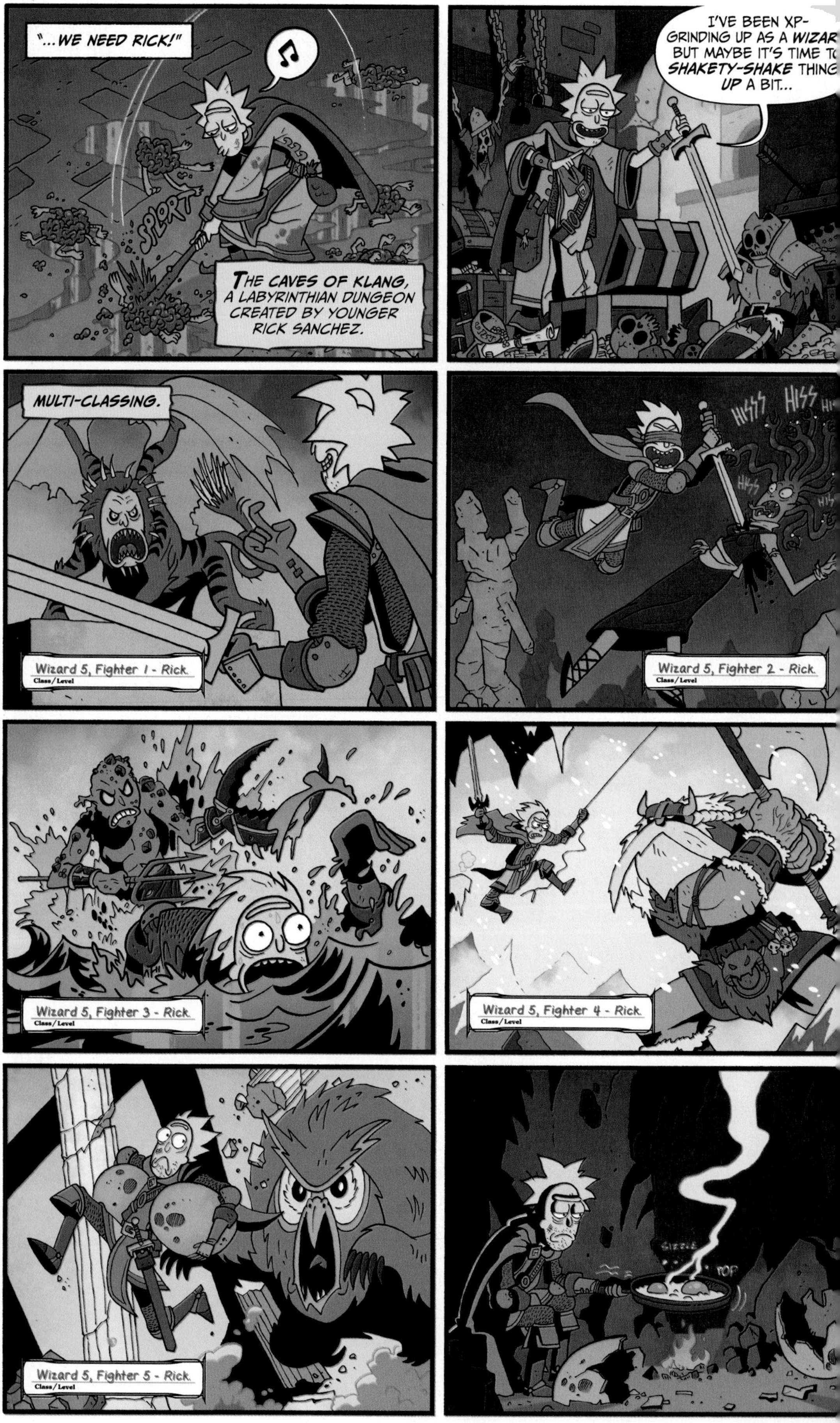
"...WE NEED RICK!"
♫
SPLORT
THE CAVES OF KLANG, A LABYRINTHIAN DUNGEON CREATED BY YOUNGER RICK SANCHEZ.
I'VE BEEN XP-GRINDING UP AS A WIZAR BUT MAYBE IT'S TIME T SHAKETY-SHAKE THING UP A BIT...
MULTI-CLASSING.
Wizard 5, Fighter 1 - Rick.
Class/Level
HISS HISS
Wizard 5, Fighter 2 - Rick.
Class/Level
Wizard 5, Fighter 3 - Rick.
Class/Level
Wizard 5, Fighter 4 - Rick.
Class/Level
Wizard 5, Fighter 5 - Rick.
Class/Level

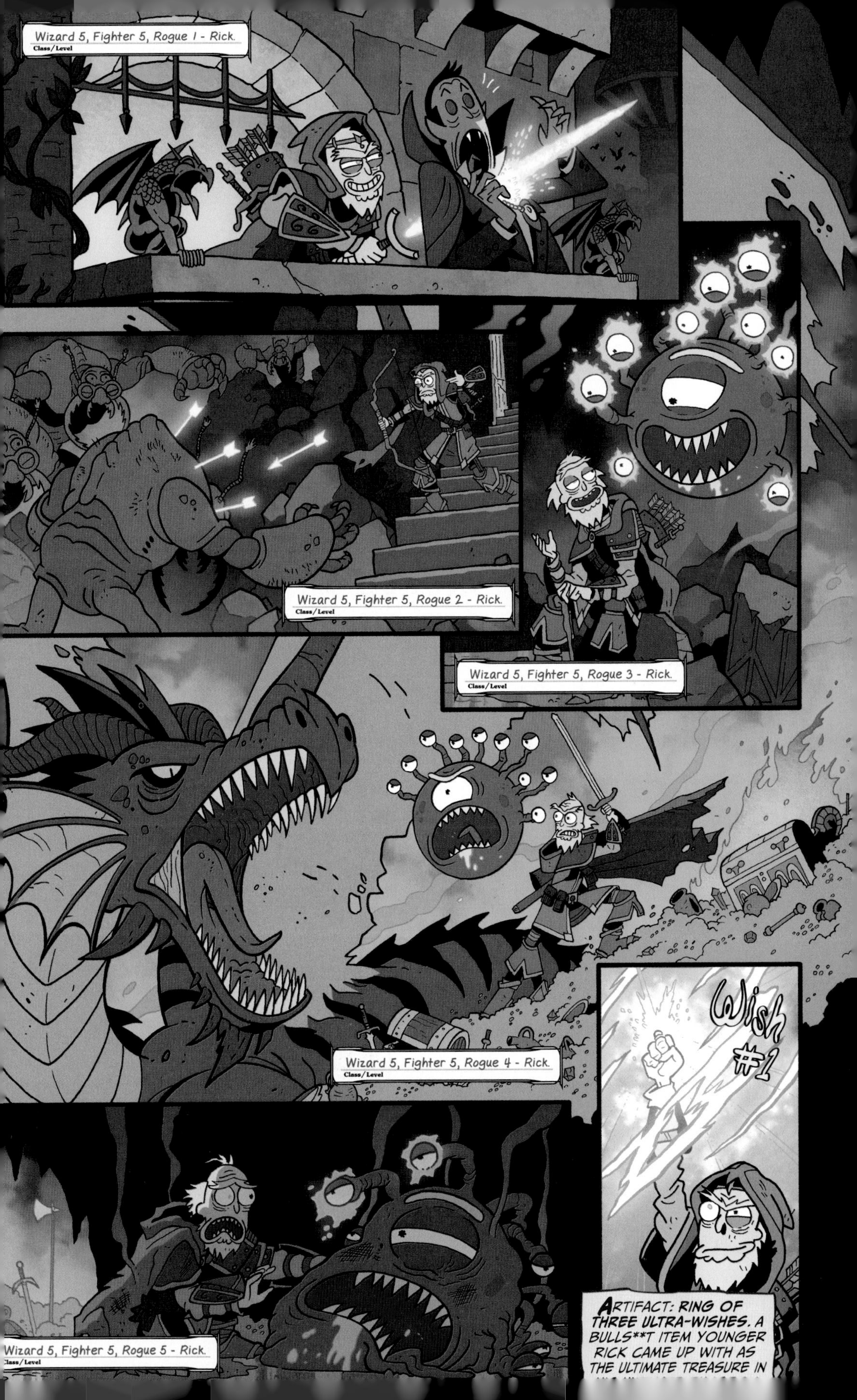

Wizard 5, Fighter 5, Rogue 1 - Rick.
Class/Level
Wizard 5, Fighter 5, Rogue 2 - Rick.
Class/Level
Wizard 5, Fighter 5, Rogue 3 - Rick.
Class/Level
Wizard 5, Fighter 5, Rogue 4 - Rick.
Class/Level
Wizard 5, Fighter 5, Rogue 5 - Rick.
Class/Level
Wish #1
ARTIFACT: RING OF THREE ULTRA-WISHES. A BULLS**T ITEM YOUNGER RICK CAME UP WITH AS THE ULTIMATE TREASURE IN

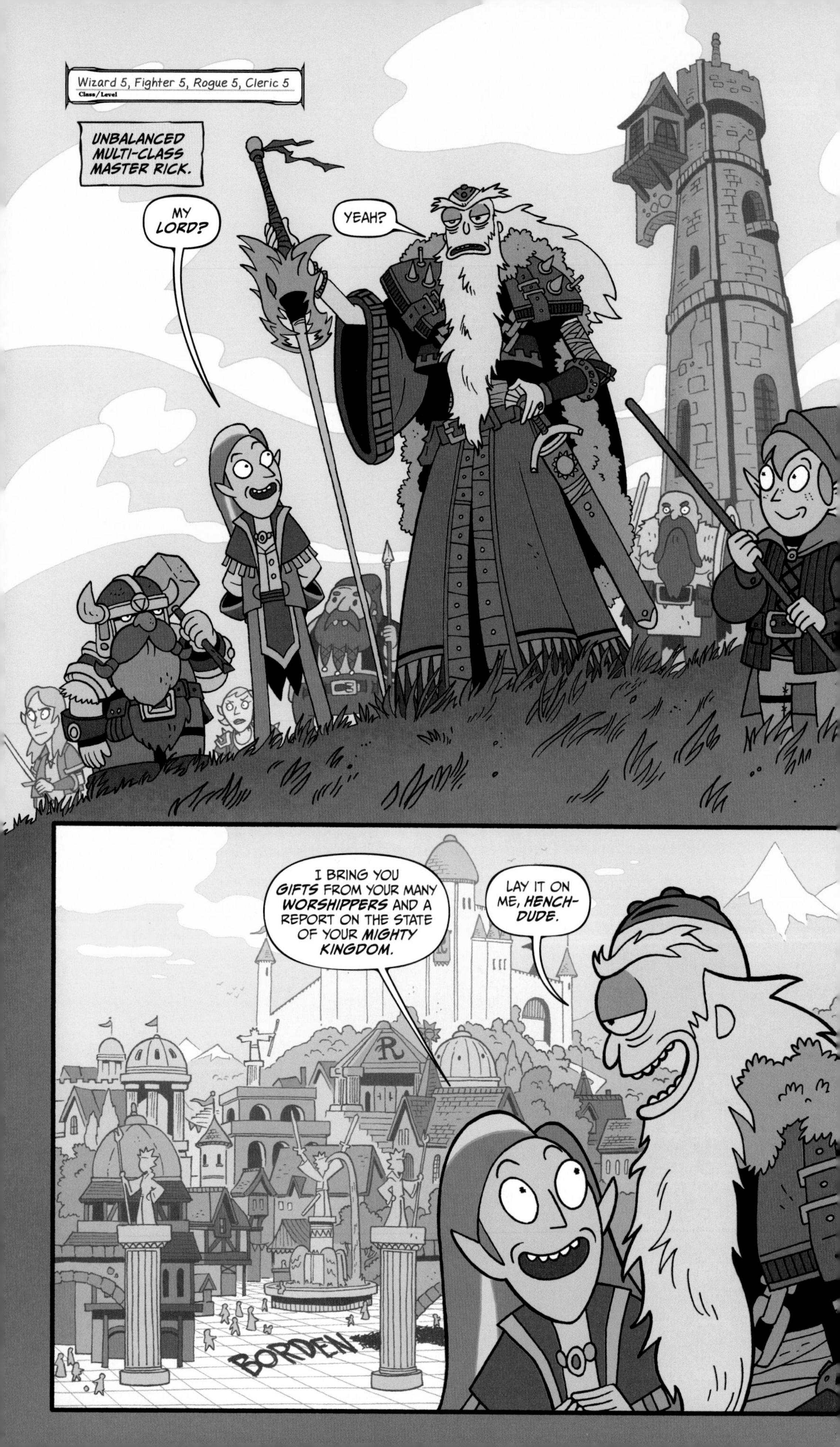

Wizard 5, Fighter 5, Rogue 5, Cleric 5
Class/Level
UNBALANCED MULTI-CLASS MASTER RICK.
MY LORD?
YEAH?
I BRING YOU GIFTS FROM YOUR MANY WORSHIPPERS AND A REPORT ON THE STATE OF YOUR MIGHTY KINGDOM.
LAY IT ON ME, HENCH-DUDE.
BORDEN

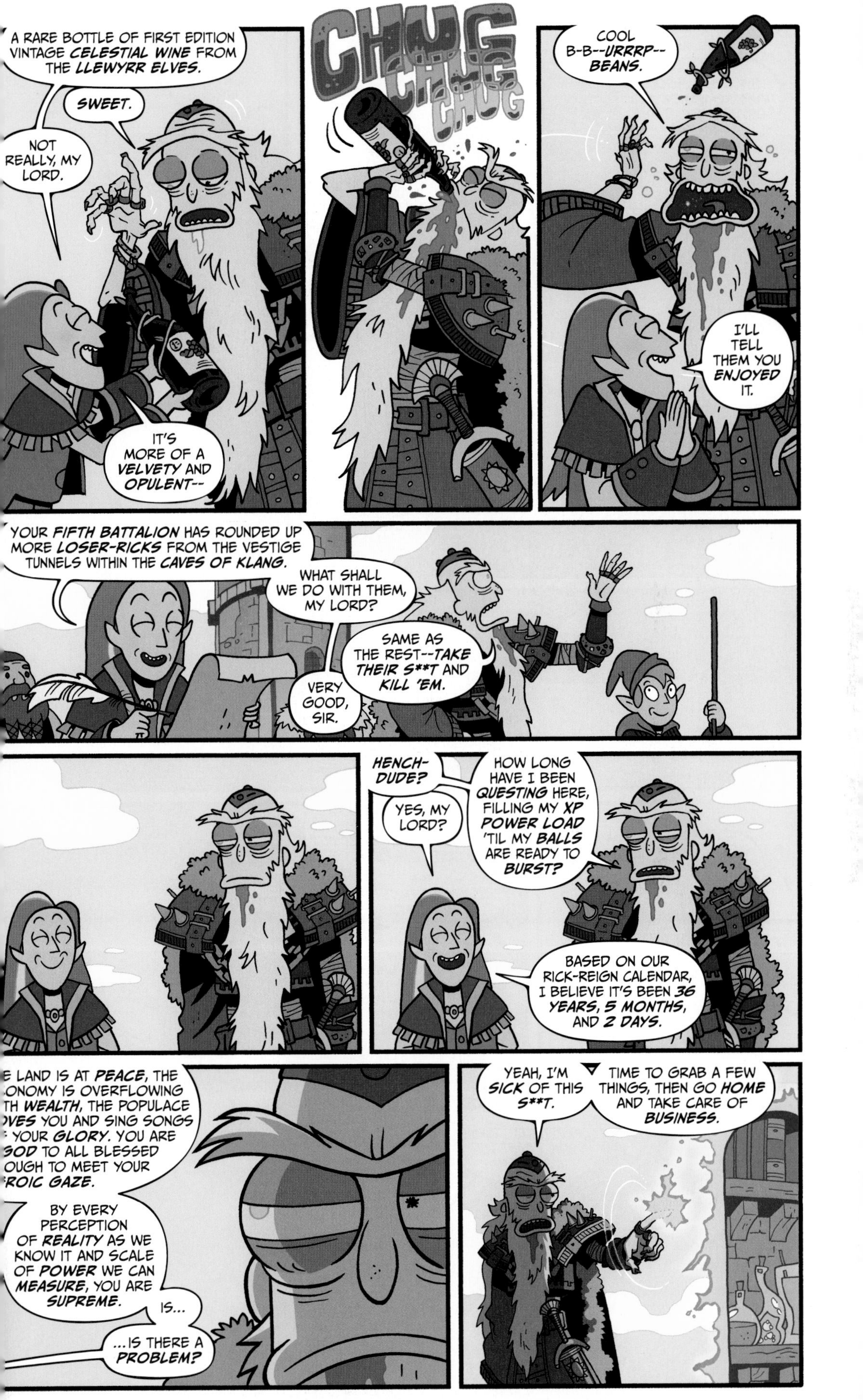
A RARE BOTTLE OF FIRST EDITION VINTAGE CELESTIAL WINE FROM THE LLEWYRR ELVES.
SWEET.
NOT REALLY, MY LORD.
IT'S MORE OF A VELVETY AND OPULENT--
CHUG CHUG CHUG
COOL B-B--URRRP--BEANS.
I'LL TELL THEM YOU ENJOYED IT.
YOUR FIFTH BATTALION HAS ROUNDED UP MORE LOSER-RICKS FROM THE VESTIGE TUNNELS WITHIN THE CAVES OF KLANG.
WHAT SHALL WE DO WITH THEM, MY LORD?
SAME AS THE REST--TAKE THEIR S**T AND KILL 'EM.
VERY GOOD, SIR.
HENCH-DUDE?
YES, MY LORD?
HOW LONG HAVE I BEEN QUESTING HERE, FILLING MY XP POWER LOAD 'TIL MY BALLS ARE READY TO BURST?
BASED ON OUR RICK-REIGN CALENDAR, I BELIEVE IT'S BEEN 36 YEARS, 5 MONTHS, AND 2 DAYS.
E LAND IS AT PEACE, THE ONOMY IS OVERFLOWING TH WEALTH, THE POPULACE OVES YOU AND SING SONGS YOUR GLORY. YOU ARE GOD TO ALL BLESSED OUGH TO MEET YOUR ROIC GAZE.
BY EVERY PERCEPTION OF REALITY AS WE KNOW IT AND SCALE OF POWER WE CAN MEASURE, YOU ARE SUPREME.
IS...
...IS THERE A PROBLEM?
YEAH, I'M SICK OF THIS S**T.
TIME TO GRAB A FEW THINGS, THEN GO HOME AND TAKE CARE OF BUSINESS.

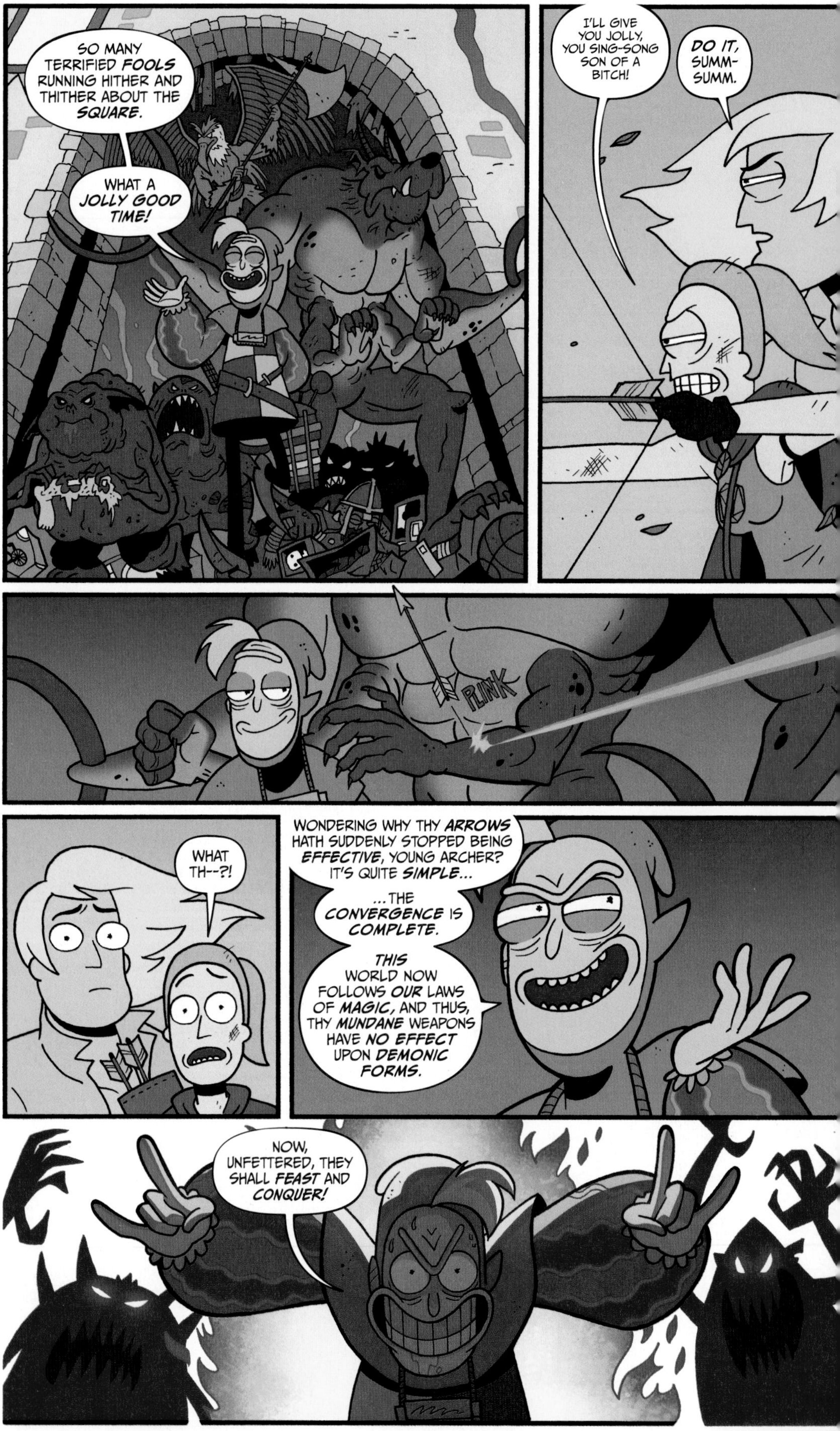
SO MANY TERRIFIED FOOLS RUNNING HITHER AND THITHER ABOUT THE SQUARE.
WHAT A JOLLY GOOD TIME!
I'LL GIVE YOU JOLLY, YOU SING-SONG SON OF A BITCH!
DO IT, SUMM-SUMM.
PLINK
WHAT TH--?!
WONDERING WHY THY ARROWS HATH SUDDENLY STOPPED BEING EFFECTIVE, YOUNG ARCHER? IT'S QUITE SIMPLE...
...THE CONVERGENCE IS COMPLETE.
THIS WORLD NOW FOLLOWS OUR LAWS OF MAGIC, AND THUS, THY MUNDANE WEAPONS HAVE NO EFFECT UPON DEMONIC FORMS.
NOW, UNFETTERED, THEY SHALL FEAST AND CONQUER!

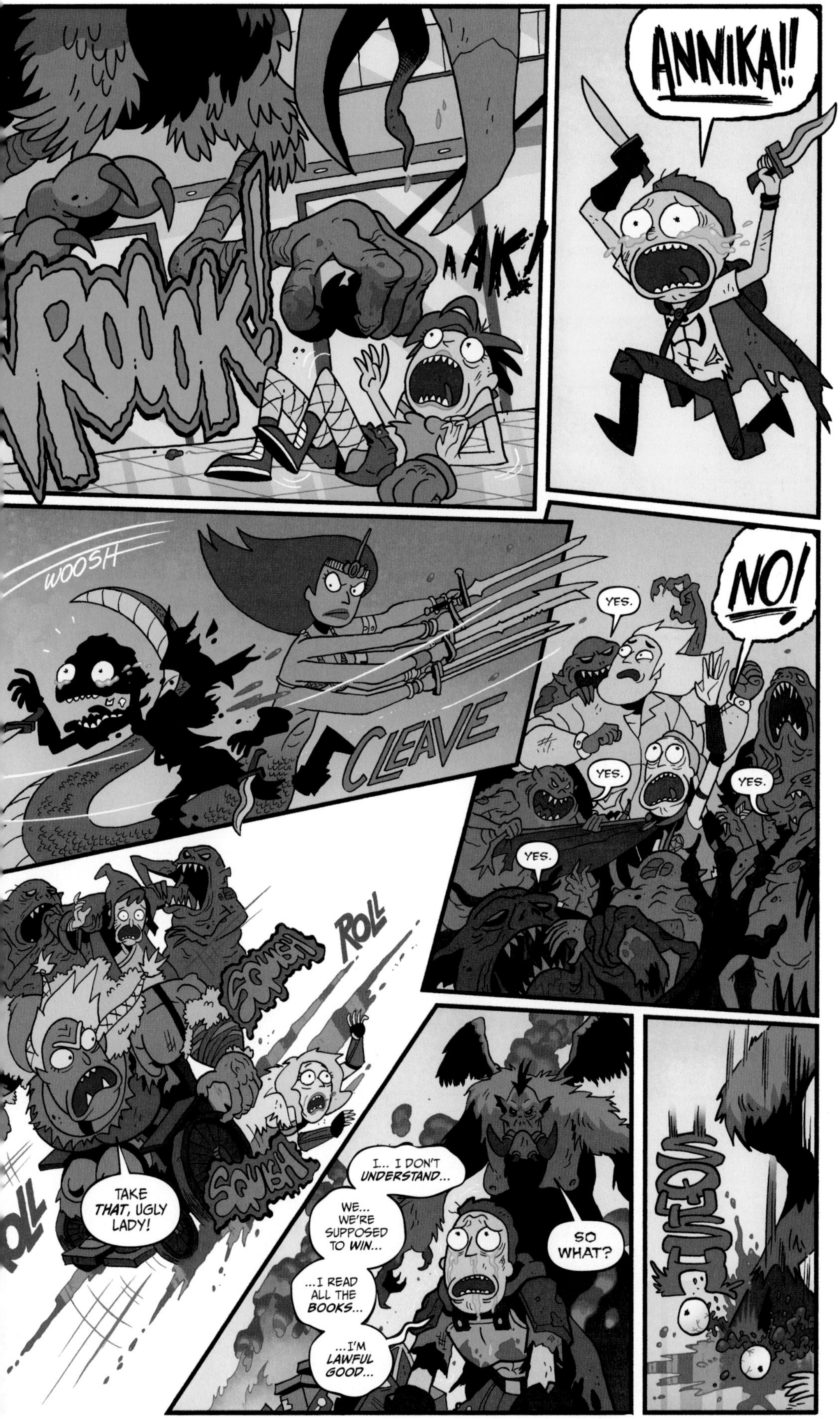
ROOOK!
AAK!
ANNIKA!!
WOOSH
CLEAVE
YES.
NO!
YES.
YES.
YES.
ROLL
SQUISH
TAKE THAT, UGLY LADY!
SQUISH
ROLL
I... I DON'T UNDERSTAND...
WE... WE'RE SUPPOSED TO WIN...
...I READ ALL THE BOOKS...
...I'M LAWFUL GOOD...
SO WHAT?
SQUISH

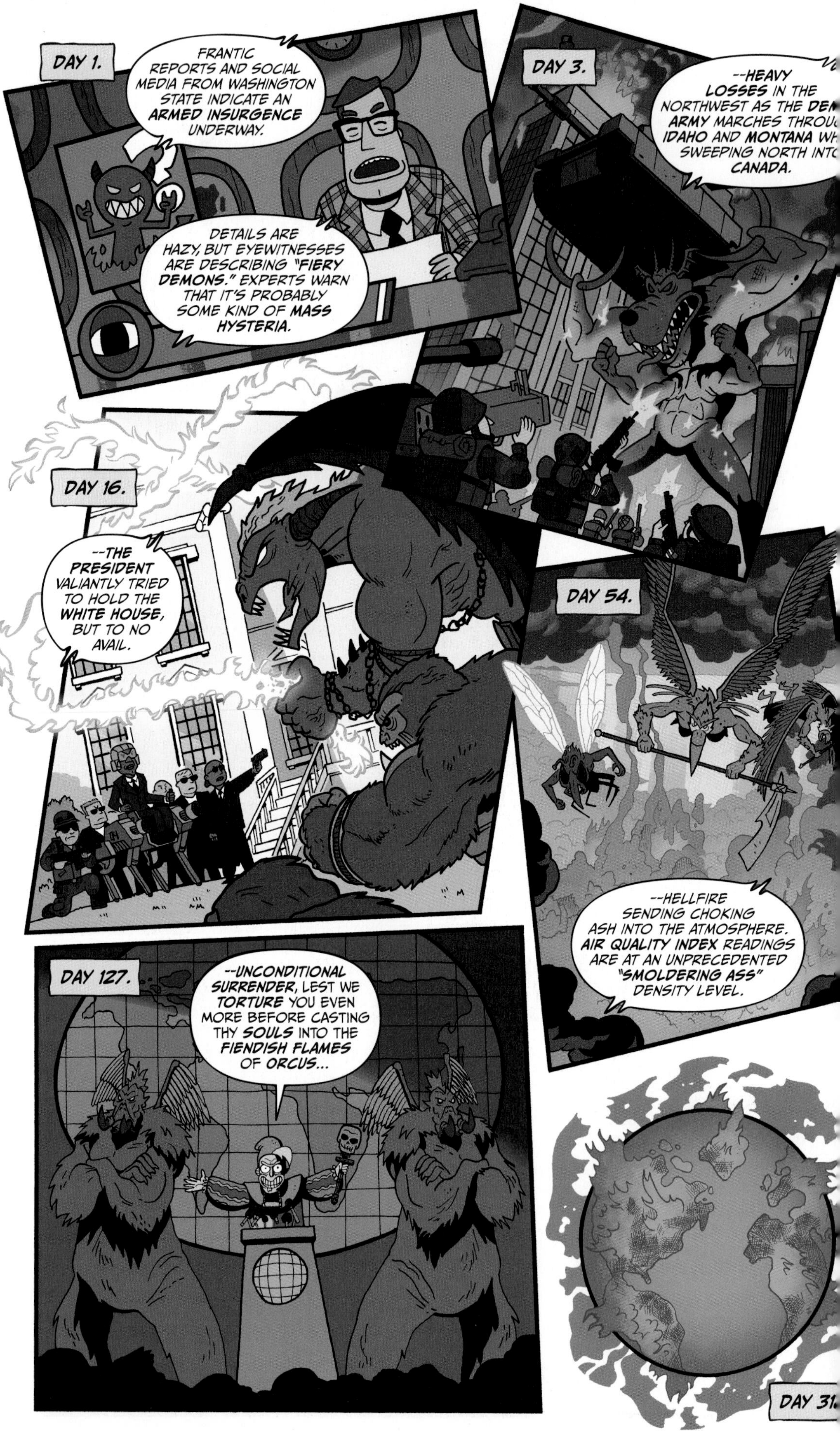
DAY 1.
FRANTIC REPORTS AND SOCIAL MEDIA FROM WASHINGTON STATE INDICATE AN ARMED INSURGENCE UNDERWAY.
DETAILS ARE HAZY, BUT EYEWITNESSES ARE DESCRIBING "FIERY DEMONS." EXPERTS WARN THAT IT'S PROBABLY SOME KIND OF MASS HYSTERIA.
DAY 3.
--HEAVY LOSSES IN THE NORTHWEST AS THE DEM ARMY MARCHES THROU IDAHO AND MONTANA WH SWEEPING NORTH INTO CANADA.
DAY 16.
--THE PRESIDENT VALIANTLY TRIED TO HOLD THE WHITE HOUSE, BUT TO NO AVAIL.
DAY 54.
--HELLFIRE SENDING CHOKING ASH INTO THE ATMOSPHERE. AIR QUALITY INDEX READINGS ARE AT AN UNPRECEDENTED "SMOLDERING ASS" DENSITY LEVEL.
DAY 127.
--UNCONDITIONAL SURRENDER, LEST WE TORTURE YOU EVEN MORE BEFORE CASTING THY SOULS INTO THE FIENDISH FLAMES OF ORCUS...
DAY 31

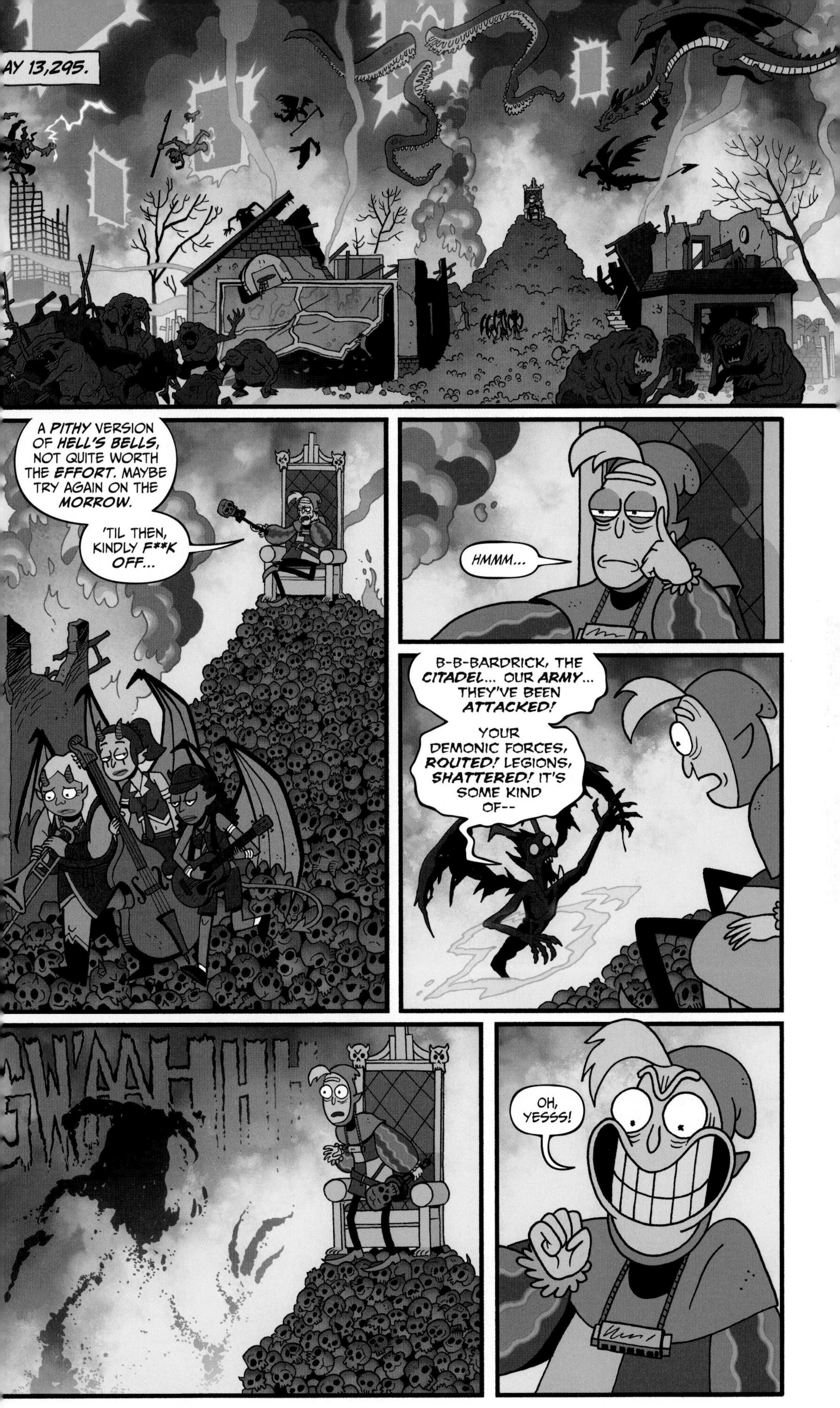
AY 13,295.
A PITHY VERSION OF HELL'S BELLS, NOT QUITE WORTH THE EFFORT. MAYBE TRY AGAIN ON THE MORROW.
'TIL THEN, KINDLY F**K OFF...
HMMM...
B-B-BARDRICK, THE CITADEL... OUR ARMY... THEY'VE BEEN ATTACKED!
YOUR DEMONIC FORCES, ROUTED! LEGIONS, SHATTERED! IT'S SOME KIND OF--
GWAAHH
OH, YESSS!

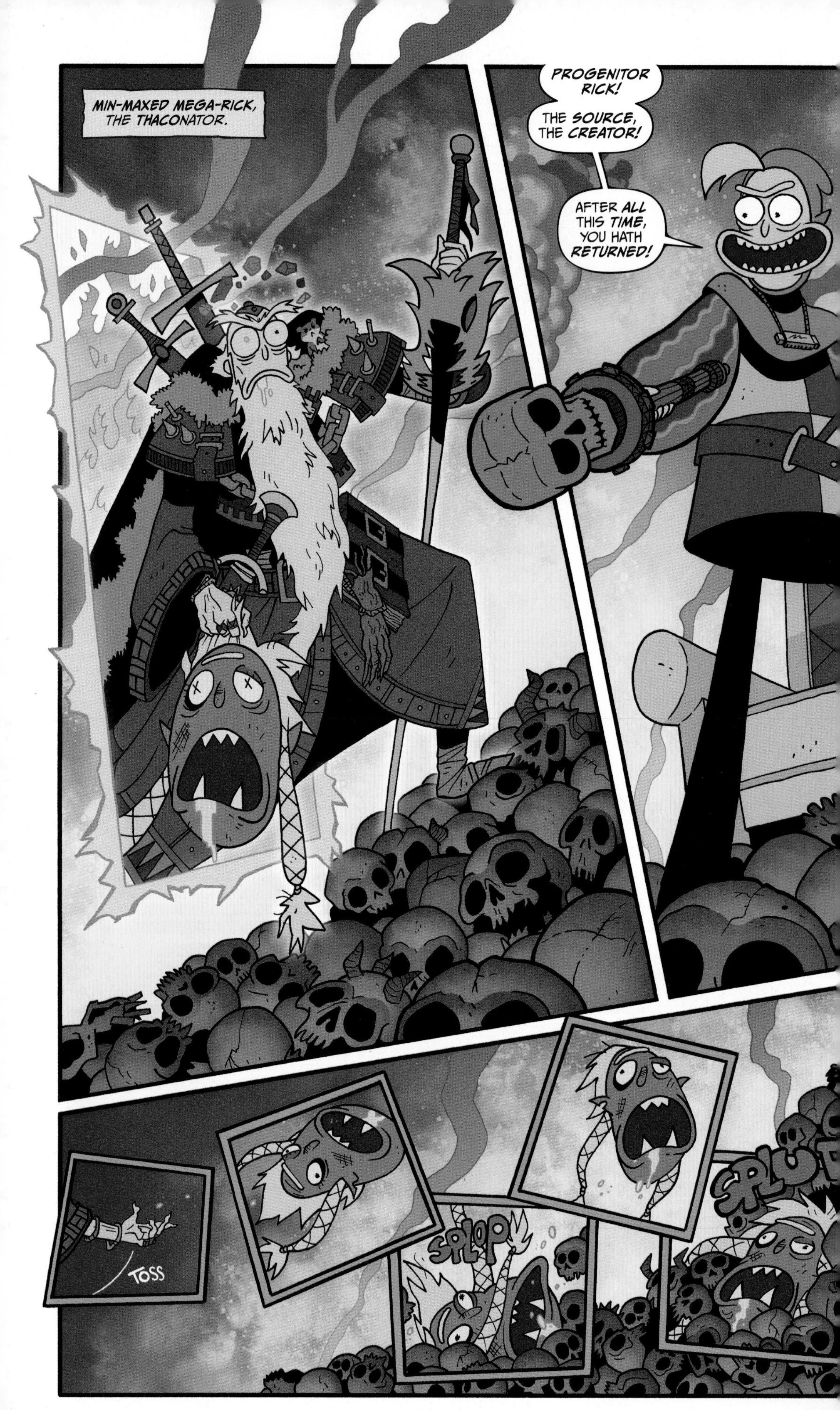

MIN-MAXED MEGA-RICK, THE THACONATOR.
PROGENITOR RICK!
THE SOURCE, THE CREATOR!
AFTER ALL THIS TIME, YOU HATH RETURNED!
TOSS
SPLOP
SPLU

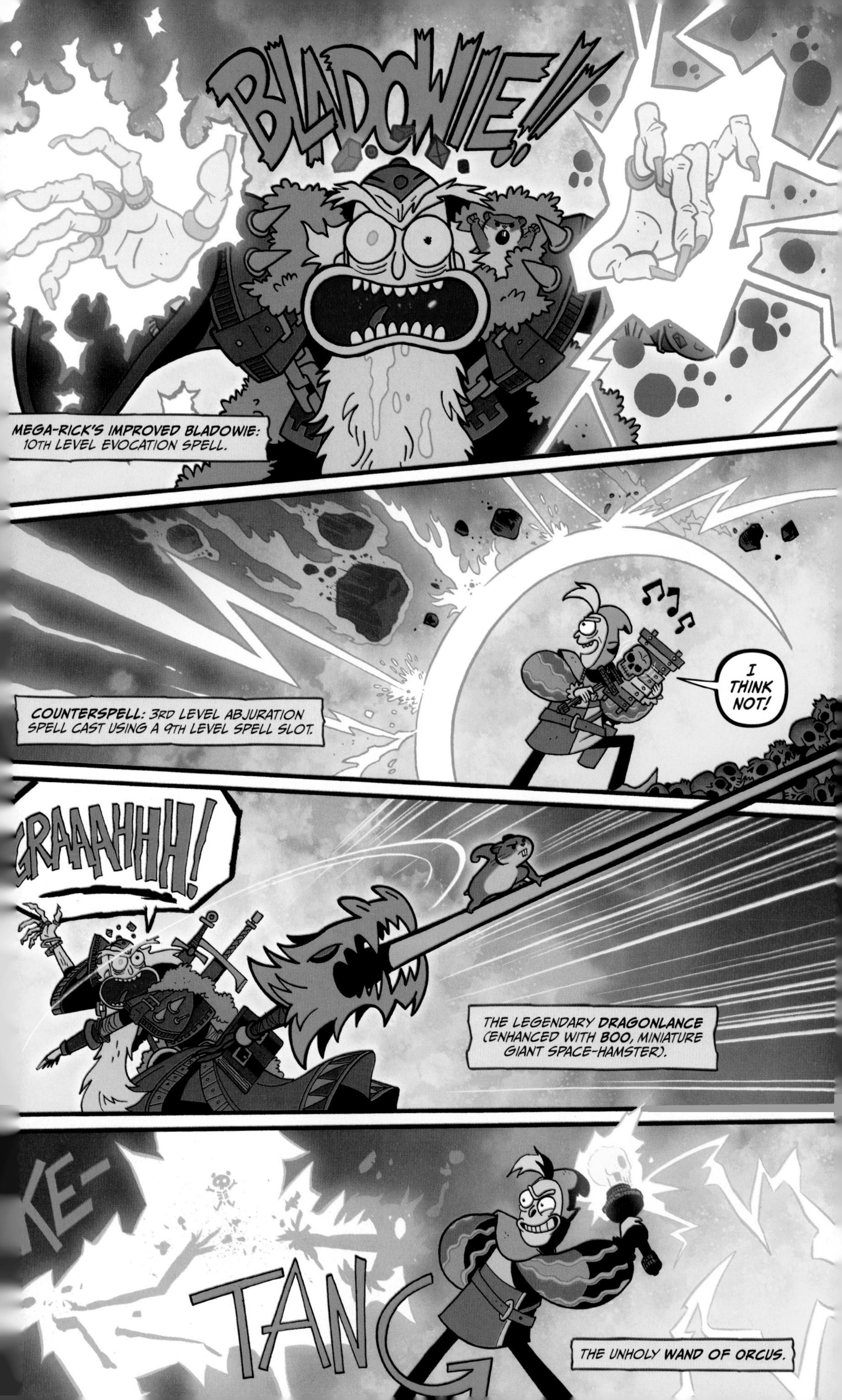
BLADOWIE!!
MEGA-RICK'S IMPROVED BLADOWIE: 10TH LEVEL EVOCATION SPELL.
COUNTERSPELL: 3RD LEVEL ABJURATION SPELL CAST USING A 9TH LEVEL SPELL SLOT.
I THINK NOT!
GRAAAHHH!
THE LEGENDARY DRAGONLANCE (ENHANCED WITH BOO, MINIATURE GIANT SPACE-HAMSTER).
KE-
TANG
THE UNHOLY WAND OF ORCUS.

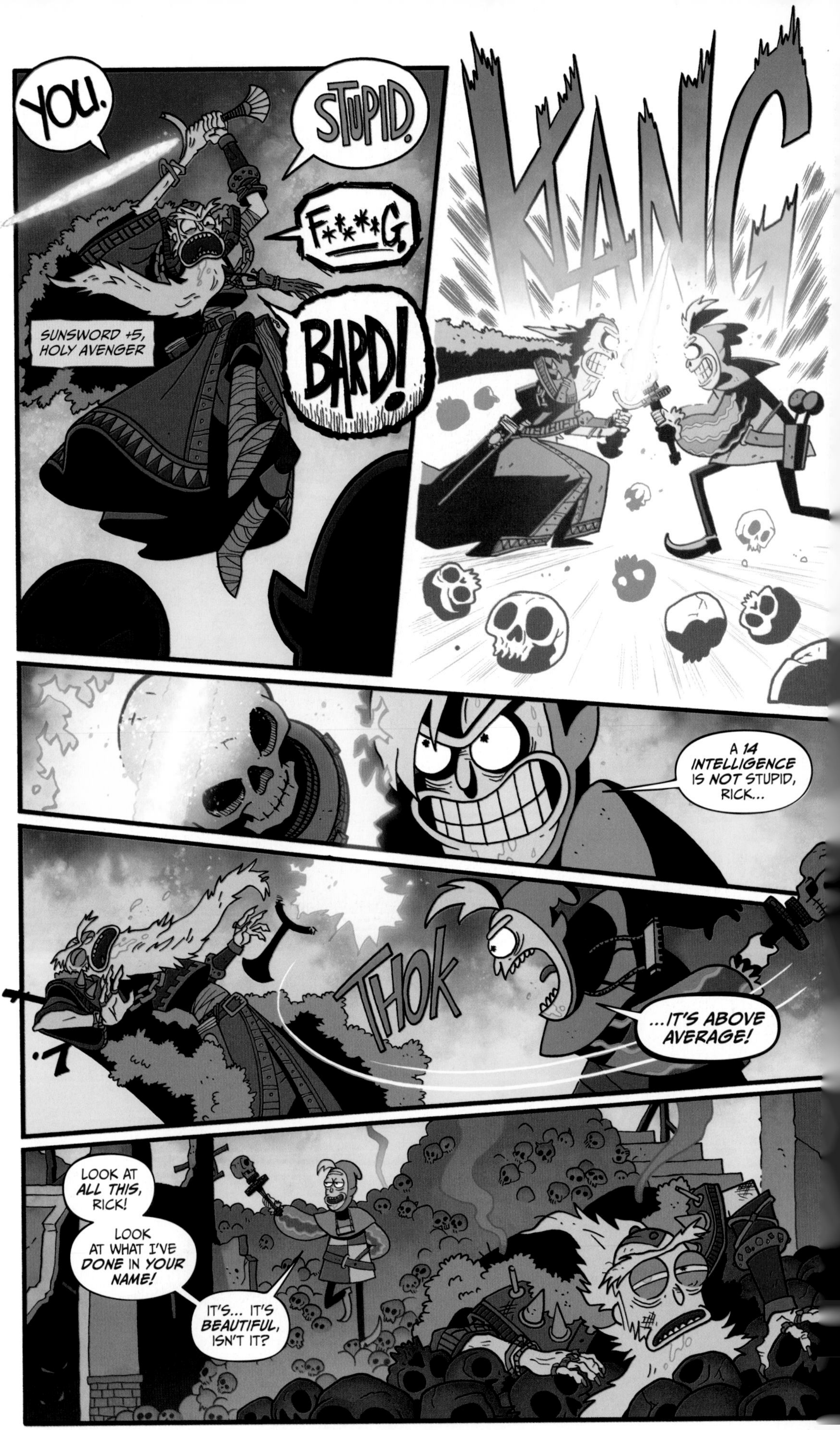
YOU.
STUPID.
F*%*G.
BARD!
SUNSWORD +5, HOLY AVENGER
KANG
A 14 INTELLIGENCE IS NOT STUPID, RICK...
THOK
...IT'S ABOVE AVERAGE!
LOOK AT ALL THIS, RICK!
LOOK AT WHAT I'VE DONE IN YOUR NAME!
IT'S... IT'S BEAUTIFUL, ISN'T IT?

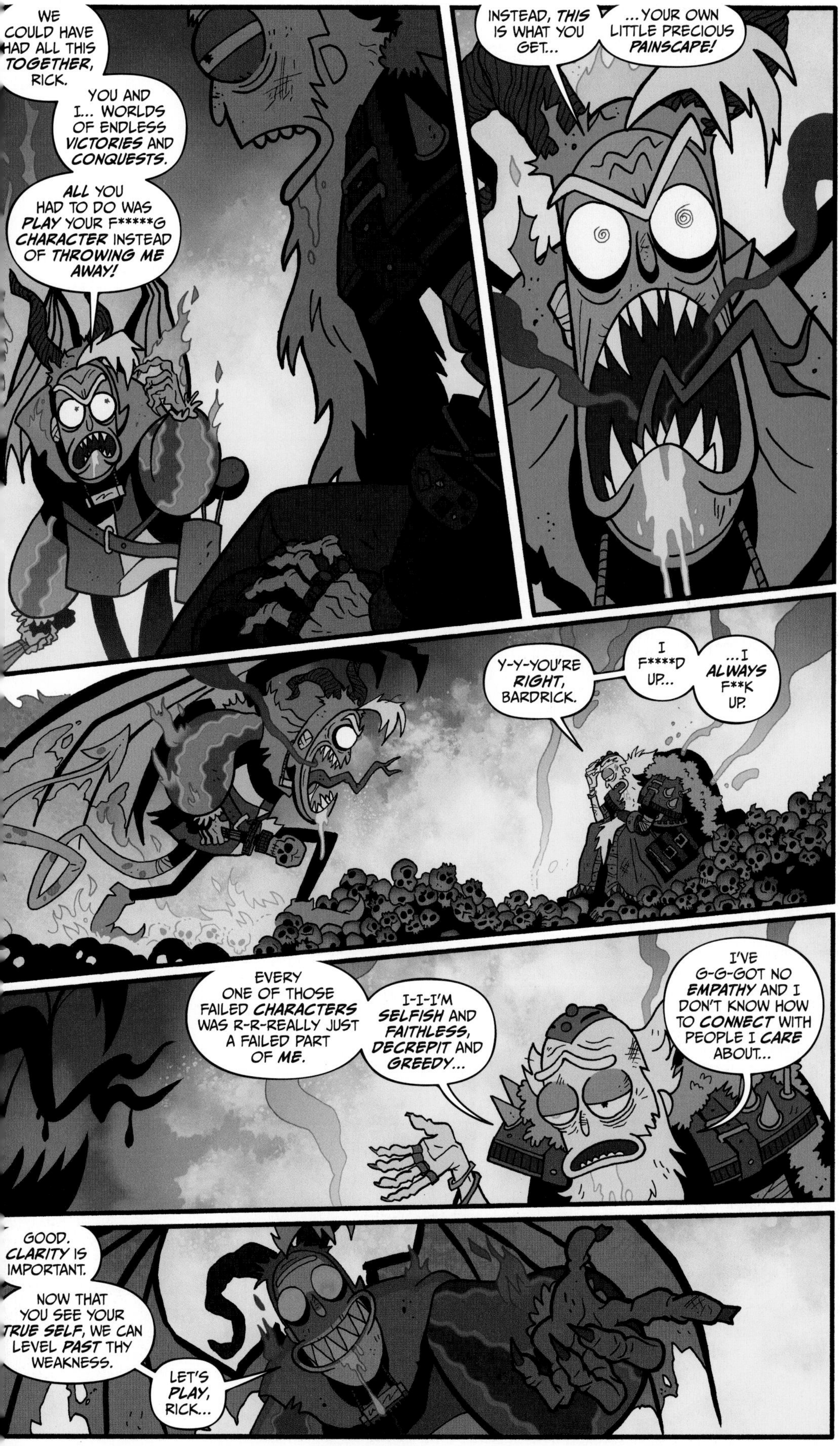
WE COULD HAVE HAD ALL THIS TOGETHER, RICK.
YOU AND I... WORLDS OF ENDLESS VICTORIES AND CONQUESTS.
ALL YOU HAD TO DO WAS PLAY YOUR F*****G CHARACTER INSTEAD OF THROWING ME AWAY!
INSTEAD, THIS IS WHAT YOU GET...
...YOUR OWN LITTLE PRECIOUS PAINSCAPE!
Y-Y-YOU'RE RIGHT, BARDRICK.
I F****D UP...
...I ALWAYS F**K UP.
EVERY ONE OF THOSE FAILED CHARACTERS WAS R-R-REALLY JUST A FAILED PART OF ME.
I-I-I'M SELFISH AND FAITHLESS, DECREPIT AND GREEDY...
I'VE G-G-GOT NO EMPATHY AND I DON'T KNOW HOW TO CONNECT WITH PEOPLE I CARE ABOUT...
GOOD. CLARITY IS IMPORTANT.
NOW THAT YOU SEE YOUR TRUE SELF, WE CAN LEVEL PAST THY WEAKNESS.
LET'S PLAY, RICK...

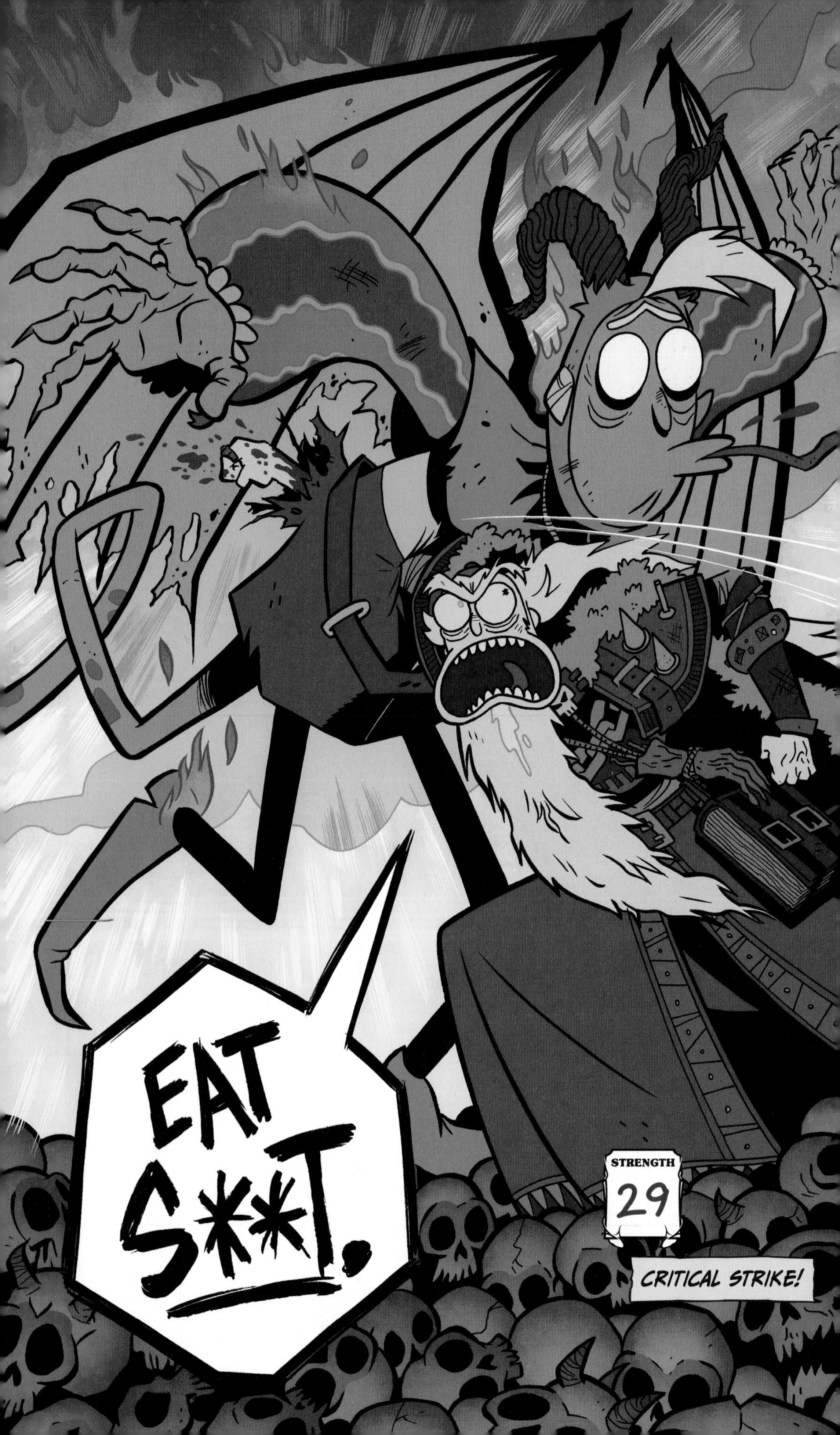
EAT S**T.
STRENGTH
29
CRITICAL STRIKE!

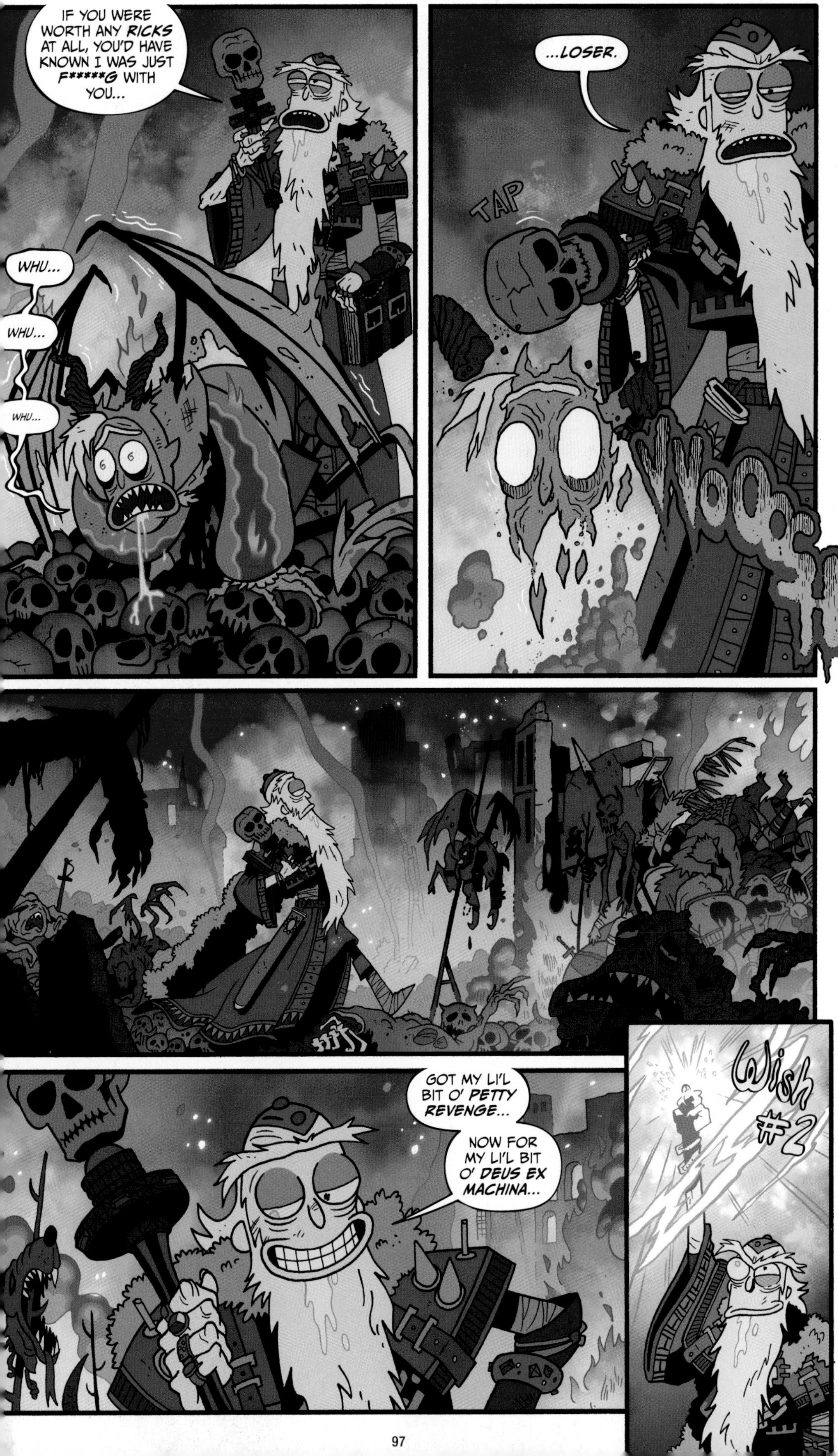
IF YOU WERE WORTH ANY RICKS AT ALL, YOU'D HAVE KNOWN I WAS JUST F*****G WITH YOU...
WHU...
WHU...
WHU...
...LOSER.
TAP
WOOSH
GOT MY LI'L BIT O' PETTY REVENGE...
NOW FOR MY LI'L BIT O' DEUS EX MACHINA...
Wish #2

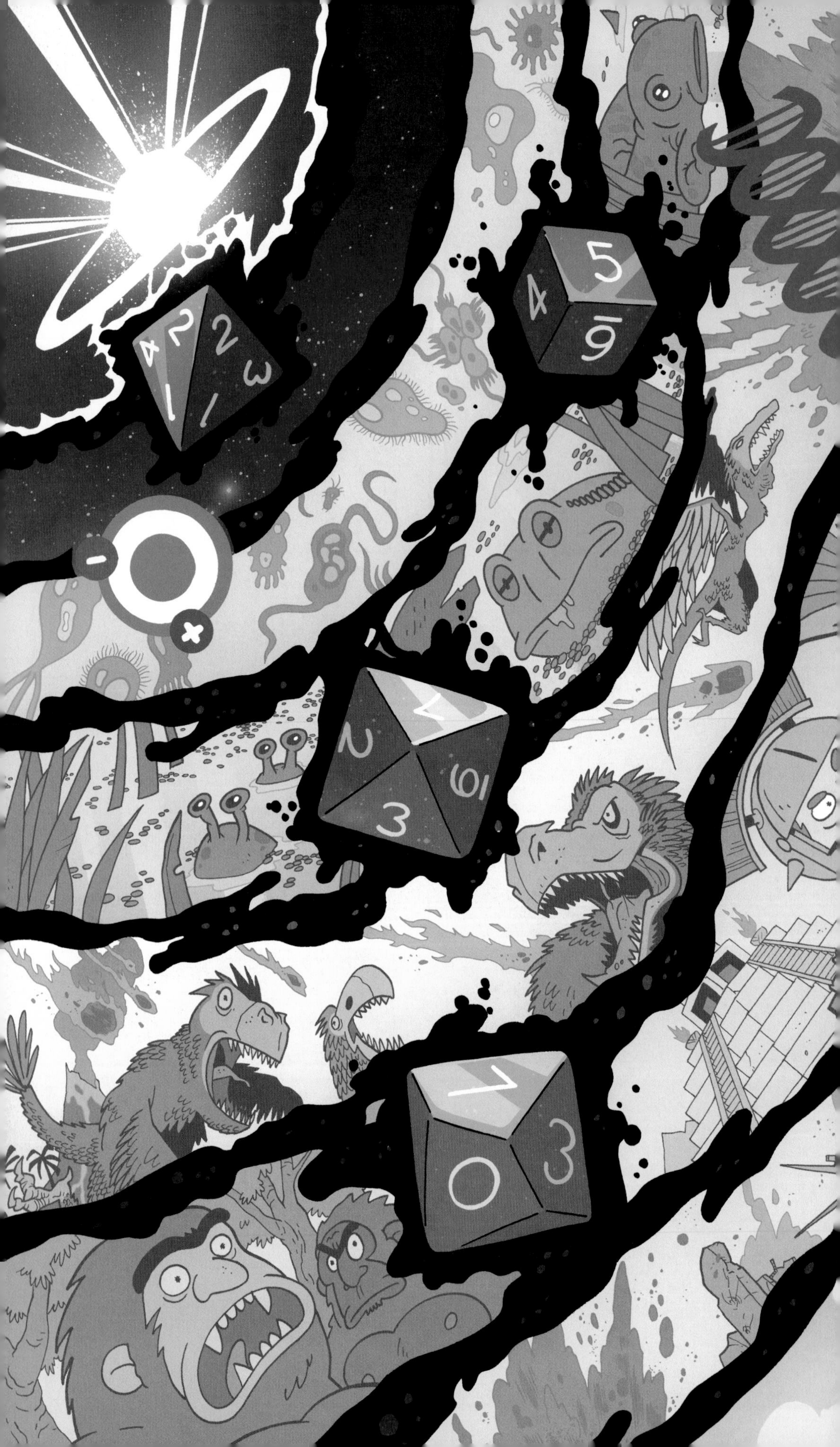

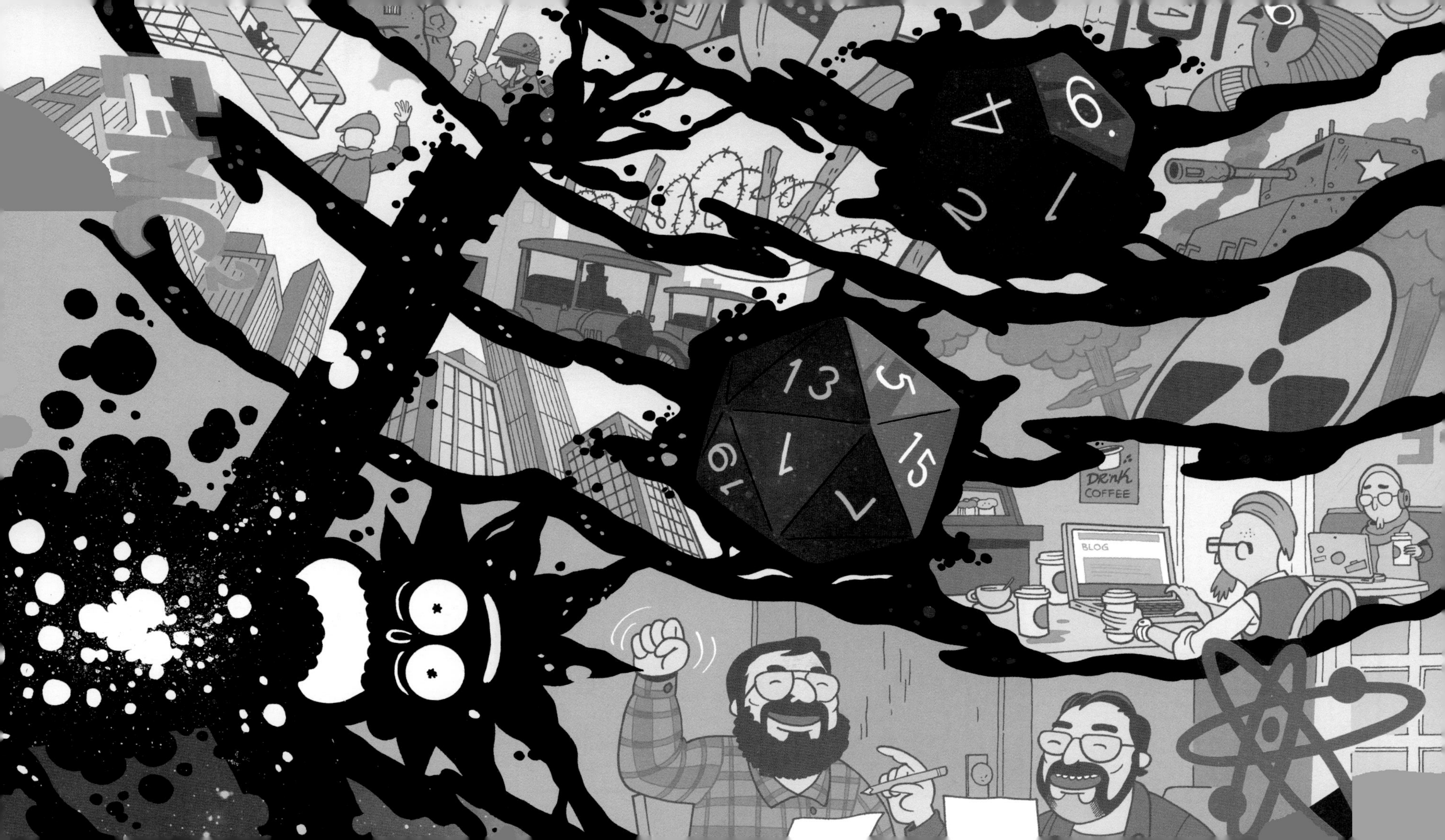
DRINK COFFEE
BLOG

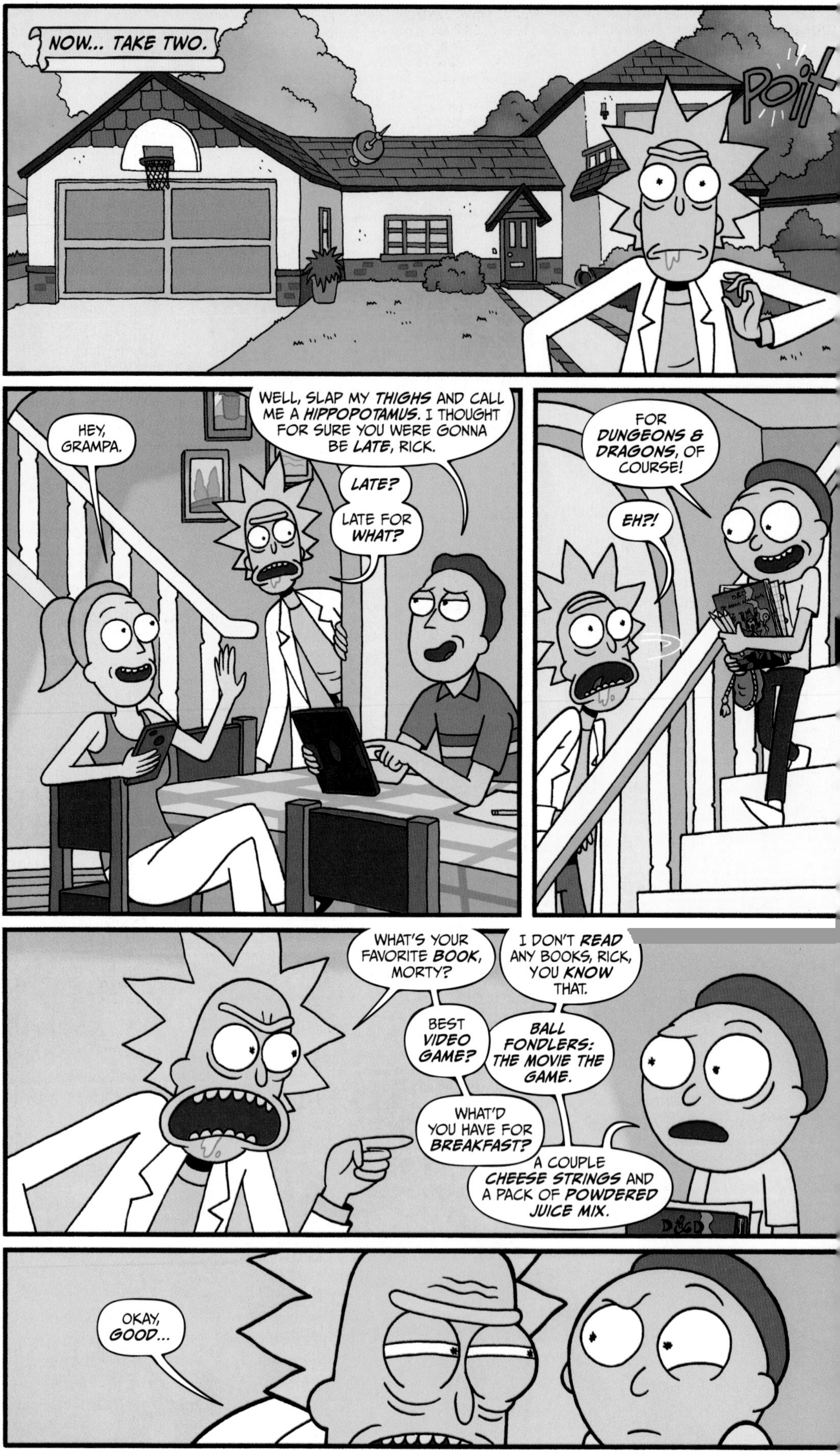
NOW... TAKE TWO.
POIT
HEY, GRAMPA.
WELL, SLAP MY THIGHS AND CALL ME A HIPPOPOTAMUS. I THOUGHT FOR SURE YOU WERE GONNA BE LATE, RICK.
LATE?
LATE FOR WHAT?
FOR DUNGEONS & DRAGONS, OF COURSE!
EH?!
WHAT'S YOUR FAVORITE BOOK, MORTY?
I DON'T READ ANY BOOKS, RICK, YOU KNOW THAT.
BEST VIDEO GAME?
BALL FONDLERS: THE MOVIE THE GAME.
WHAT'D YOU HAVE FOR BREAKFAST?
A COUPLE CHEESE STRINGS AND A PACK OF POWDERED JUICE MIX.
D&D
OKAY, GOOD...

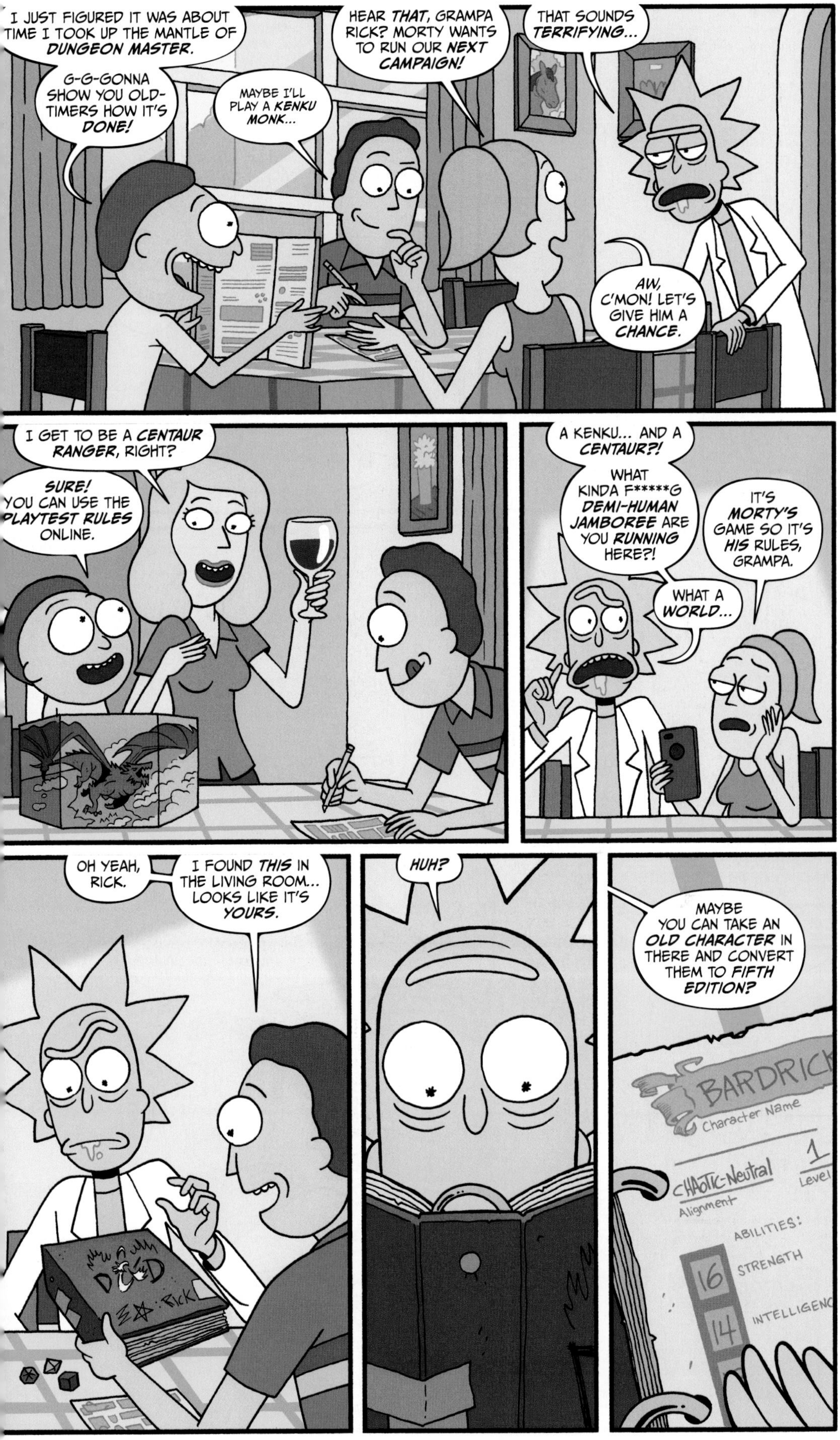
I JUST FIGURED IT WAS ABOUT TIME I TOOK UP THE MANTLE OF DUNGEON MASTER.
G-G-GONNA SHOW YOU OLD-TIMERS HOW IT'S DONE!
MAYBE I'LL PLAY A KENKU MONK...
HEAR THAT, GRAMPA RICK? MORTY WANTS TO RUN OUR NEXT CAMPAIGN!
THAT SOUNDS TERRIFYING...
AW, C'MON! LET'S GIVE HIM A CHANCE.
I GET TO BE A CENTAUR RANGER, RIGHT?
SURE! YOU CAN USE THE PLAYTEST RULES ONLINE.
A KENKU... AND A CENTAUR?!
WHAT KINDA F*****G DEMI-HUMAN JAMBOREE ARE YOU RUNNING HERE?!
IT'S MORTY'S GAME SO IT'S HIS RULES, GRAMPA.
WHAT A WORLD...
OH YEAH, RICK.
I FOUND THIS IN THE LIVING ROOM... LOOKS LIKE IT'S YOURS.
D&D
RICK
HUH?
MAYBE YOU CAN TAKE AN OLD CHARACTER IN THERE AND CONVERT THEM TO FIFTH EDITION?
BARDRICK
Character Name
CHAOTIC-Neutral
Alignment
1
Level
ABILITIES:
16
STRENGTH
14

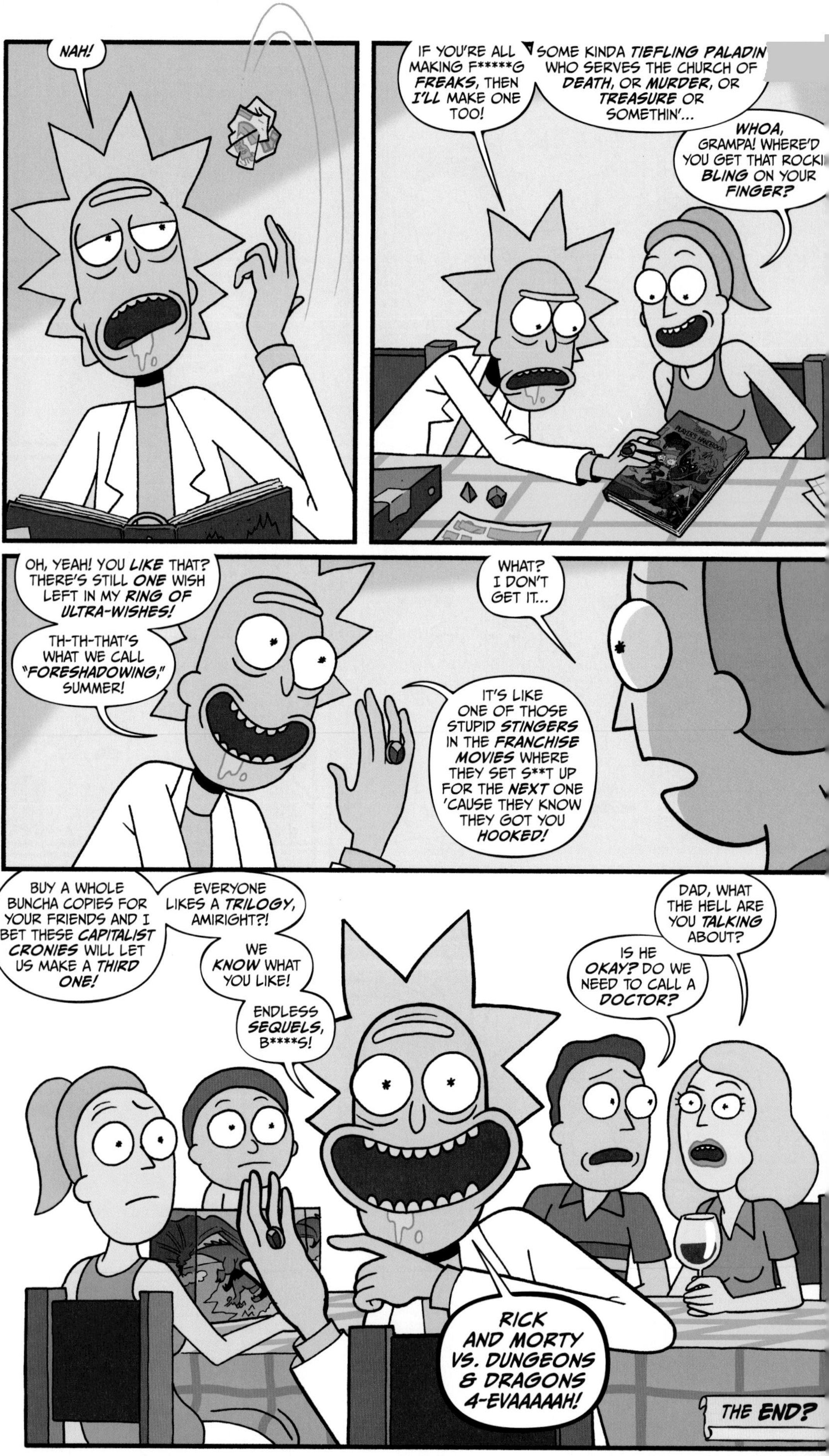
NAH!
IF YOU'RE ALL MAKING F*****G FREAKS, THEN I'LL MAKE ONE TOO!
SOME KINDA TIEFLING PALADIN WHO SERVES THE CHURCH OF DEATH, OR MURDER, OR TREASURE OR SOMETHIN'...
WHOA, GRAMPA! WHERE'D YOU GET THAT ROCKI BLING ON YOUR FINGER?
OH, YEAH! YOU LIKE THAT? THERE'S STILL ONE WISH LEFT IN MY RING OF ULTRA-WISHES!
TH-TH-THAT'S WHAT WE CALL "FORESHADOWING," SUMMER!
WHAT? I DON'T GET IT...
IT'S LIKE ONE OF THOSE STUPID STINGERS IN THE FRANCHISE MOVIES WHERE THEY SET S**T UP FOR THE NEXT ONE 'CAUSE THEY KNOW THEY GOT YOU HOOKED!
BUY A WHOLE BUNCHA COPIES FOR YOUR FRIENDS AND I BET THESE CAPITALIST CRONIES WILL LET US MAKE A THIRD ONE!
EVERYONE LIKES A TRILOGY, AMIRIGHT?!
WE KNOW WHAT YOU LIKE!
ENDLESS SEQUELS, B****S!
DAD, WHAT THE HELL ARE YOU TALKING ABOUT?
IS HE OKAY? DO WE NEED TO CALL A DOCTOR?
RICK AND MORTY VS. DUNGEONS & DRAGONS 4-EVAAAAAH!
THE END?

Rick and Morty vs. Dungeons & Dragons

vs.

DUNGEONS & DRAGONS
II: Painscape

Cover Gallery

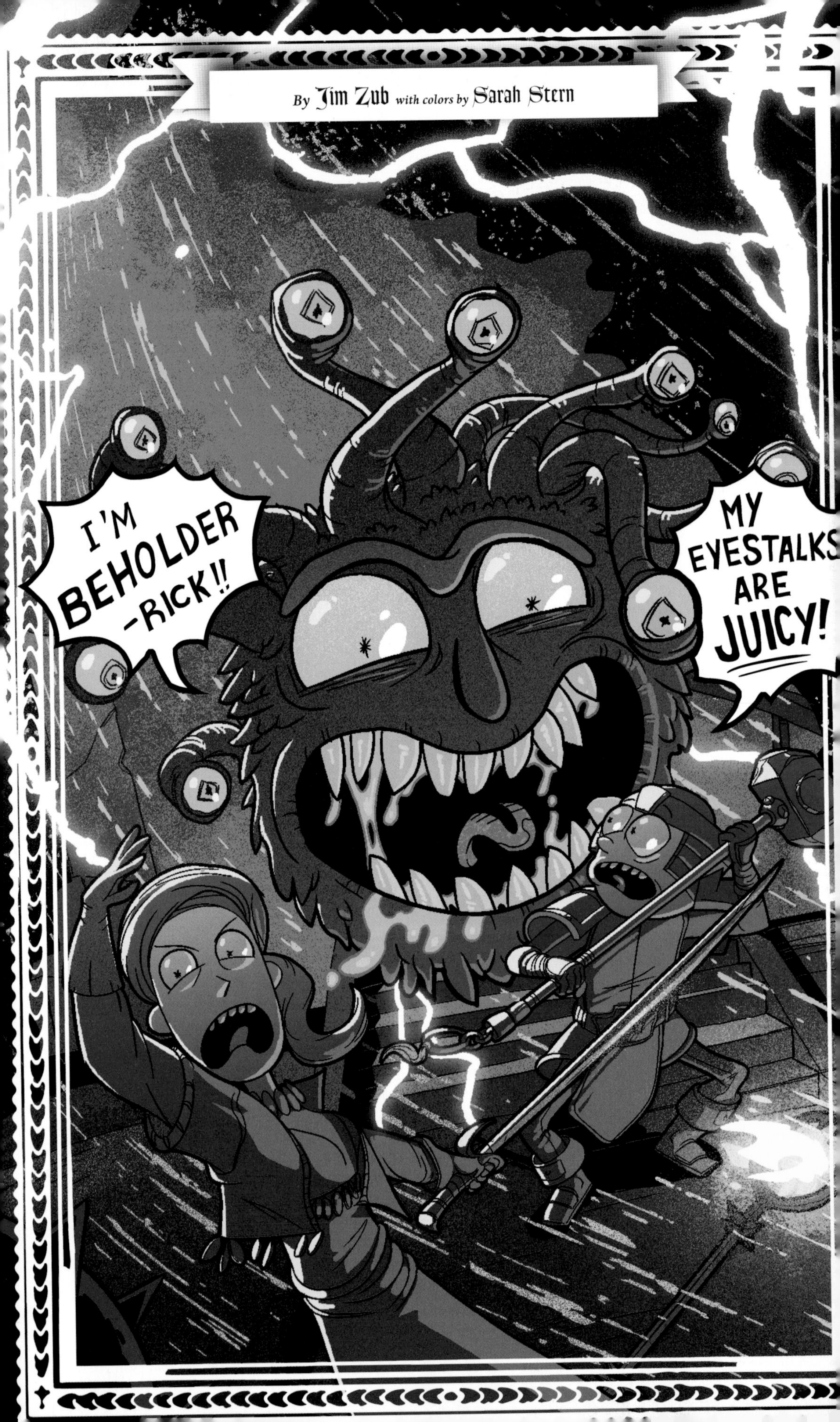
By Jim Zub with colors by Sarah Stern
I'M BEHOLDER-RICK!!
MY EYESTALKS ARE JUICY!

Blank Character Sheet Cover

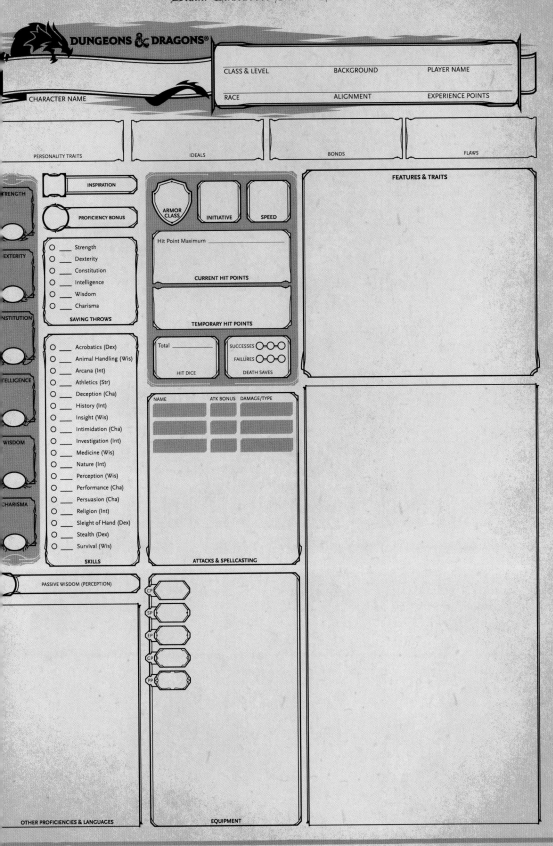

DUNGEONS & DRAGONS®

CHARACTER NAME

CLASS & LEVEL | BACKGROUND | PLAYER NAME

RACE | ALIGNMENT | EXPERIENCE POINTS

PERSONALITY TRAITS

IDEALS

BONDS

FLAWS

TRENGTH

EXTERITY

NSTITUTION

TELLIGENCE

WISDOM

CHARISMA

INSPIRATION

PROFICIENCY BONUS

O ___ Strength
O ___ Dexterity
O ___ Constitution
O ___ Intelligence
O ___ Wisdom
O ___ Charisma

SAVING THROWS

O ___ Acrobatics (Dex)
O ___ Animal Handling (Wis)
O ___ Arcana (Int)
O ___ Athletics (Str)
O ___ Deception (Cha)
O ___ History (Int)
O ___ Insight (Wis)
O ___ Intimidation (Cha)
O ___ Investigation (Int)
O ___ Medicine (Wis)
O ___ Nature (Int)
O ___ Perception (Wis)
O ___ Performance (Cha)
O ___ Persuasion (Cha)
O ___ Religion (Int)
O ___ Sleight of Hand (Dex)
O ___ Stealth (Dex)
O ___ Survival (Wis)

SKILLS

ARMOR CLASS

INITIATIVE

SPEED

Hit Point Maximum ____________

CURRENT HIT POINTS

TEMPORARY HIT POINTS

Total ____________

HIT DICE

SUCCESSES O-O-O

FAILURES O-O-O

DEATH SAVES

NAME	ATK BONUS	DAMAGE/TYPE

ATTACKS & SPELLCASTING

FEATURES & TRAITS

PASSIVE WISDOM (PERCEPTION)

OTHER PROFICIENCIES & LANGUAGES

CP

SP

EP

GP

PP

EQUIPMENT

By Jim Zub and Troy Little

DUNGEONS & DRAGONS®

Wizard Rick		
CHARACTER NAME		
Wizard 5	Sage	Rick Sanchez
CLASS & LEVEL	BACKGROUND	PLAYER NAME
Human	Chaotic Neutral	6,500
RACE	ALIGNMENT	EXPERIENCE POINTS

PERSONALITY TRAITS	IDEALS	BONDS	FLAWS
I've got a spell for every situation.	Unlocking the secrets of the universe is its own reward.	Don't tell anyone, but I kinda wish my family was here questing with me.	This Elvish wine taste pretty damn good...

Ability	Modifier	Score
STRENGTH	+0	10
DEXTERITY	+1	13
CONSTITUTION	+2	15
INTELLIGENCE	+4	19
WISDOM	+1	13
CHARISMA	+0	10

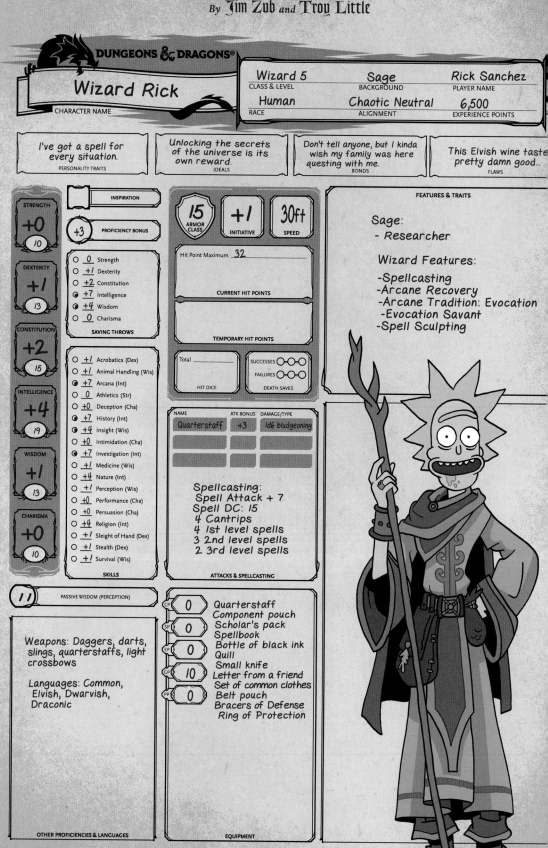

INSPIRATION

+3 PROFICIENCY BONUS

SAVING THROWS

- ○ 0 Strength
- ○ +1 Dexterity
- ○ +2 Constitution
- ● +7 Intelligence
- ● +4 Wisdom
- ○ 0 Charisma

SKILLS

- ○ +1 Acrobatics (Dex)
- ○ +1 Animal Handling (Wis)
- ● +7 Arcana (Int)
- ○ 0 Athletics (Str)
- ○ +0 Deception (Cha)
- ● +7 History (Int)
- ● +4 Insight (Wis)
- ○ +0 Intimidation (Cha)
- ● +7 Investigation (Int)
- ○ +1 Medicine (Wis)
- ○ +4 Nature (Int)
- ○ +1 Perception (Wis)
- ○ +0 Performance (Cha)
- ○ +0 Persuasion (Cha)
- ○ +4 Religion (Int)
- ○ +1 Sleight of Hand (Dex)
- ○ +1 Stealth (Dex)
- ○ +1 Survival (Wis)

11 PASSIVE WISDOM (PERCEPTION)

ARMOR CLASS	INITIATIVE	SPEED
15	+1	30ft

Hit Point Maximum 32

CURRENT HIT POINTS

TEMPORARY HIT POINTS

Total

HIT DICE

SUCCESSES

FAILURES

DEATH SAVES

NAME	ATK BONUS	DAMAGE/TYPE
Quarterstaff	+3	1d6 bludgeoning

Spellcasting:
Spell Attack + 7
Spell DC: 15
4 Cantrips
4 1st level spells
3 2nd level spells
2 3rd level spells

ATTACKS & SPELLCASTING

FEATURES & TRAITS

Sage:
- Researcher

Wizard Features:

-Spellcasting
-Arcane Recovery
-Arcane Tradition: Evocation
-Evocation Savant
-Spell Sculpting

Weapons: Daggers, darts, slings, quarterstaffs, light crossbows

Languages: Common, Elvish, Dwarvish, Draconic

OTHER PROFICIENCIES & LANGUAGES

CP	0
SP	0
EP	0
GP	10
PP	0

Quarterstaff
Component pouch
Scholar's pack
Spellbook
Bottle of black ink
Quill
Small knife
Letter from a friend
Set of common clothes
Belt pouch
Bracers of Defense
Ring of Protection

EQUIPMENT

By Derek Charm

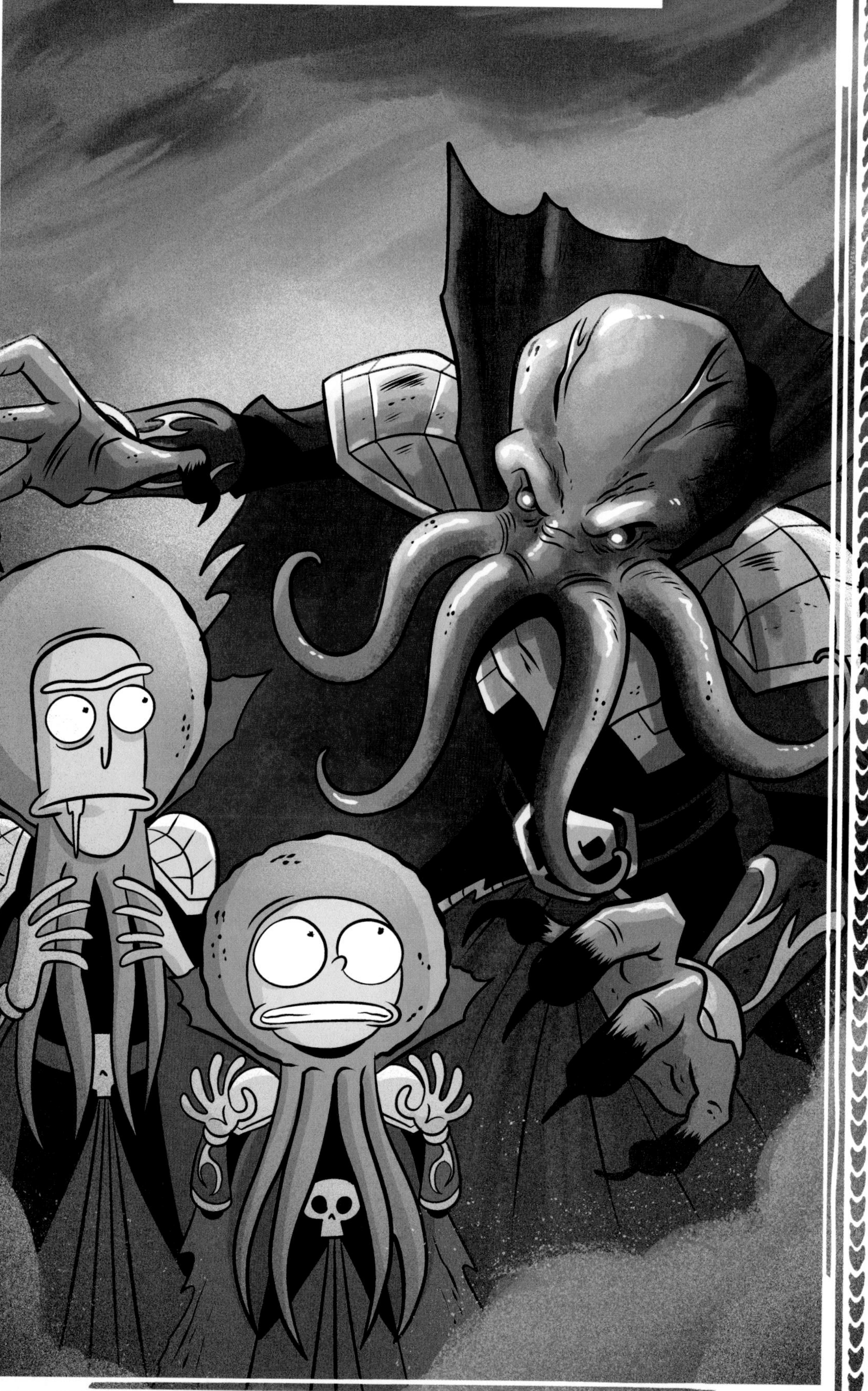

By Mikey Spano

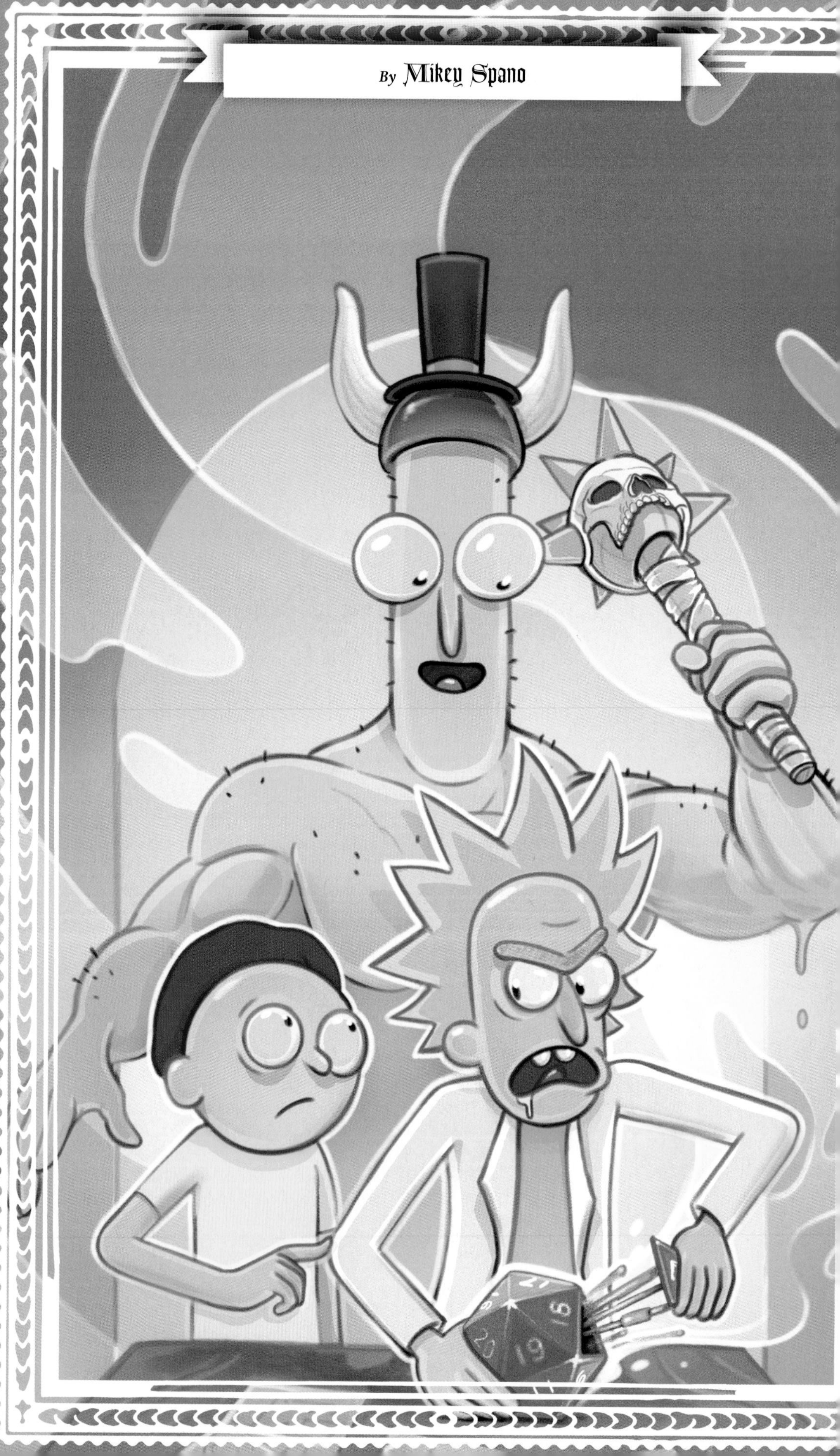

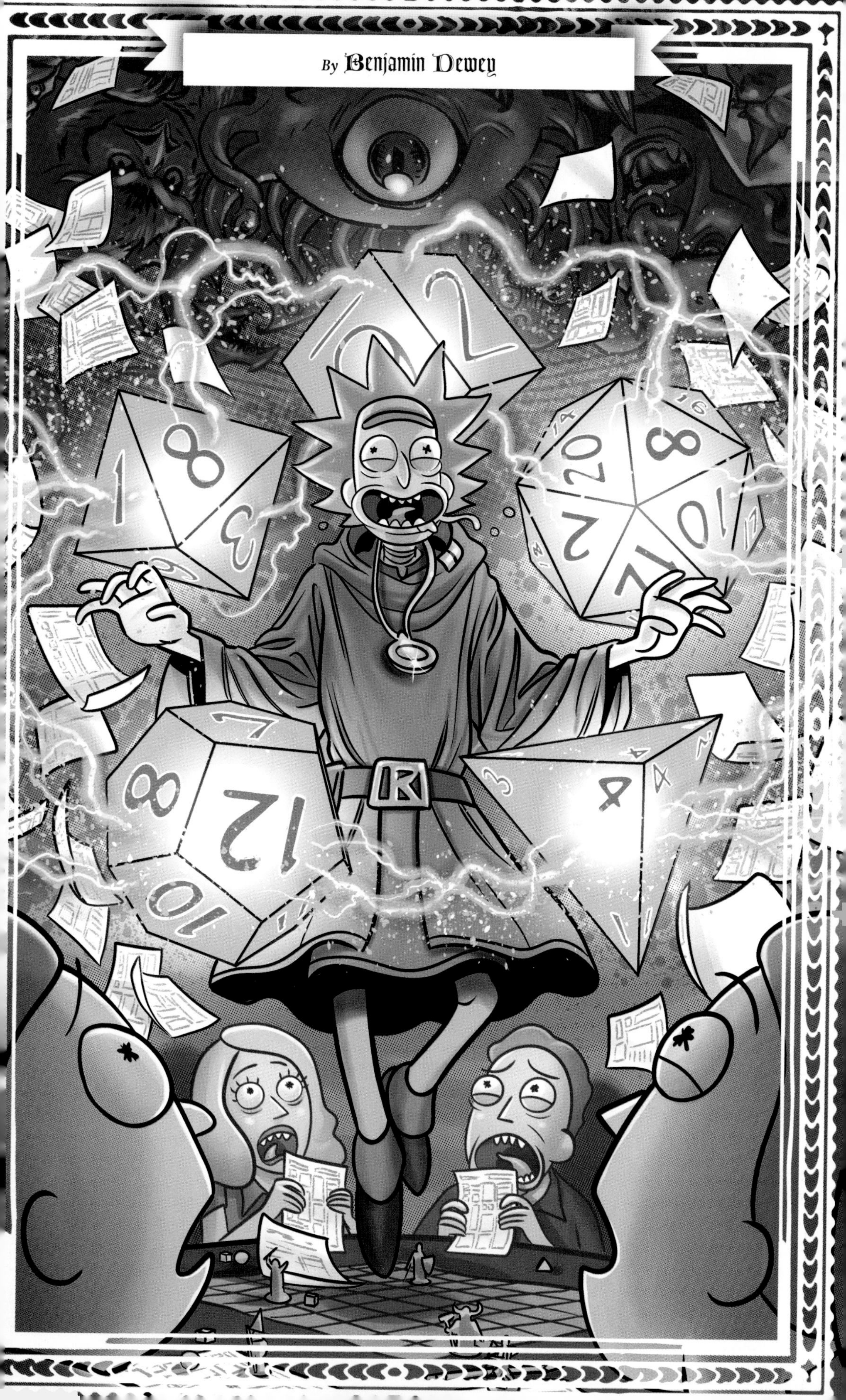
By Benjamin Dewey

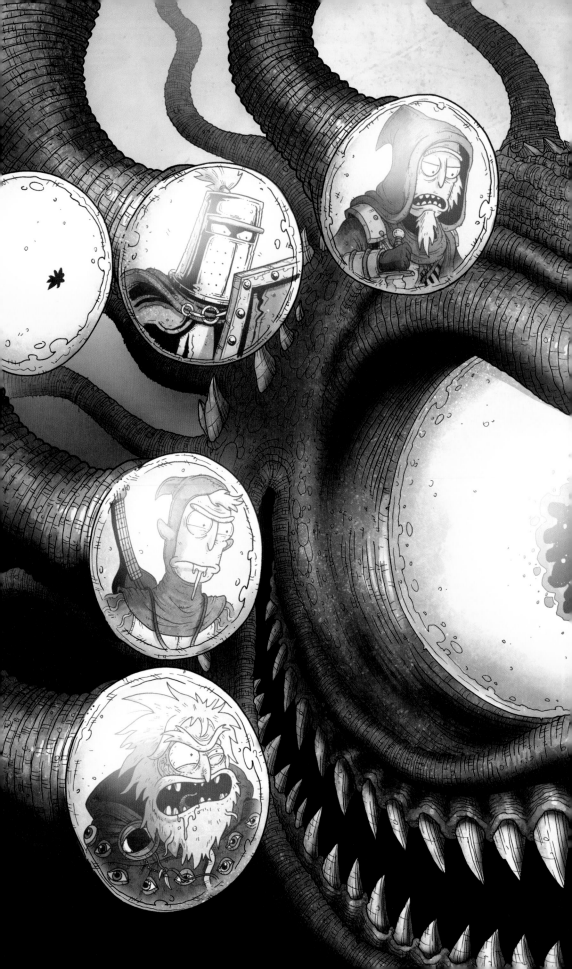

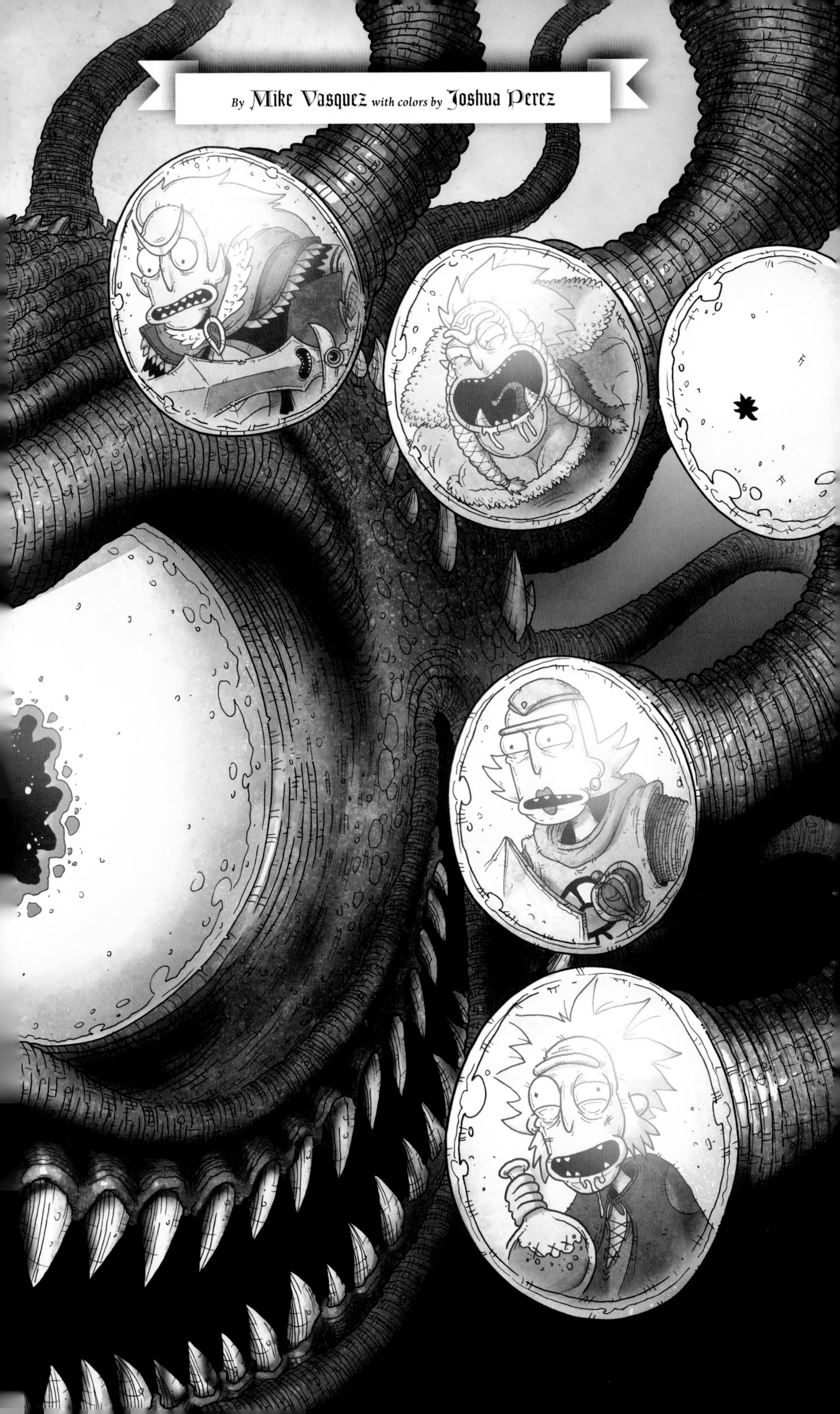
By Mike Vasquez with colors by Joshua Perez

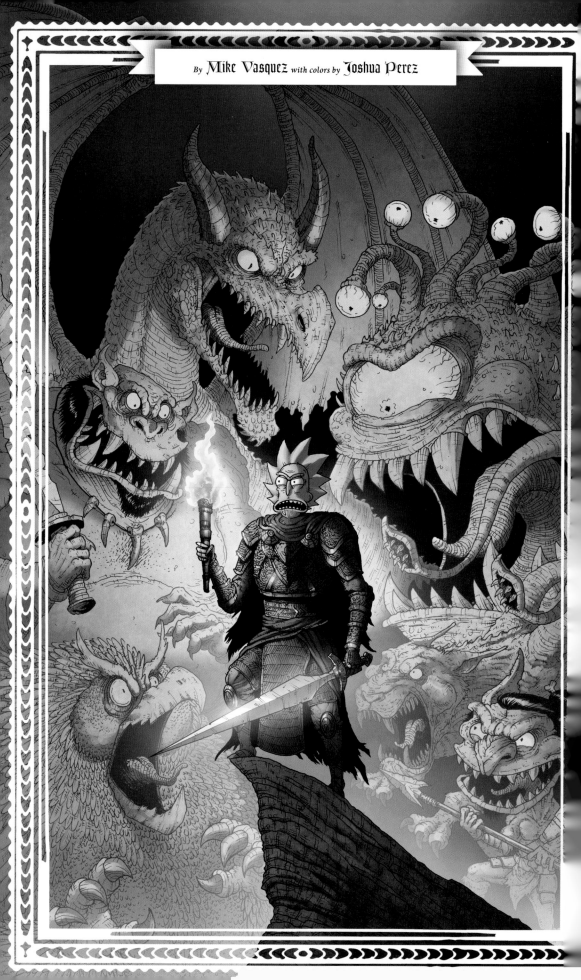

By Mike Vasquez *with colors by* Joshua Perez

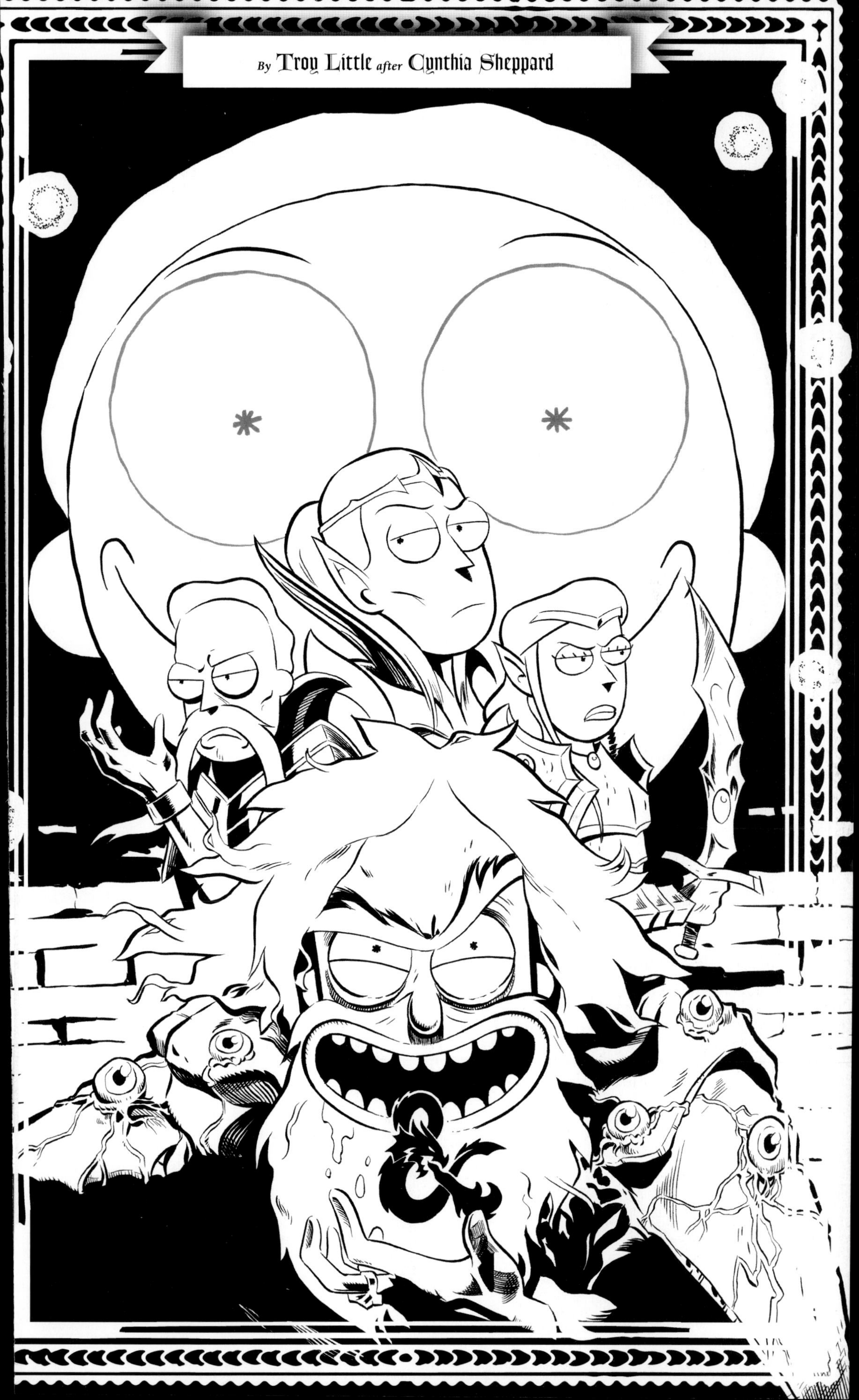
By Troy Little after Cynthia Sheppard

By Julia Scott

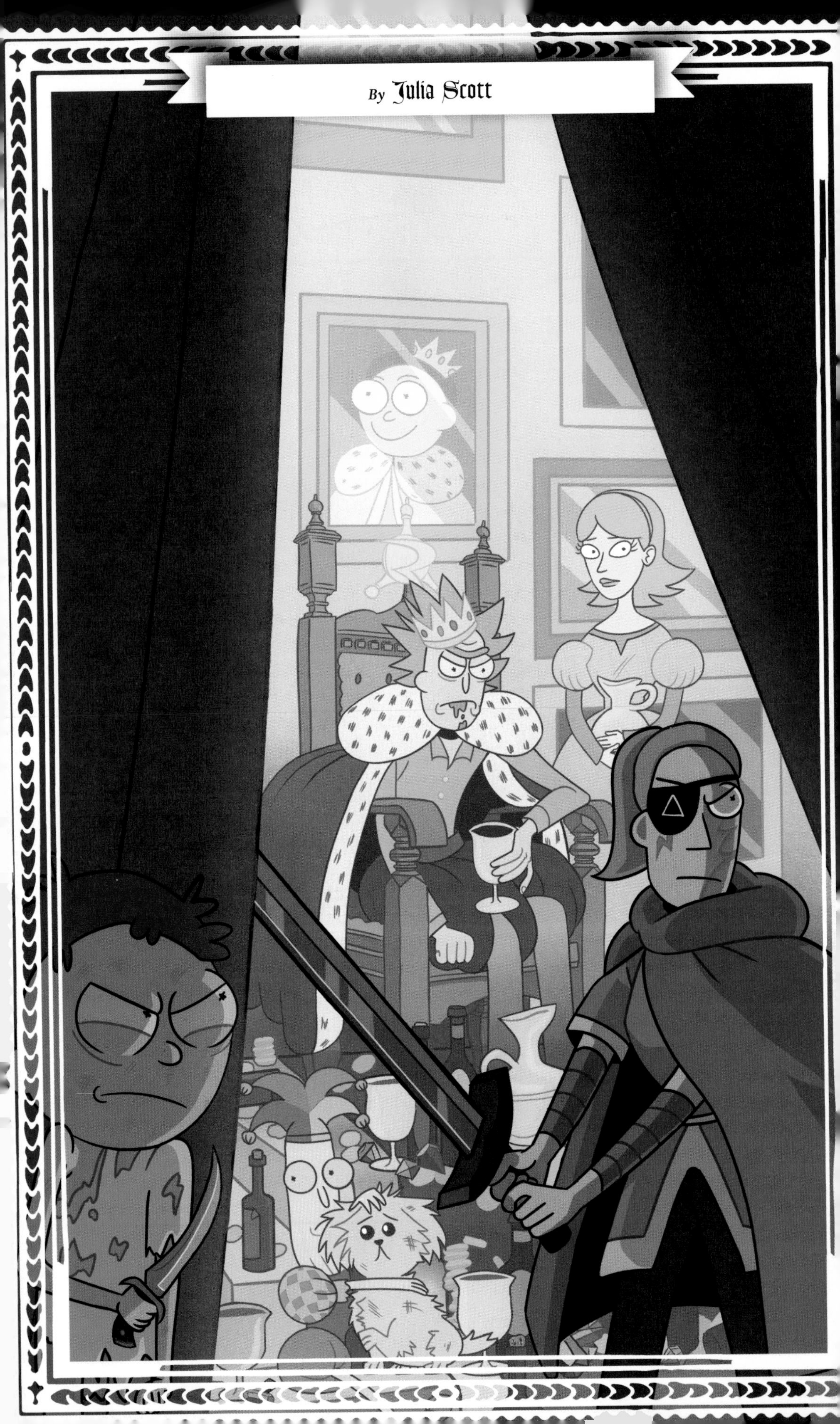

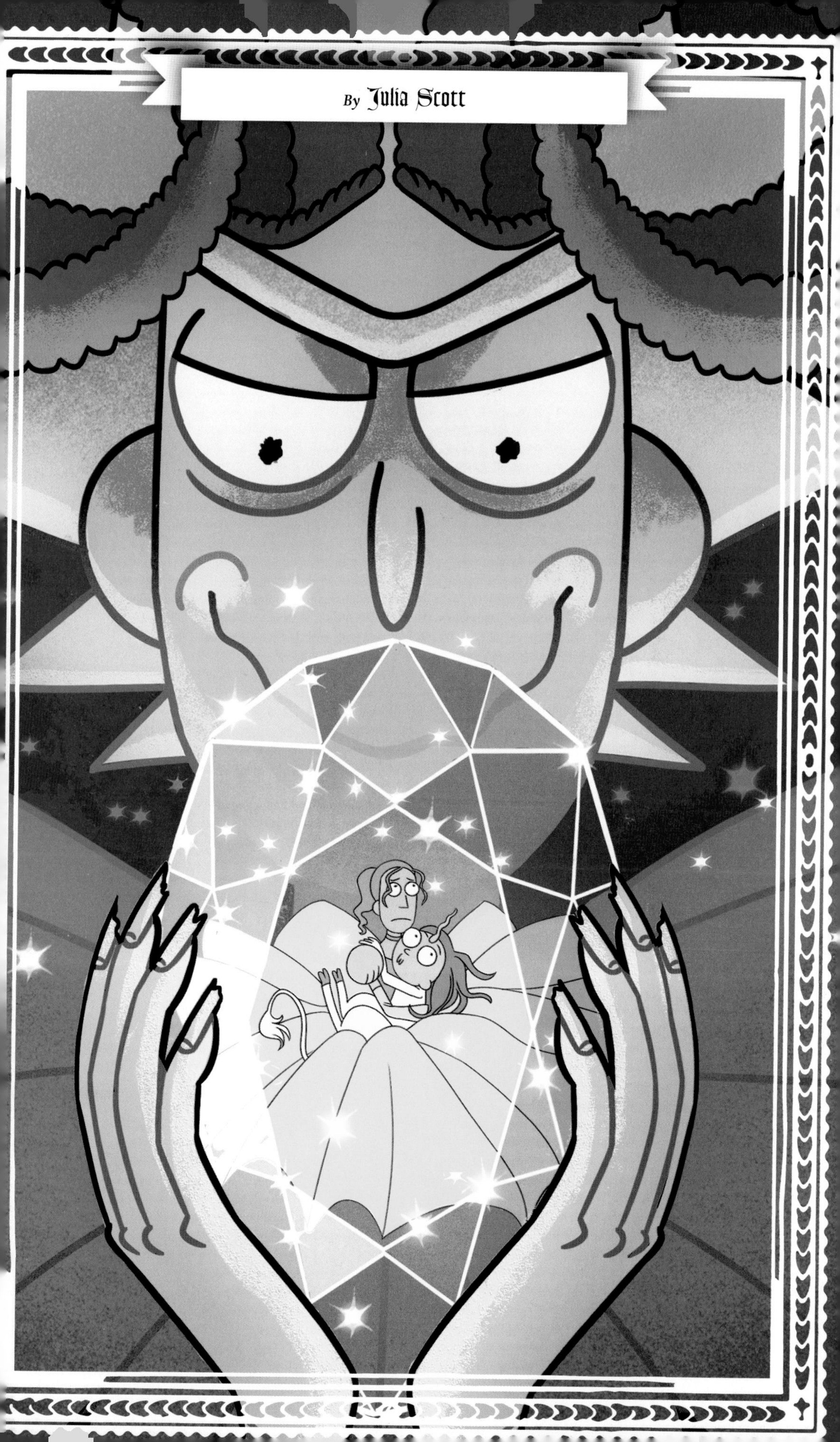
By Julia Scott

By Nicole Goux

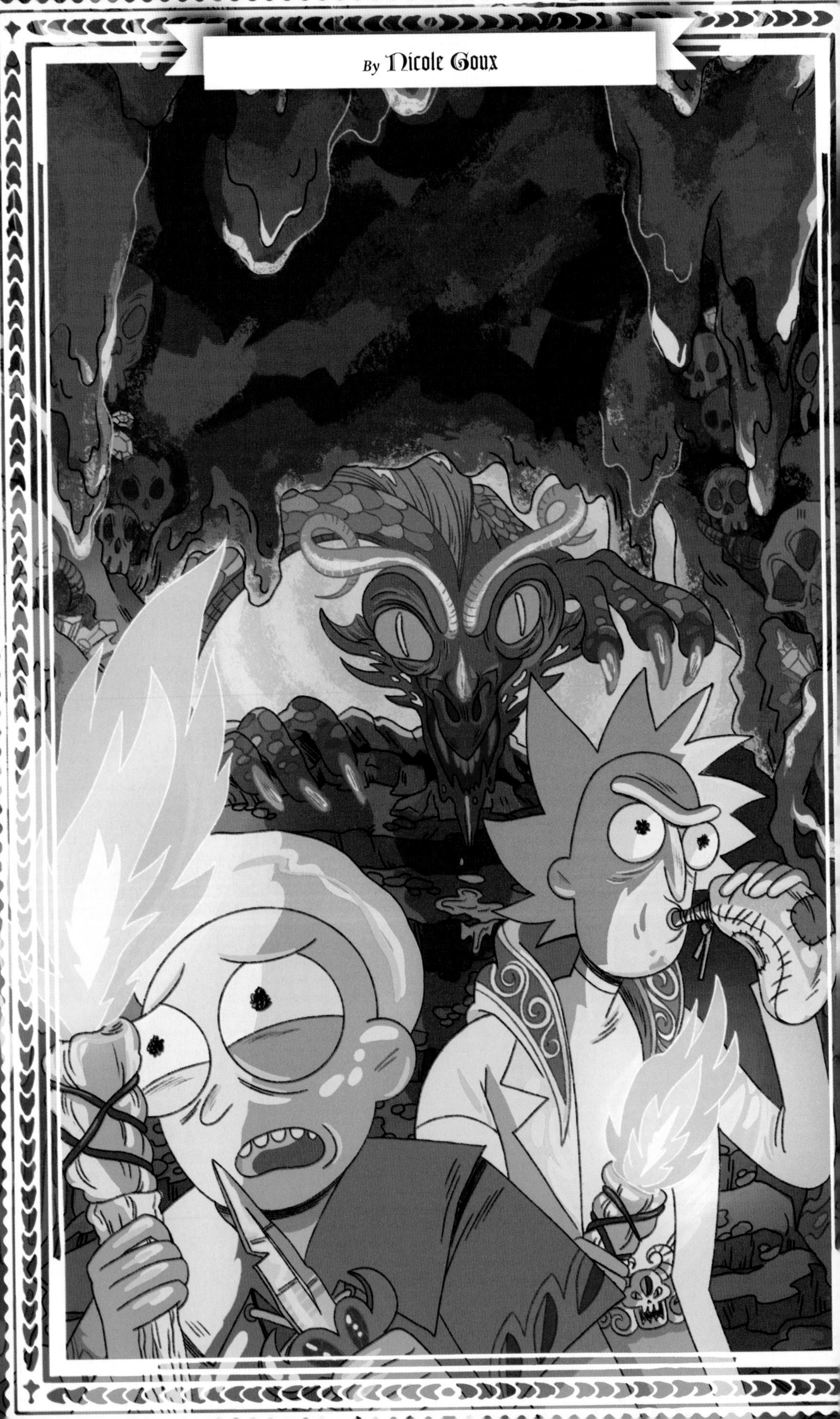

By Jim Zub and Troy Little

DUNGEONS & DRAGONS®

CHARACTER NAME: Wizard-Fighter Rick

Wizard 5, Fighter 5	Sage	Rick Sanchez
CLASS & LEVEL	BACKGROUND	PLAYER NAME
Human	Chaotic Neutral	64,000
RACE	ALIGNMENT	EXPERIENCE POINTS

don't think you're stupid, I *know* you are.
PERSONALITY TRAITS

Knowledge is the only thing I respect, at least until I figure out what you know, and then you're screwed.
IDEALS

Loyalty is for the weak. Companionship is for the stupid.
BONDS

Dwarven ale is a blessing and a curse.
FLAWS

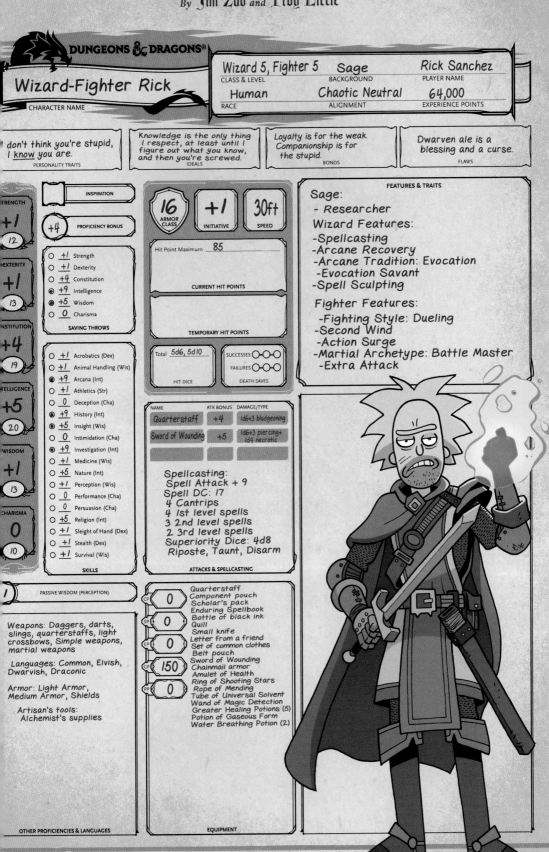

STRENGTH +1 / 12

DEXTERITY +1 / 13

CONSTITUTION +4 / 19

INTELLIGENCE +5 / 20

WISDOM +1 / 13

CHARISMA 0 / 10

INSPIRATION

+4 PROFICIENCY BONUS

SAVING THROWS
- +1 Strength
- +1 Dexterity
- +4 Constitution
- ● +9 Intelligence
- ● +5 Wisdom
- 0 Charisma

SKILLS
- +1 Acrobatics (Dex)
- +1 Animal Handling (Wis)
- ● +9 Arcana (Int)
- +1 Athletics (Str)
- 0 Deception (Cha)
- ● +9 History (Int)
- ● +5 Insight (Wis)
- 0 Intimidation (Cha)
- ● +9 Investigation (Int)
- +1 Medicine (Wis)
- +5 Nature (Int)
- +1 Perception (Wis)
- 0 Performance (Cha)
- 0 Persuasion (Cha)
- ● +5 Religion (Int)
- +1 Sleight of Hand (Dex)
- +1 Stealth (Dex)
- +1 Survival (Wis)

1 PASSIVE WISDOM (PERCEPTION)

16 ARMOR CLASS

+1 INITIATIVE

30ft SPEED

Hit Point Maximum 85

CURRENT HIT POINTS

TEMPORARY HIT POINTS

Total 5d6, 5d10
HIT DICE

DEATH SAVES
SUCCESSES ○○○
FAILURES ○○○

NAME	ATK BONUS	DAMAGE/TYPE
Quarterstaff	+4	1d6+3 bludgeoning
Sword of Wounding	+5	1d6+3 piercing+ 1d4 necrotic

Spellcasting:
Spell Attack + 9
Spell DC: 17
4 Cantrips
4 1st level spells
3 2nd level spells
2 3rd level spells
Superiority Dice: 4d8
Riposte, Taunt, Disarm

ATTACKS & SPELLCASTING

CP 0
SP 0
EP 0
GP 150
PP 0

Quarterstaff
Component pouch
Scholar's pack
Enduring Spellbook
Bottle of black ink
Quill
Small knife
Letter from a friend
Set of common clothes
Belt pouch
Sword of Wounding
Chainmail armor
Amulet of Health
Ring of Shooting Stars
Rope of Mending
Tube of Universal Solvent
Wand of Magic Detection
Greater Healing Potions (5)
Potion of Gaseous Form
Water Breathing Potion (2)

EQUIPMENT

FEATURES & TRAITS

Sage:
- Researcher

Wizard Features:
- Spellcasting
- Arcane Recovery
- Arcane Tradition: Evocation
- Evocation Savant
- Spell Sculpting

Fighter Features:
- Fighting Style: Dueling
- Second Wind
- Action Surge
- Martial Archetype: Battle Master
- Extra Attack

Weapons: Daggers, darts, slings, quarterstaffs, light crossbows, Simple weapons, martial weapons

Languages: Common, Elvish, Dwarvish, Draconic

Armor: Light Armor, Medium Armor, Shields

Artisan's tools: Alchemist's supplies

OTHER PROFICIENCIES & LANGUAGES

By Mady G.

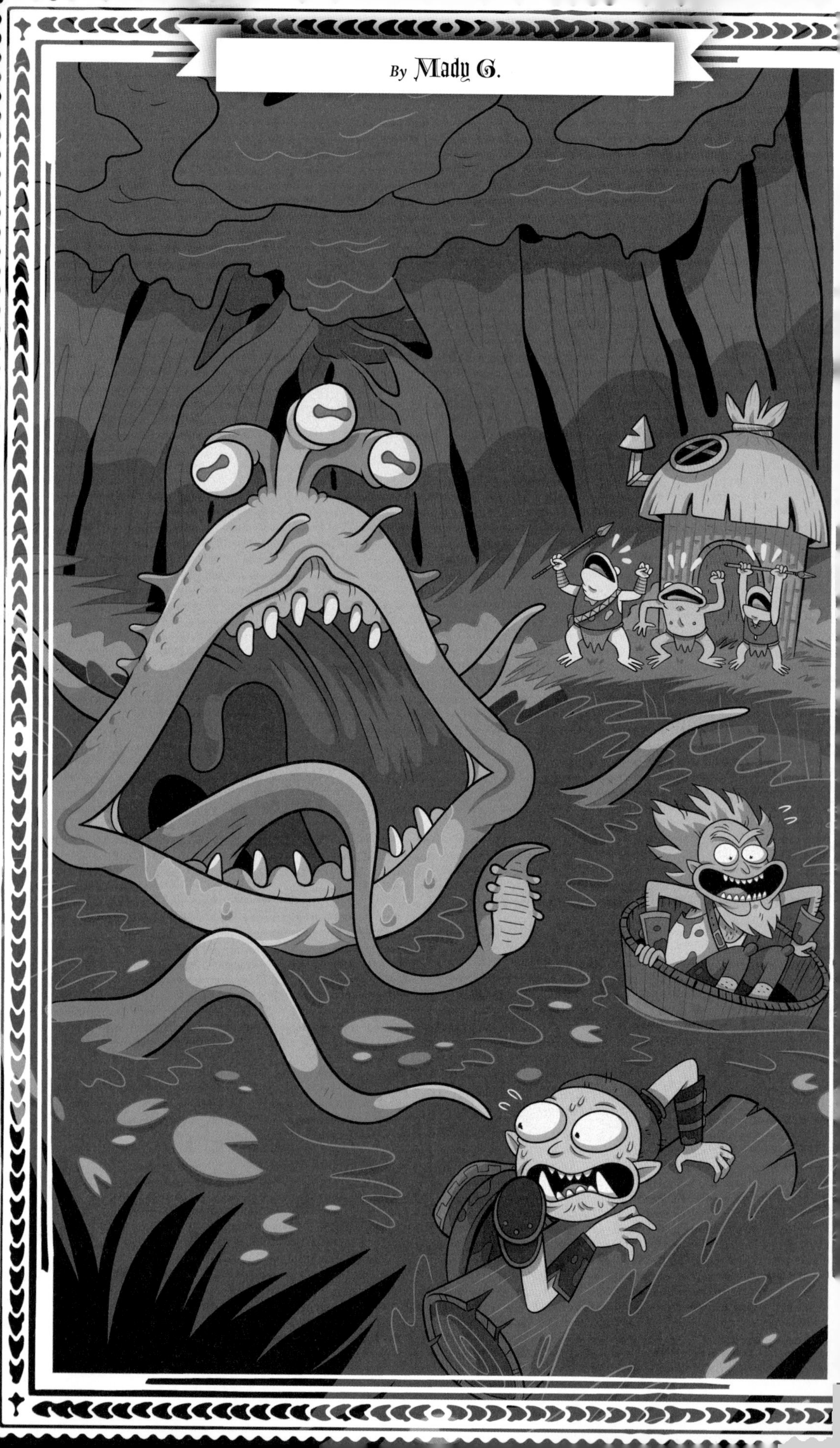

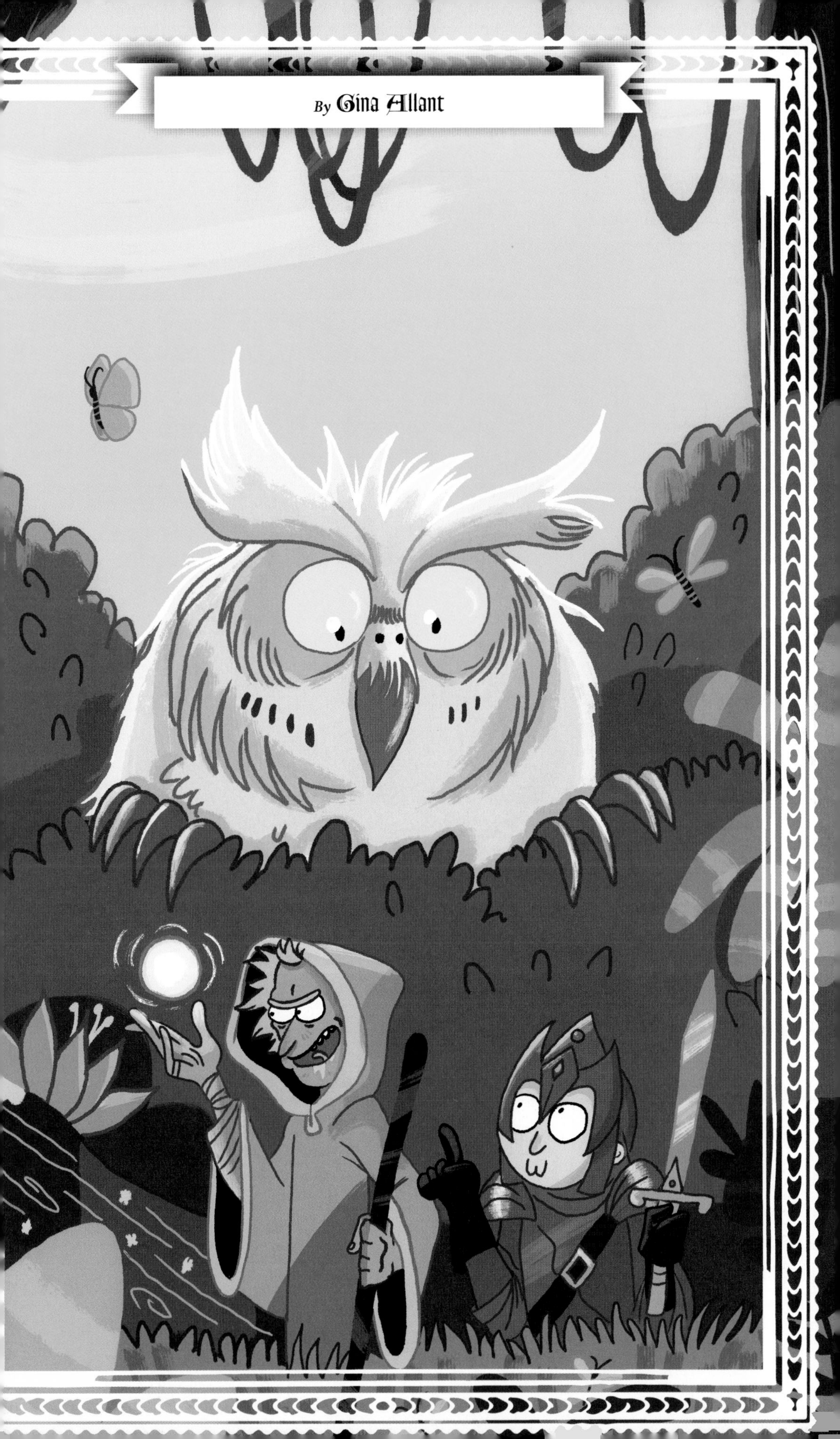
By Gina Allant

By Jim Zub and Troy Little

DUNGEONS & DRAGONS®

Wizard-Fighter-Rogue Rick
CHARACTER NAME

CLASS & LEVEL	BACKGROUND	PLAYER NAME
Wizard 5, Fighter 5, Rogue 5	Sage	Rick Sanchez

RACE	ALIGNMENT	EXPERIENCE POINTS
Human	Chaotic Neutral	165,000

PERSONALITY TRAITS: I'm right. I'm always right.

IDEALS: If you're not strong enough to keep it, then it was never yours.

BONDS: The XP grind and I now understand each other.

FLAWS: Satyr whiskey marginally num the pain of knowing too much and being surrounded by fools

Ability	Modifier	Score
STRENGTH	+1	12
DEXTERITY	+2	14
CONSTITUTION	+2	15
INTELLIGENCE	+5	20
WISDOM	+1	13
CHARISMA	0	10

INSPIRATION

+5 PROFICIENCY BONUS

SAVING THROWS
- ○ +1 Strength
- ○ +2 Dexterity
- ○ +2 Constitution
- ● +10 Intelligence
- ● +6 Wisdom
- ○ 0 Charisma

SKILLS
- ○ +2 Acrobatics (Dex)
- ○ +1 Animal Handling (Wis)
- ● +15 Arcana (Int)
- ○ +1 Athletics (Str)
- ○ 0 Deception (Cha)
- ● +10 History (Int)
- ● +6 Insight (Wis)
- ○ 0 Intimidation (Cha)
- ● +10 Investigation (Int)
- ○ +1 Medicine (Wis)
- ○ +5 Nature (Int)
- ○ +1 Perception (Wis)
- ○ 0 Performance (Cha)
- ○ 0 Persuasion (Cha)
- ○ +5 Religion (Int)
- ○ +2 Sleight of Hand (Dex)
- ● +12 Stealth (Dex)
- ○ +1 Survival (Wis)

11 PASSIVE WISDOM (PERCEPTION)

OTHER PROFICIENCIES & LANGUAGES

Weapons: Daggers, darts, slings, quarterstaffs, light crossbows, Simple weapons, martial weapons

Languages: Common, Elvish, Dwarvish, Draconic, Thieves' Cant

Armor: Light Armor, Medium Armor, Shields

Artisan's tools: Alchemist's supplies

Thieves' Tools, Disguise Kit, Poisoner's Kit

16 ARMOR CLASS | +2 INITIATIVE | 30ft SPEED

Hit Point Maximum 107

CURRENT HIT POINTS

TEMPORARY HIT POINTS

HIT DICE: Total 5d6, 5d10, 5d8

DEATH SAVES: SUCCESSES ○-○-○ FAILURES ○-○-○

ATTACKS & SPELLCASTING

NAME	ATK BONUS	DAMAGE/TYPE
Longsword +3	+10	1d6+7 piercing
Sword of Wounding	+5	1d8+2 piercing

Spellcasting:
Spell Attack + 10
Spell DC: 18
4 Cantrips
4 1st level spells
3 2nd level spells
2 3rd level spells
Superiority Dice: 4d8
Riposte, Taunt, Disarm
Sneak Attack: 3d6

EQUIPMENT

CP 0 | SP 0 | EP 0 | GP 500 | PP 0

Cloak
Thieves' Tools
Boots of Speed
Beads of Force (4)
Bag of Holding
Enduring Spellbook
Rope of Climbing
Component pouch
+3 Defender Longsword
Mithril Chainmail armor
Superior Healing Potions (5)
Potions of Heroism (2)
Potion of Invulnerability (1)
Longbow
Quiver of Ehlonna
20 Arrows +2
20 Arrows +1

FEATURES & TRAITS

Sage:
- Researcher

Wizard Features:
- Spellcasting
- Arcane Recovery
- Arcane Tradition: Evocation
- Evocation Savant
- Spell Sculpting

Fighter Features:
- Fighting Style: Dueling
- Second Wind
- Action Surge
- Martial Archetype: Battle Master
- Extra Attack

Rogue Features:
- Expertise
- Sneak Attack
- Thieves' Cant
- Cunning Action
- Roguish Archetype: Assassin
- Uncanny Dodge

By Sheri Groleau

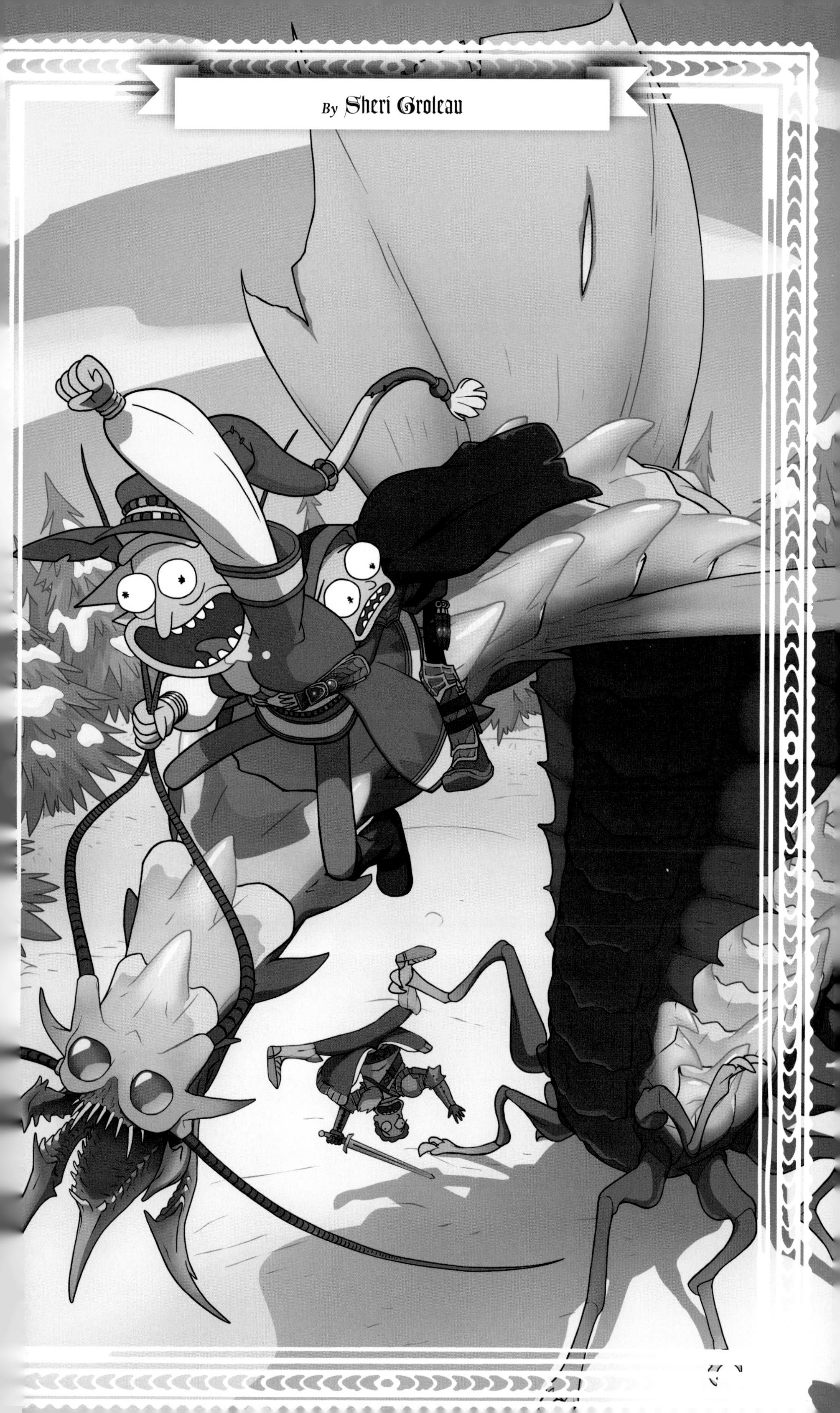

By Kendra Wells

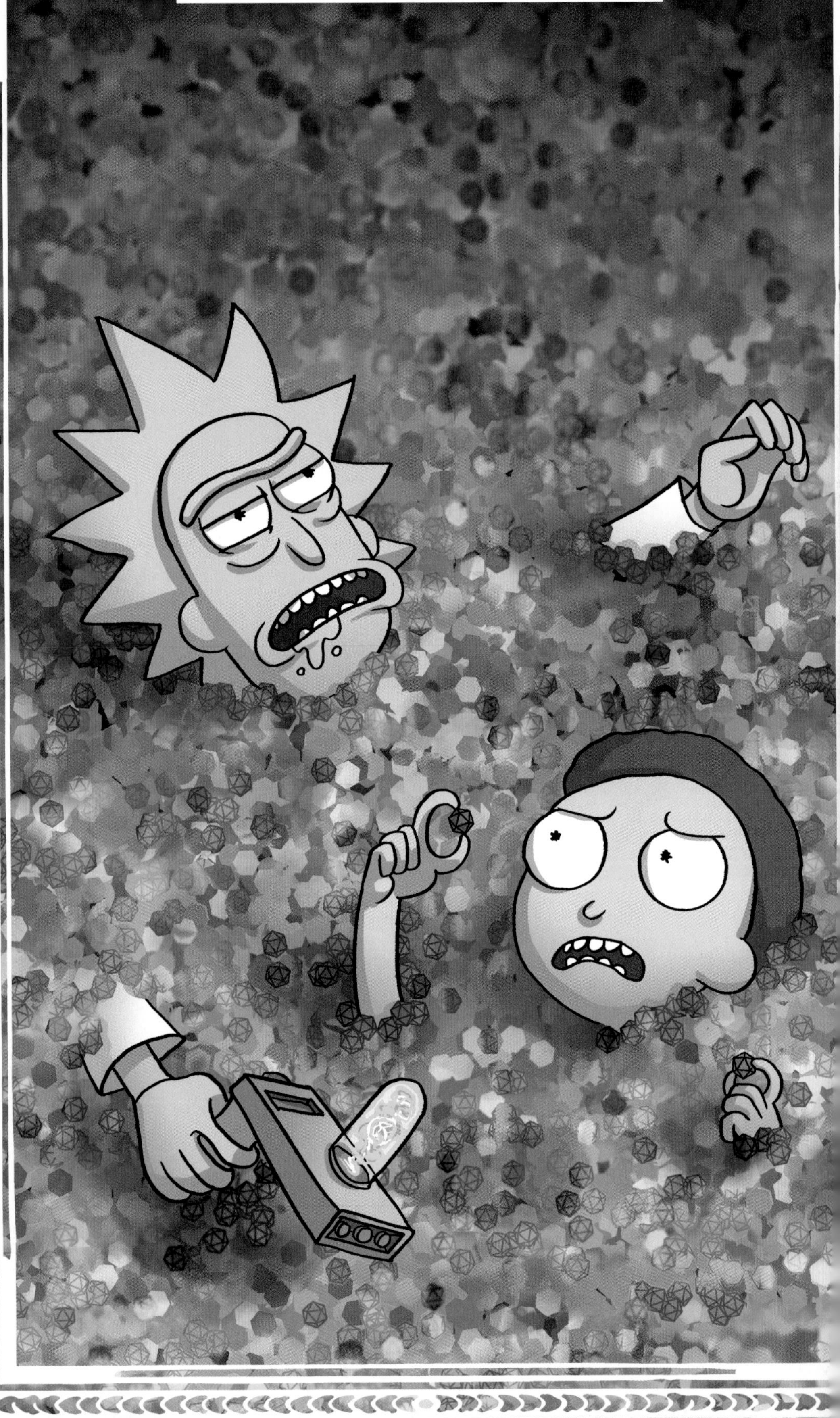

By **Jim Zub** and **Troy Little**

DUNGEONS & DRAGONS®

Wizard 5, Fighter 5, Rogue 5, Cleric 5	Sage	Rick Sanchez
CLASS & LEVEL	BACKGROUND	PLAYER NAME
Human	Chaotic Neutral	355,000
RACE	ALIGNMENT	EXPERIENCE POINTS

Wizard-Fighter-Rogue-CleRick

CHARACTER NAME

PERSONALITY TRAITS
I'm a one-man army and I crap platinum pieces.

IDEALS
I found divine magic by worshipping myself, so bow down and pay homage, baby!

BONDS
If you cross me, there's no dimension far enough away to save you.

FLAWS
These artifacts are ITCHY.

INSPIRATION

+6 PROFICIENCY BONUS

23 ARMOR CLASS

+4 INITIATIVE

30ft SPEED

Hit Point Maximum **142**

CURRENT HIT POINTS

TEMPORARY HIT POINTS

STRENGTH +9 / 29
DEXTERITY +4 / 18
CONSTITUTION -4 / 19
INTELLIGENCE -4 / 19
WISDOM +2 / 14
CHARISMA -0 / 10

SAVING THROWS
- +9 Strength
- +4 Dexterity
- +4 Constitution
- +10 Intelligence (●)
- +8 Wisdom (●)
- 0 Charisma

SKILLS
- +4 Acrobatics (Dex)
- +2 Animal Handling (Wis)
- +16 Arcana (Int) (●)
- +9 Athletics (Str)
- +0 Deception (Cha)
- +10 History (Int) (●)
- +8 Insight (Wis) (●)
- +0 Intimidation (Cha)
- +10 Investigation (Int) (●)
- +2 Medicine (Wis)
- +4 Nature (Int)
- +2 Perception (Wis)
- +0 Performance (Cha)
- +0 Persuasion (Cha)
- +4 Religion (Int)
- +9 Sleight of Hand (Dex)
- +16 Stealth (Dex) (●)
- +2 Survival (Wis)

PASSIVE WISDOM (PERCEPTION)

Total **5d6, 5d10, 10d8**

HIT DICE

DEATH SAVES
SUCCESSES ○○○
FAILURES ○○○

NAME	ATK BONUS	DAMAGE/TYPE
Dragon Lance	+15	1d12+11 piercing
Sun Blade	+15	1d8+4 radiant
Oathbow	+10	1d8+4 piercing

Spellcasting:
Spell Attack + 10
Spell DC: 18
4 Cantrips
4 1st level spells
3 2nd level spells
3 3rd level spells
3 4th level spells
2 5th level spells
Superiority Dice: 4d8
Riposte, Taunt, Disarm
Sneak Attack: 3d6
Channel Divinity: 1 use
Dragon Lance
Sun Blade
Necklace of Fireballs
Longsword +4 lifestealing
Sword of Kas: +5 shortsword, +5d12 on crit (19/20),
+2d10 against allies and former allies, gives concealment,
crit damage against Vecna, invisible, Poison/radiant attack,
target slide, +5 item bonus to defense.

ATTACKS & SPELLCASTING

OTHER PROFICIENCIES & LANGUAGES
...eapons: Daggers, darts, slings, ...arterstaffs, light crossbows, ...ple weapons, martial weapons

...nguages: Common, Elvish, ...varvish, Draconic, Thieves' Cant

...mor: Light Armor, Medium Armor, ...ields, Heavy Armor

...tisan's tools: Alchemist's supplies

...ieves' Tools, Disguise Kit, ...soner's Kit

CP ∞
SP ∞
EP ∞
GP ∞
PP ∞

EQUIPMENT
Adamantine Platemail Armor of Invulnerability (+5)
Amulet of Health
Amulet of Proof against Detection and Location
Backpack of Holding
Belt of Storm Giant Strength
Books of Levitation
Deck of Many Things
Disguise Kit
Dragonlance
Figurine of Wondrous Power - Boo the Hamster
Hand of Vecna
Headband of Intellect
Ioun Stone- Greater absorption
Ioun Stone- Mastery
Ioun Stone- Protection
Ioun Stone- Regeneration
Necklace of Fireballs
Manual of Stone Golems
Pearl of Power
Periapt of Health
Ring of Animal Influence
Ring of Evasion
Ring of Free Action
Ring of Mind Shielding
Ring of Spell Storing
Ring of Spell Turning
Ring of Three Mega-Wishes
Rod of Resurrection
Sword of Kas
Sun Blade

FEATURES & TRAITS

Sage:
- Researcher

Wizard Features:
- Spellcasting
- Arcane Recovery
- Arcane Tradition: Evocation
  - Evocation Savant
  - Spell Sculpting

Fighter Features:
- Fighting Style: Dueling
- Second Wind
- Action Surge
- Martial Archetype: Battle Master
- Extra Attack

Rogue Features:
- Expertise
- Sneak Attack
- Thieves' Cant
- Cunning Action
- Roguish Archetype: Assassin
- Uncanny Dodge

Cleric Features:
- Spellcasting
- Divine Domain: Rick!
- Channel Divinity
- Destroy Undead

Made a wish to be able to attune to any number of items.

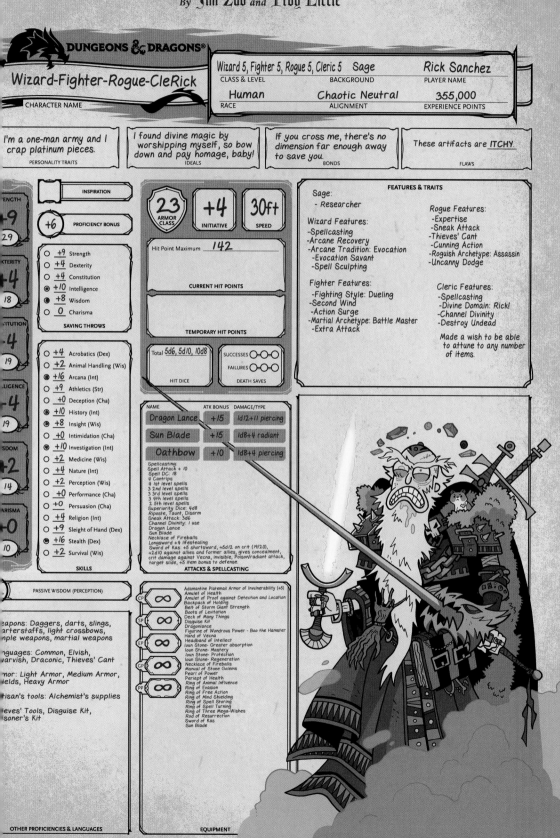

By Tess Stone

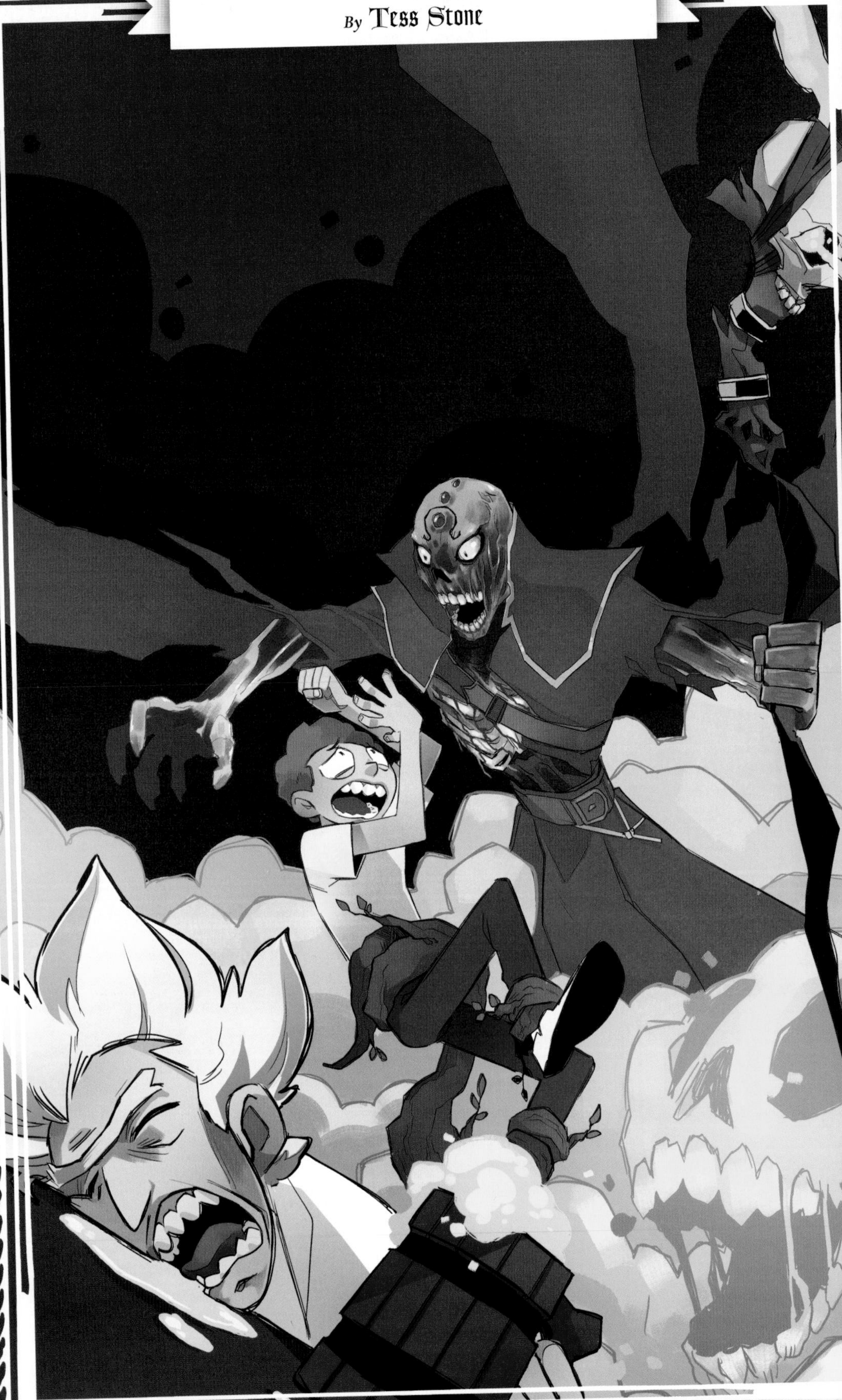

Dan Harmon is the Emmy® winning creator/executive producer of the comedy series *Community*, as well as the co-creator/executive producer of Adult Swim's *Rick and Morty*™.

Justin Roiland grew up in Manteca, California, where he did the basic stuff children do. Later in life he traveled to Los Angeles. Justin also really hates writing about himself in the third person. I hate this. That's right. It's me. I've been writing this whole thing. Hi. The cat's out of the bag. It's just you and me now. There never was a third person.

Jim Zub is a Canadian writer whose favorite D&D characters are rogues and rangers. Over the past ten years he's written a slew of sword and sorcery and superhero comics, including *Conan the Barbarian, Dungeons & Dragons, Skullkickers, Pathfinder, The Avengers,* and this fine book right here. If you cut him, he bleeds d20s.

Troy Little, three-time Eisner, Ringo and Harvey nominee, has worked with IDW, Oni Press, and Top Shelf on such books as the award-winning adaption of *Fear & Loathing in Las Vegas, Rick & Morty vs. Dungeons & Dragons, The Powerpuff Girls, Radically Rearranged Ronin Ragdolls* with Kevin Eastman, as well as his creator-owned books, *Chiaroscuro* and the *Angora Napkin series*. He lives in PEI, Canada.

Leonardo Ito was hired off a tweet asking, "Whose face do I need to punch in order to color Rick and Morty vs D&D?" He has a deep passion for cartoons and is proud to have contributed to many of his dream projects, including the Batman Animated franchise, *Powerpuff Girls, Sonic the Hedgehog, Teenage Mutant Ninja Turtles,* and, of course, *Rick and Morty vs. Dungeons & Dragons.* He thinks Rick is a lunatic but is afraid to say it out loud.

Chris Crank letters a bunch of books put out by Image, Dark Horse, and Oni Press. He also has a podcast with Mike Norton (*crankcast.net*) and makes music (*sonomorti.bandcamp.com*).

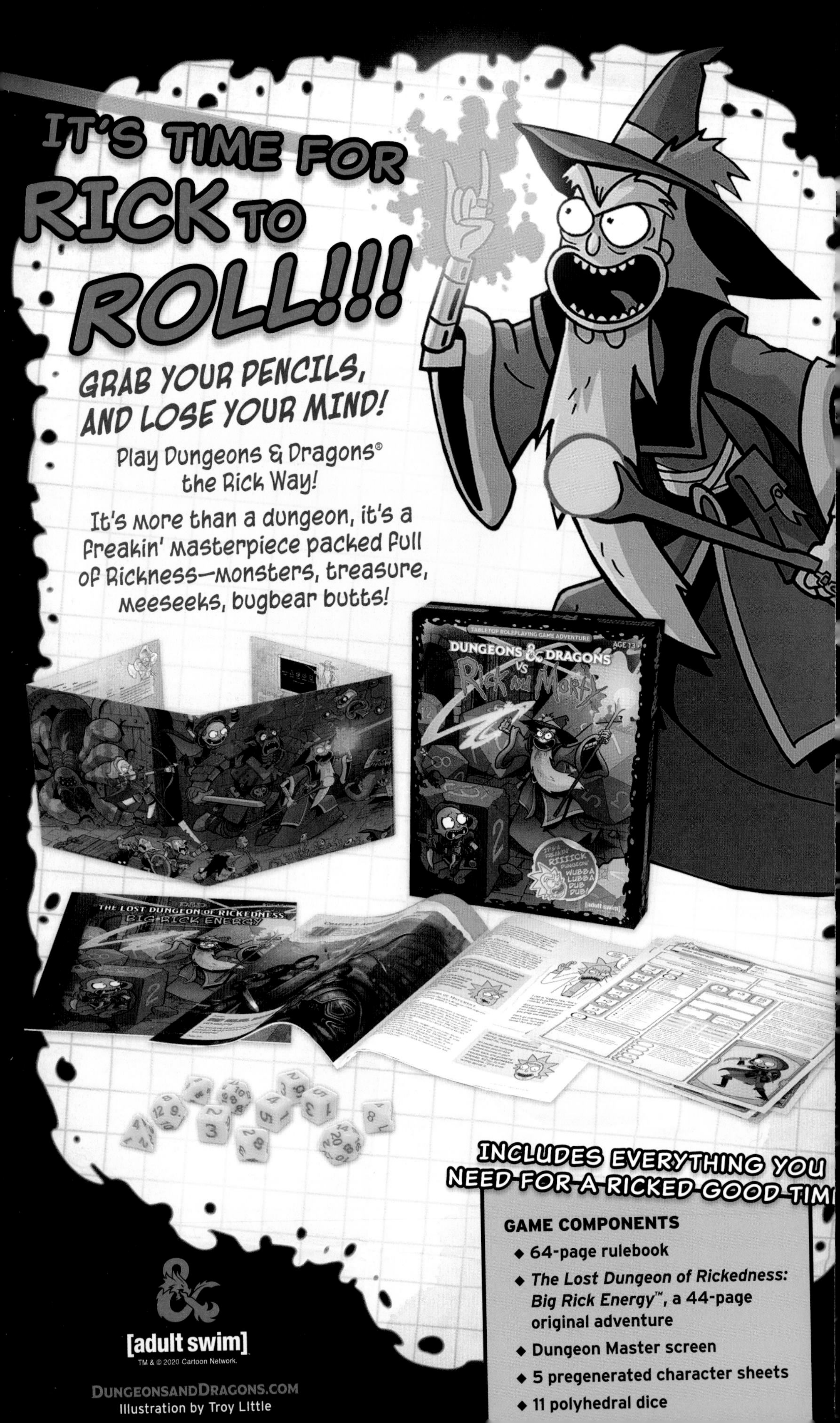
IT'S TIME FOR RICK TO ROLL!!!
GRAB YOUR PENCILS, AND LOSE YOUR MIND!
Play Dungeons & Dragons® the Rick Way!
It's more than a dungeon, it's a freakin' masterpiece packed full of Rickness—monsters, treasure, meeseeks, bugbear butts!
TABLETOP ROLEPLAYING GAME ADVENTURE
DUNGEONS & DRAGONS VS Rick and Morty
AGE 13+
IT'S A FREAKIN' RIIIICK DUNGEON! WUBBA LUBBA DUB DUB!
[adult swim]
THE LOST DUNGEON OF RICKEDNESS: BIG RICK ENERGY
INCLUDES EVERYTHING YOU NEED FOR A RICKED GOOD TIM
GAME COMPONENTS
◆ 64-page rulebook
◆ The Lost Dungeon of Rickedness: Big Rick Energy™, a 44-page original adventure
◆ Dungeon Master screen
◆ 5 pregenerated character sheets
◆ 11 polyhedral dice
[adult swim]
TM & © 2020 Cartoon Network.
DUNGEONSANDDRAGONS.COM
Illustration by Troy Little

More Books From Oni Press

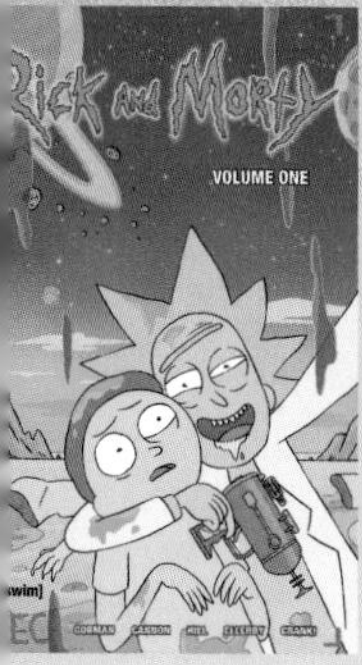

VOLUME ONE

:K AND MORTY™, VOL. 1
Zac Gorman, CJ Cannon,
Marc Ellerby, and more
28 pages, softcover, color
ISBN 978-1-62010-281-7

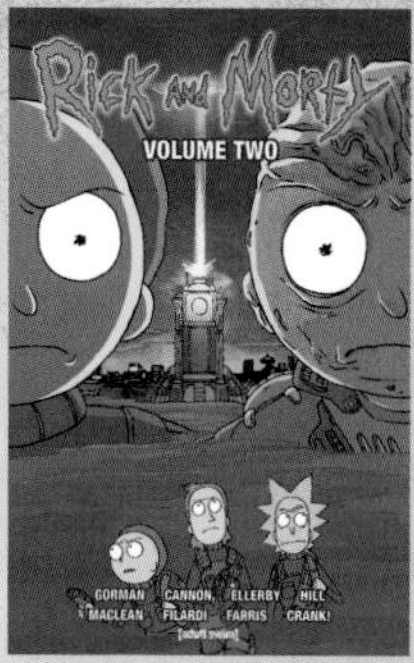

VOLUME TWO

RICK AND MORTY™, VOL. 2
By Zac Gorman, CJ Cannon,
Marc Ellerby, and more
128 pages, softcover, color
ISBN 978-1-62010-319-7

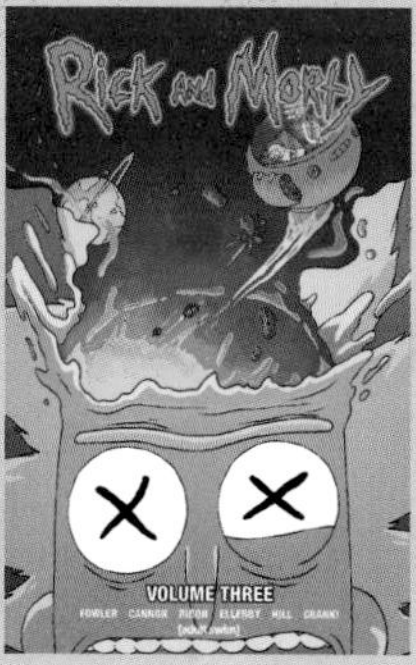

VOLUME THREE

RICK AND MORTY™, VOL. 3
By Tom Fowler, CJ Cannon,
Marc Ellerby, and more
128 pages, softcover, color
ISBN 978-1-62010-343-2

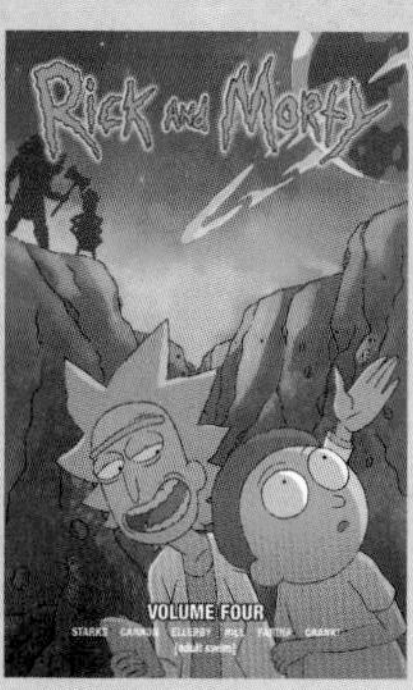

VOLUME FOUR

RICK AND MORTY™, VOL. 4
By Kyle Starks, CJ Cannon,
Marc Ellerby, and more
128 pages, softcover, color
ISBN 978-1-62010-377-7

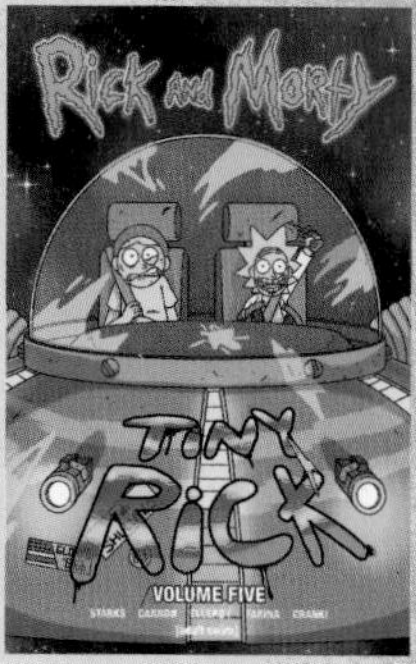

TINY RICK
VOLUME FIVE

RICK AND MORTY™, VOL. 5
By Kyle Starks, CJ Cannon,
Marc Ellerby, and more!
128 pages, softcover, color
ISBN 978-1-62010-416-3

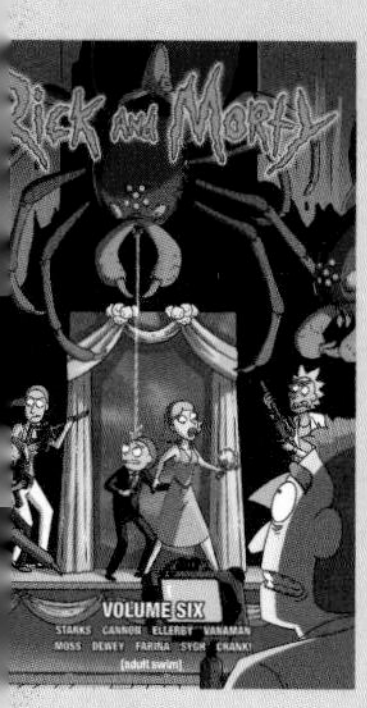

VOLUME SIX

K AND MORTY™, VOL. 6
y Kyle Starks, CJ Cannon,
Marc Ellerby, and more
28 pages, softcover, color
ISBN 978-1-62010-452-1

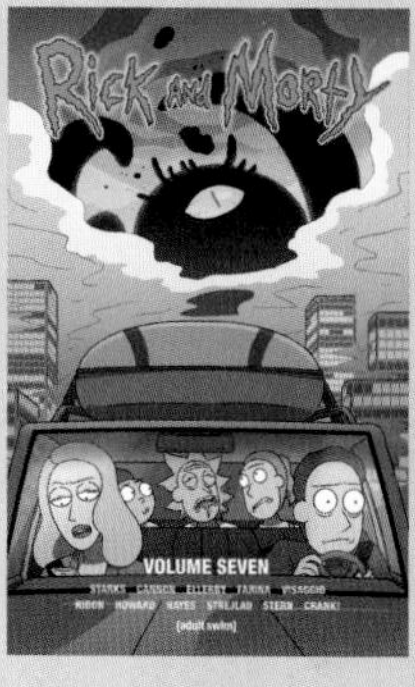

VOLUME SEVEN

RICK AND MORTY™, VOL. 7
By Kyle Starks, CJ Cannon,
Marc Ellerby, and more
128 pages, softcover, color
ISBN 978-1-62010-509-2

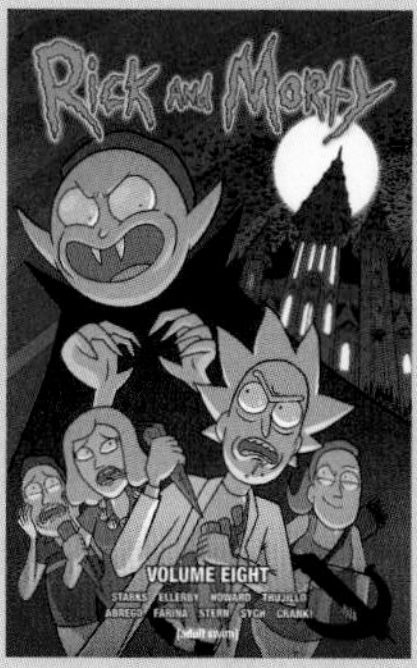

VOLUME EIGHT

RICK AND MORTY™, VOL. 8
By Kyle Starks, Tini Howard,
Marc Ellerby, and more
128 pages, softcover, color
ISBN 978-1-62010-549-8

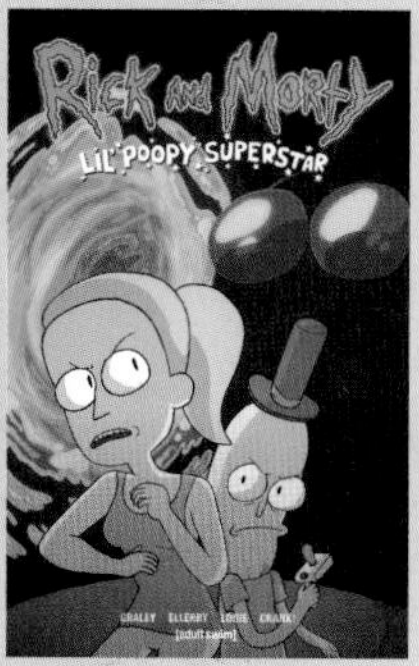

LIL' POOPY SUPERSTAR

RICK AND MORTY™:
LIL' POOPY SUPERSTAR
By Sarah Graley, Marc Ellerby,
and Mildred Louis
128 pages, softcover, color
ISBN 978-1-62010-374-6

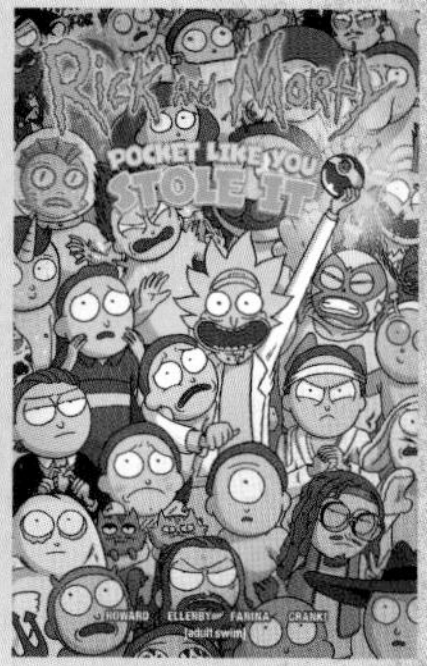

POCKET LIKE YOU STOLE IT

RICK AND MORTY™:
POCKET LIKE YOU STOLE IT
By Tini Howard, Marc Ellerby,
and Katy Farina
128 pages, softcover, color
ISBN 978-1-62010-474-3

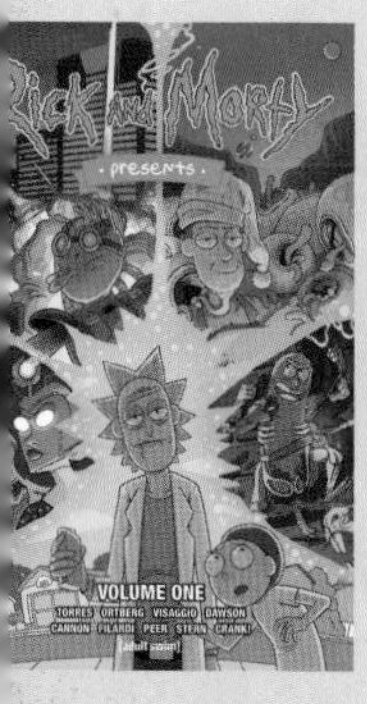

presents
VOLUME ONE

RICK AND MORTY™
PRESENTS, VOL. 1
J. Torres, Daniel Ortberg,
CJ Cannon, and more,
36 pages, softcover, color
SBN 978-1-62010-552-8

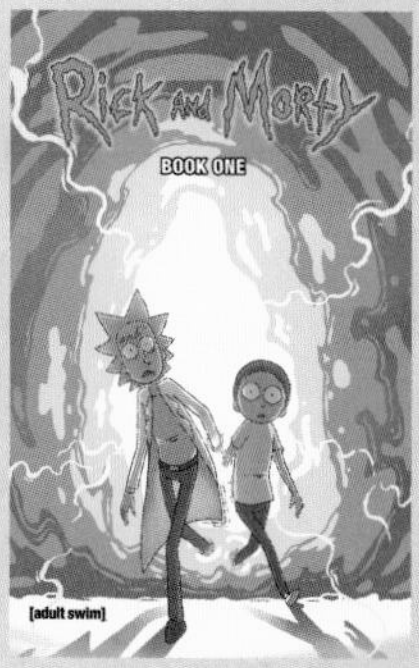

BOOK ONE
[adult swim]

RICK AND MORTY™
DELUXE EDITION, BOOK 1
By Zac Gorman, CJ Cannon,
Marc Ellerby, and more,
296 pages, hardcover, color
ISBN 978-1-62010-360-9

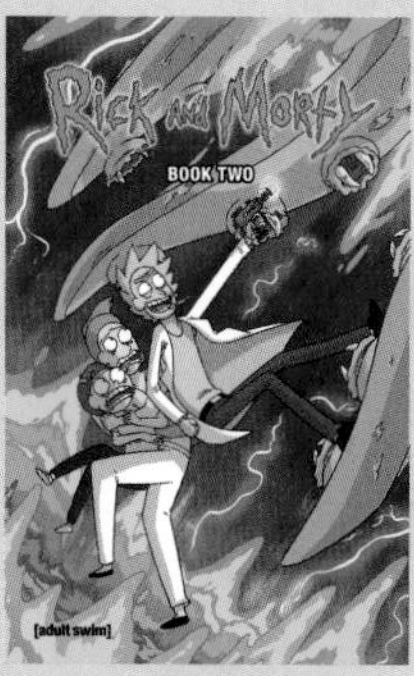

BOOK TWO
[adult swim]

RICK AND MORTY™
DELUXE EDITION, BOOK 2
By Tom Fowler, Kyle Starks,
CJ Cannon, Marc Ellerby,
and more, 288 pages,
hardcover, color
ISBN 978-1-62010-439-2

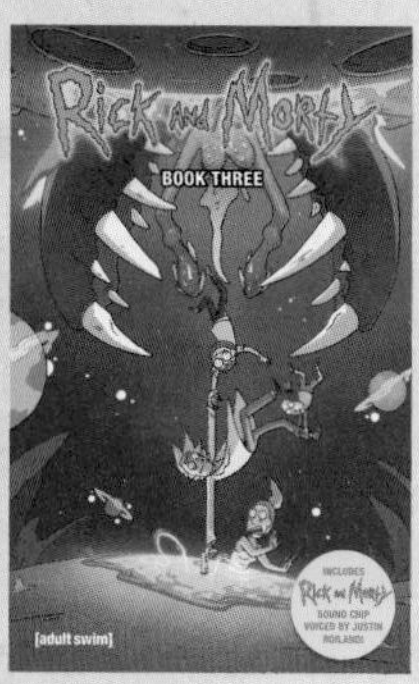

BOOK THREE
[adult swim]

RICK AND MORTY™
DELUXE EDITION, BOOK 3
By Kyle Starks, CJ Cannon,
Marc Ellerby, Sarah Graley, and
more, 288 pages,
hardcover, color
ISBN 978-1-62010-535-1

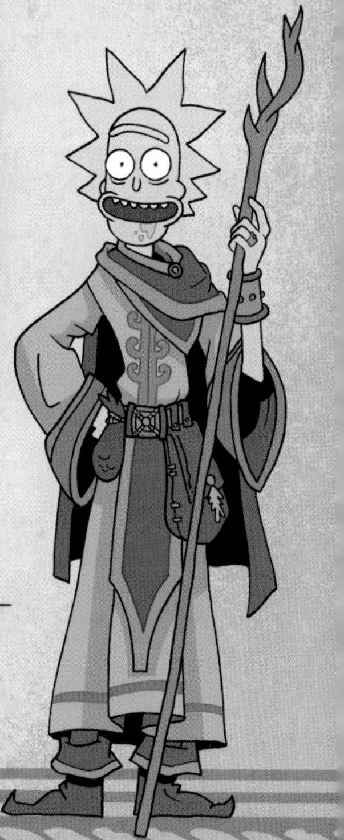

ONI PRESS

For more information on these and other fine Oni Press comic books and graphic novels visit *www.onipress.com*. To find a comic specialty store in your area visit *www.comicshops.us*.

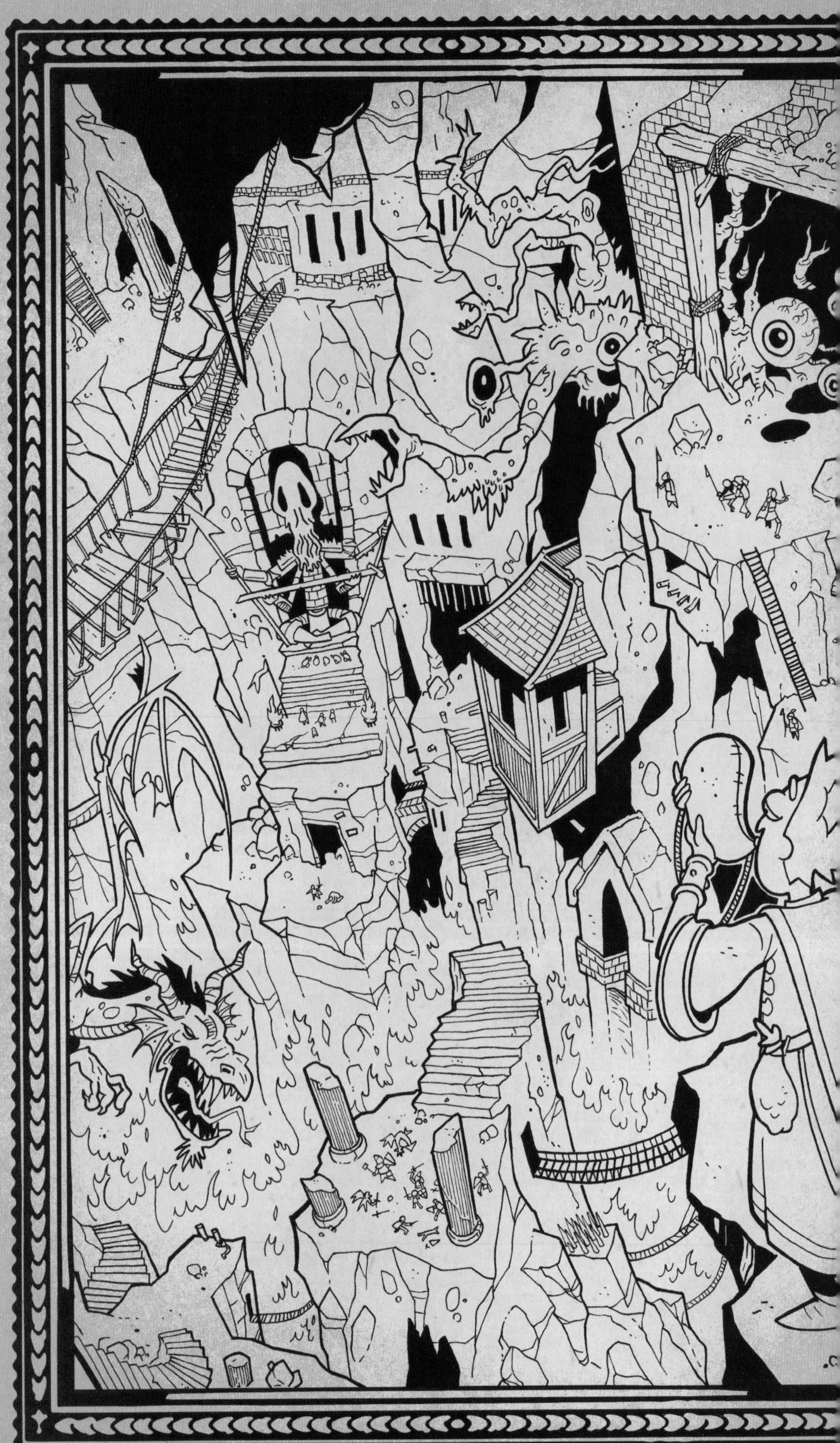